T0355929

Project Objectives Management

Aligning Targets, Delivering Results, and Adapting to Changes

Reitse van der Wekken

Apress®

Project Objectives Management: Aligning Targets, Delivering Results, and Adapting to Changes

Reitse van der Wekken
Delft, The Netherlands

ISBN-13 (pbk): 979-8-8688-0955-2   ISBN-13 (electronic): 979-8-8688-0956-9
https://doi.org/10.1007/979-8-8688-0956-9

Copyright © 2024 by Reitse van der Wekken

Managing Director, Apress Media LLC: Welmoed Spahr
Acquisitions Editor: Shivangi Ramachandran
Development Editor: James Markham
Project Manager: Jessica Vakili
Copy Editor: Kim Burton

Cover designed by eStudioCalamar

Illustrations by D. van der Drift and R. van der Wekken

Distributed to the book trade worldwide by Apress Media, LLC, 1 New York Plaza, New York, NY 10004, U.S.A. Phone 1-800-SPRINGER, fax (201) 348-4505, e-mail orders-ny@springer-sbm.com, or visit www.springeronline.com. Apress Media, LLC is a California LLC and the sole member (owner) is Springer Science + Business Media Finance Inc (SSBM Finance Inc). SSBM Finance Inc is a **Delaware** corporation.

For information on translations, please e-mail booktranslations@springernature.com; for reprint, paperback, or audio rights, please e-mail bookpermissions@springernature.com.

Apress titles may be purchased in bulk for academic, corporate, or promotional use. eBook versions and licenses are also available for most titles. For more information, reference our Print and eBook Bulk Sales web page at http://www.apress.com/bulk-sales.

Any source code or other supplementary material referenced by the author in this book is available to readers on GitHub (https://github.com/Apress). For more detailed information, please visit https://www.apress.com/gp/services/source-code.

If disposing of this product, please recycle the paper

To Saari and Petter

You grew up with me writing anytime, anywhere

And to Marieke

*Without you, I would have finished this book
ten years earlier :-)*

Table of Contents

About the Author

Reitse van der Wekken is a project manager at Allseas, a leading contractor in the global offshore energy market, where he manages innovative offshore platform decommissioning and installation projects, mostly located in the North Sea in Europe. He lives with his wife and two children in the city of Delft in The Netherlands, and if not reading or writing or relaxing with his family and friends, you might find him at sea doing offshore sailing. This book and the project management method introduced in it result from more than two decades of interest in and writing about project objectives management, a topic that highly interests and challenges him daily as a project management professional.

In 1996, he received a master's degree in mechanical engineering at the Delft University of Technology in The Netherlands. After that, he worked as a project manager on international projects at German multinational Siemens, delivering automation, control, and electrical systems for harbor cranes. Reitse started experiencing and exploring various challenges with project targets and expectations from internal and external stakeholders while working at a project supplier—the organization that prepares and delivers the project result, as opposed to the project customer that implements and uses the project result. He became a senior project manager within three years in China, where he experienced other perspectives on stakeholders and project objectives, and finally manager of the cranes project management department in

The Netherlands. Meanwhile, inspired by the book *The Goal* by the late business consultant Eliyahu Goldratt, he started using "future of the company" concepts in coaching and evaluating employees.

Driven by a long-term interest in offshore engineering and construction, Reitse moved on to Allseas in 2012. Since then, he has continued researching and writing about project objectives management.

Preface

A profound but often neglected challenge of project teams is their daily struggle with prioritization and conflict on their project between, on the one hand, the direct or customer-imposed targets and expectations and, on the other hand, the remaining targets and expectations of other stakeholders within their organization.

At the start of a project, various formal targets and expectations are established and captured in a contract or project charter, such as managing the project within available time and budget and providing the expected project result to its customer. However, during the project, various other stakeholders impose their (sometimes informal) targets and expectations on the project; for example, strict cost claim management, training new employees on the project, complying with society's expectations, trial of new innovative products or services, capturing useful lessons learned, or even active development on the project of improved process assets for future projects.

In many cases, such internal or external, direct or indirect, formal or informal targets and expectations conflict with each other, or their achievement is driven only by coincidence (for example, the random personal motivation of an employee) instead of deliberately planned and pursued by the organization; or priorities among these targets and expectations are not always clear, or worse not clearly defined, or worst not defined at all. Usually, such targets and expectations are combined with day-to-day challenges on the project, such as internal and external communication, unexpected changes, cost increases, continuous competition with other projects for (human) resources, or even private circumstances of project team members.

All these challenges seem even bigger at the project supplier level, where important targets and expectations of its organization (many long-term) are often overshadowed by the urgent (usually short-term) targets and expectations of the project's customer.

A solution for this challenge within project management for the project supplier starts with key questions: What is project success? How do we achieve project success? How is project success linked to the success of the organizations involved? How are project targets and expectations, often called *project objectives*, linked to project success, and how do we manage these objectives? What is the special difference between managing project objectives for the customer or the supplier of the project? What is the project supplier's specific challenge in managing project objectives? How can the project supplier overcome and manage this challenge?

This book introduces methods to answer these questions and provide the project supplier with solutions for these challenges.

Why should you learn about another method when many project management methods exist, such as Prince2, Six Sigma, or Agile? Because most of these project management methods focus on overall project management processes and procedures covering all aspects of a project, but limited guidance is provided for managing project objectives within a project and its organization. And even less guidance is provided specifically for the project supplier.

And what about the additional effort to maintain another process within the organization? Instead of extra work, this method provides a productive complement to existing organizational (project) management processes without major changes or excessive additional workload. In fact, many key components of the method are already present in one form or another within many project organizations, although possibly with limited coherence, process, or urgency. The method integrates a day-to-day high awareness, urgency, and focus on managing all project objectives within the project and project organization, to provide maximum benefit for the organization.

The method is of specific benefit to project suppliers, who deliver the project result to their customers. More specifically of benefit to a project supplier with a small to medium-sized organization, having limited resources (such as sufficient competent personnel) in combination with a multi-project environment, or without extensive and matured organizational project management procedures within their organization, or growing fast in size or revenue, or operating in a turbulent, continuously changing, and competitive business field. In contrast, at medium to large organizations, usually more suitable and effective processes are already in place, captured within matured organizational structures, based on years of practice and experience, developed, and maintained by a dedicated organizational department.

This book introduces a method by answering the relevant why, where, what, and how questions about changes to the project supplier's organization and its project execution practices.

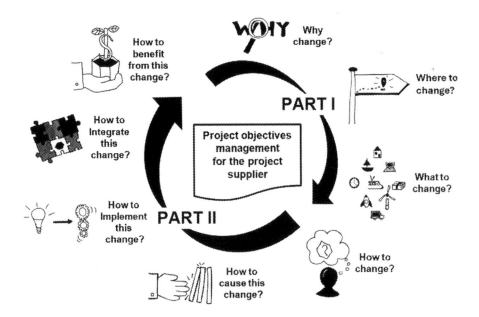

This step-by-step introduction gives insight into the method's philosophy and principles, a prerequisite for successful implementation and use within the project supplier's organization. While going through each successive chapter and question, the required "change" transforms into the "method" itself.

PART I

Why, Where, and What?

Part I of this book addresses needed change in a project supplier's organization and project execution practices.

Chapter 1 analyzes the customer and supplier perspectives on project objectives, focusing on why change is needed in the first place. Chapter 2 discusses the goal of the project supplier, focusing on where to change. Chapter 3 identifies various generic productive aspects of project subjects, focusing on what to change.

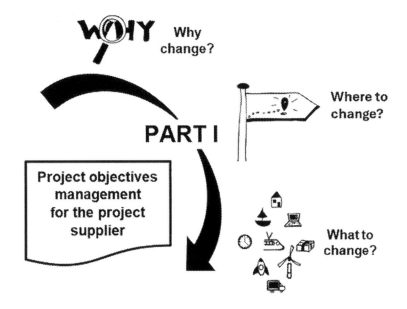

CHAPTER 1

The Customer Perspective: Why Change?

Why are changes to the project supplier's organization and its project execution practices needed?

The first step is to determine why this change is needed.

Project Management Success and Objectives

"Julie!" John Jr. raises his voice. "If you don't listen to your own management team, then please listen to me for once."

She remains silent, so he pushes on. "We need to stop some of your innovation projects immediately. We still don't cover any costs with expected revenue, the cost continues to grow, and there is still no return on investment expected in the near future. But worse, we have immediate and severe cash flow issues as we speak!"

"Come on, John, we always manage ... you always manage ... just as Dad did." Julie pleads.

"Not this time, now we got ourselves in real trouble. Our bank has refused any more loans, even short term, since yesterday. We don't have enough cash to pay our employee wages at the end of this month!"

"What? Call them right now. This is unacceptable! How long have we, has Dad, been banking with them?" Julie exclaims.

"Julie!" John fires back while standing up but keeps his hands firm on the table.

"This is not about quick fixes anymore. We keep making the same mistakes again and again without learning from them. Our profit margins remain too low, we are understaffed, and the staff we have is overworked and not motivated anymore. Some of our best employees are leaving us as we speak. We have no idea where we are heading with our company, we have no clear vision and no clue if we can be profitable at what we currently do, let alone with our innovations. We jeopardize our company's future ... our employee's future ... our future. We jeopardize all that Dad has built up!"

John is out of breath and shaking. He sits down and takes a few seconds to let his anger pass.

Julie is startled and looks upset at her brother. He never shouts. She still sees him shaking. She wants to say something but hesitates and looks down at the floor. Seconds pass by in silence. Julie's gaze is captured by a worn-down part of the carpet next to the table leg. Then, her gaze wanders off to the stain next to it. Looking around she notices more scuffs and stains all over the floor. Now her gaze follows a path of scuffs and stains toward the wall on the other side of the room and up to the window and its shades ... the same sorry state ... old, worn-down, definitely ready for a makeover. When was the last time this room got a redecoration, Julie thinks. This is where we receive our guests, stakeholders, investors, clients, suppliers, and even new job applicants! Not something to be proud of, or any good for our business. I guess Dad expected us to have settled down his business by now, including a completely reno-vated office. He had even allocated a budget for that, but that's gone now. Nice job of making Dad proud, she thinks sadly.

John also looks at the carpet as if he knows what Julie thinks and says emotionally.

"But instead of helping us ... the only thing you care about is your projects."

Another silence in the board room of Smith Electrical Services, just minutes after their management team reluctantly walked out for a coffee break. They left them alone for another one of their many heated discussions.

Several minutes pass. Then, Julie let's out a deep sigh and looks up at her brother.

"I know John ... I know ... I'm sorry."

Smith Electrical Services, or SES, is one of the larger electrical service and installation providers in their district, specializing in buildings and residential projects. SES provides consul-tancy, engineering, delivery, installation, maintenance, and upgrade services of electrical systems, communication, light-ing, heating, ventilation, and air conditioning, and recently also, new technologies such as solar power, other alternative power systems, and automation for buildings and larger resi-dential projects. SES grew from a small company established by John Smith Sr. in the 1980s to a medium-sized company with 150 employees, and now, after a couple of years taken over by his daughter Julie and son John Smith Jr.

Technical director Julie Smith has a strong passion and vision to develop and build the affordable, sustainable, carbon-neutral, and highly automated house of the future, which some say is more important for her than the company. But although managing director John Jr. supports his sister to lead SES into the future, he struggles with Julie's many, too many in his opinion, innovation projects. A lot of investment costs. However, the market seems not ready for this technology yet. He also thinks these internal developments distract SES too much from its core business and add to its already numerous challenges inside and outside the company.

"Yes ... well, it's not as simple as that anymore."

"What do you mean?" Julie is confused now and looks surprised at him.

"Come on, Julie, I don't say it often, but you know I share your vision too."

John looks in the distance, and another silence follows. Julie feels that her brother is about to continue and waits.

"But you know, there is a big difference between having a vision and pursuing that vision in the right way. It's just not working the way we do it now at SES, not without putting our whole company at risk. It's not coherent and too risky, and it's on top of many other challenges and threats we have as we speak."

"So now what?" Julie asks with a reluctant smile.

Another silence follows, but then she continues.

"I wish Dad was here now. He would know what to do."

"Yes, probably he would." Junior answers. "But our future depends on whether we can manage ourselves. You and me, and our management team, and our employees."

Another silence, and John looks at his sister, but now he waits, sure that she wants to say something.

"Actually," Julie hesitates but admits. "I have an idea, but I didn't dare to tell you ... yet."

"I already suspected you did, so just tell me," John answers with a reassuring smile.

"We need to find a way to fulfill our vision, our company's vision, combined with a smooth-running and healthy company, ready for our future. But we can't fix this ourselves anymore. Certainly not just the two of us, or our management team, or our employees, who already have too much on their plates as is. We need outside help from an expert, someone with a fresh, objective, and creative view. I know you are no fan of consultants like Dad, but that's how I see it."

John gets upset but just manages to avoid a roll with his eyes.

"And I'm sure you already have someone in mind as well."

"Well, yes, actually, I have. He is who got me started thinking in the first place. Do you remember Collin?"

John thinks for a couple of seconds.

"From college?"

"Yes."

"He came over to the house during weekends with some of your college friends, right?"

"Yes, he did."

"I liked that guy, smart but also a good listener, as I remember. It's been a long time since I have seen him, though?"

"Yeah, well, somehow we lost touch. But I accidentally ran into him a couple of weeks ago in the city, and we talked over lunch. It turns out he is a management coach now, specializing in change processes within project organizations, and he uses an interesting project management method."

"Collin is a consultant now?" John asks with a smirk but suddenly looks at the door.

"Wait a minute, what time is it? We have our team still waiting for us outside! Let's invite them back in and tell them that we have an idea that we want to share with them in more detail during the next management meeting. And come have dinner tonight at our place so you can tell me all about Collin and what you two have been up to already."

"Sounds like a plan!" Julie responds with a relieved smile.

And so it was done. John and Julie had a couple of preparatory one-on-one sessions to agree on their way forward. Thereafter, they had a first meeting with Collin over dinner. First, catching up on some old stories from their study time, but soon they started talking business. Then and there they agreed that due to its importance for SES, both Julie and John would personally drive this change project within SES, which for Collin settled an important commitment and success factor for this major change process. This was followed by a detailed intake meeting at their office to discuss what exactly their objectives were and what they expected from Collin. He prepared a proposal for his consulting, which was soon thereafter accepted and quickly followed by the first of their many sessions during the next half year at the SES office. As per Collin's instructions, no out-of-office sessions. SES is where it happens, so where it needs to be done. Quickly, the SES employees got used to Collin walking around the office, workshop, and warehouse, talking to personnel from all departments and at all levels of the organization. He literally became part of the team, and people felt safe to tell him anything on their minds.

Project Management

"It's all about the management of your projects and the link between the success of your projects and the success of your company. So, let's begin at the beginning."

Collin kicks off their first of a series of weekly sessions and he fires his first question at Julie and John.

"Now, what is a project, and what is project management?"

Various definitions exist for projects and project management. *A Guide to the Project Management Body of Knowledge*, also known as the *PMBOK Guide*,[1] is a leading global standard of the USA-based Project Management Institute (PMI). Their global standards are the profession's foundation by ensuring that your project management knowledge and frameworks are up-to-date and consistently applied. PMI defines a project as "a temporary endeavor undertaken to create a unique result, of which the end is reached when the project's objectives have been achieved." Their *PMBOK Guide* defines project management as the application of knowledge, skills, tools, and techniques to project activities to meet the project requirements.

A project is a temporary endeavor designed to produce a unique product, service, or result with a defined beginning and end, usually time-constrained and often constrained by funding or staffing, undertaken to meet unique goals and objectives, typically to bring about beneficial change or added value.[2] The temporary nature of projects contrasts with business as usual (or operations), which are repetitive, permanent, or semi-permanent functional activities to produce products or services. Managing such distinct production approaches requires developing distinct technical skills and management strategies. Project management is leading a team to achieve goals and meet success criteria at a specified

---

[1] PMI, 2021

[2] Wikipedia, 2022

time. The primary challenge of project management is to achieve all the project goals within the given constraints. This information is usually described in project documentation created at the beginning of the development process. The primary constraints are scope, time, and budget. The secondary challenge is to optimize the allocation of necessary inputs and apply them to meet predefined objectives. In practice, the management of these two systems is often quite different and requires the development of distinct technical skills and management strategies.

In more detail, the project manager and project team use the following *project controls* to manage the project.[3]

- Time control is the task, responsibility, and authority to timely execute the project plan such that the project result is available at the agreed time.

- Money control is the task, responsibility, and authority to profitably execute the project plan, such that the project result is finished within the agreed budget.

- **Quality control** is the task, responsibility, and authority to qualitatively execute the project plan, such that the project result meets the required quality.

- **Information control** is the task, responsibility, and authority to unequivocally execute the project plan, such that the project result is documented for management, operation, and maintenance.

- **Organization control** is the task, responsibility, and authority to execute the project plan by the responsible people, such that the project result is handed over to the user for management, operation, and maintenance.

---

[3] Wijnen et al, 1984

Project Success, Success Factors, and Success Criteria

Since the 1990s, project success has become and remains a major interest and field of study within project management.[4] A 2015 bibliometric study published a portfolio of papers on project management success, covering the recent evolution of this topic over the last 15 years, from 2000 to 2014. Conclusions pointed out significant authors and journals as a relevant source of information to the project management success field. Despite the vast amount of study however, a wide difference of opinions remains, such as disagreement on what determines project success and the difference between what is recorded in literature and surveys of professionals' opinions. Past focus was mainly on the *iron triangle* consisting of time, cost and quality; however, current approaches seem more complex and undetermined. The iron triangle is now considered more a measure of efficiency than a sole measure of project success. Some recent research is based on managerial and organizational theories and reflects the multidimensional and networked nature of project success. Other research challenges the traditional division in project success and project management success by complementing it with market and social benefit successes. Yet other studies discuss the various approaches to project success and conclude that till now, there still is no consensus

---

[4] Collins and Baccarini, 2004; Thomas, 2008; Ika, 2009; Khosravi and Afshari, 2011; Müller and Jugdev, 2012; Davis, 2014; Ram, 2014; Beleiu, 2015; Carvalho, 2015; Machado and Martens, 2015; Sudhakar, 2016; Shokri-Ghasabeh and Kavousi-Chabok, 2009; Kylindri et al, 2012; Dalcher, 2012; Irvine, 2013; Ebbesen and Hope, 2013; Müller, 2012; Al-Tmeemy et al, 2010; Manana et al, 2011; Velayudhan, 2016; Turner and Zolin, 2012

on what determines project success and that new approaches led to refocusing project management goals to make them more customer and stakeholder-based, either internal or external to the company. Two very useful distinctions, however, exist in the literature on project success.[5]

First, a distinction is made between project success *criteria*, outputs against which success or failure of a project is measured, and project success *factors*, inputs into the (project) management system leading directly or indirectly to project success. Project success factors are crucial for analyzing why projects are a success or a failure but cannot be used for measuring the actual degree of success, which is the domain of project success criteria instead.

> *"Quite some theory to digest, and even more coming up during our next sessions. But, I will help you to make the theory easier to digest by drawing explanatory diagrams, as many as I need to." Collin says while he grabs a marker and turns to the first flip chart in the left corner of the room.*

> *"So, you will see me, and you, doing this a lot during our sessions, to clarify ideas by sketches. It really works! And yes, for creativity, we work with old-fashioned flip charts instead of computer presentations."*

> *"Now, here we have a project." Collin continues while he draws a rectangle, and two arrows going in and coming out of the rectangle.*

> *"With inputs and outputs, managed by project management."*

> *Above the incoming arrow, Collin writes "project success factors," and he further explains.*

> *"Project success factors are inputs into the project management system leading directly or indirectly to project success."*

> *And he continues while he writes above the outgoing arrow.*

---

[5] Basu, 2012; Beleiu, 2015; Korbijn, 2014; Almarri, 2017

"And project success criteria are outputs against which success or failure of a project is measured." (Figure 1-1)

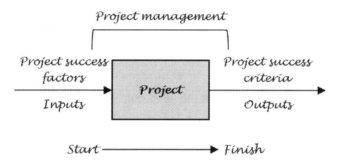

Figure 1-1. *Definition of a project and project management*

Project success factors, or critical success factors (CSFs), are frequently studied during the last two decades.[6] One study identifies 20 CSFs across 63 publications grouped under effectiveness (determined by how the project contributes to the achievement of business results) and efficiency (measured as a function of performing the scope and meeting targets of time, cost, and quality criteria of the project).

Effectiveness consists of support from upper management, clear and realistic goals, detailed and up-to-date project plan, efficient communication channels and system, involvement, and commitment of stakeholders, effective control of changes, availability of information on the history of previous projects, adequate organizational structure, effective process for hiring suppliers, qualified project team and management, adequate project management tools and methodology and project size and complexity. Efficiency consists of an experienced and competent project team, an experienced and competent project manager, a clearly defined and detailed scope, sufficient and well-allocated resources, a

---

[6] Andersen et al, 2006; Cooper and Kleinschmidt, 2007; Elattar, 2009; Müller, 2012; Ahimbisibwe et al, 2015; Saadé et al, 2015; Sudhakar, 2016; Osorio et al, 2014; Constantino et al, 2015; Ram and Corkindale, 2014

realistic timeline, effective risk management, effective project monitoring and control, and a realistic budget.

One paper introduces a decision support system to predict project performances based on project CSFs that can serve as the fundamental criteria to prevent possible causes of failures with an effective project selection process, considering company strategic objectives, project manager's experience, and the competitive environment. However, another paper questions the validity of many of the claimed CSFs and the utility of the general body of literature on CSFs, and they caution researchers who may plan to use claimed CSFs in their research to carefully examine the validity of the claim before proceeding.

PMI's *PMBOK Guide* refers to project success factors as *enterprise environmental factors*, which refer to internal and external factors surrounding or influencing a project's success. These factors may come from any or all enterprises involved in the project, may enhance or constrain project management options, and may positively or negatively influence the outcome. Enterprise environmental factors include but are not limited to, the following.

- organizational culture
- structure and processes
- government or industry standards
- infrastructure
- existing human resources
- personnel administration
- company work authorization systems
- marketplace conditions and stakeholder risk tolerances
- political climate
- organization's established communications channels

14

- commercial database

- and project management information systems

Certain *outputs* of a project, such as achieved project objectives (a measurement of project success criteria), might lead in turn to *inputs* into a future project, being project success factors (inputs that lead to project success of that succeeding project), such as acquiring useful process assets or lessons learned. An elaborate study[7] confirms the need for strict criteria to describe the achievement of success in projects. The study further investigated the relationship between performance indicators (success criteria) and value-for-money creation factors (success factors) in public-private partnership projects. Another study[8] concludes that the project management field focuses either on project success factors or project success criteria, neglecting the relationships (mechanisms) between these concepts. It can be concluded that it remains mainly unclear how success factors contribute to success criteria.

Collin draws an additional rectangle with the text "Future Project" to the right of the existing rectangle. He adds an arrow connected to the new rectangle, with the text "project success factors" above it, and explains.

"And as we learned, the outputs of one project might turn again into inputs into a future project." (Figure 1-2)

---

[7] Almarri, 2017

[8] Pankratz and Basten, 2018

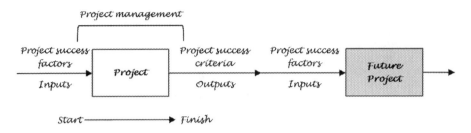

Figure 1-2. *Connected project and future project*

"Now, take this in for a moment." He says while he drinks another sip of coffee.

"We will park this topic for now and pick it up later again to further investigate project success criteria, which are linked to project objectives, in more detail."

Second, a useful distinction is made between the measurement of *project* success criteria, measured against the performance on overall objectives of the project, and measurement of *project management* success criteria, measured against the performance on project management objectives—later defined as the *project controls*—such as cost, time, quality, organization, and information. Project success deals with goal and purpose, and project management success with inputs and outputs. These overall and project management objectives together constitute the project objectives, which measure the project's success. Note that this distinction also indicates that a project can still be a success overall despite poor project management performance and vice versa.

Collin adds several elements to the diagram and says, while he points at the flip chart.

"So, project success criteria are linked to project objectives, consisting of project management objectives and overall project objectives, against which project success is measured." (Figure 1-3)

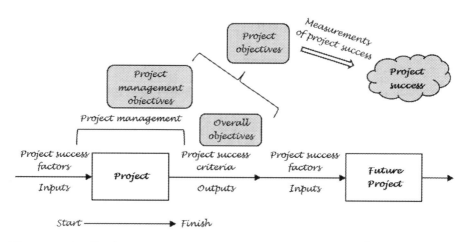

Figure 1-3. *Project, project management and project success*

"Yes, that does make it much clearer to me." John agrees after a couple of seconds, intensely studying the flip chart.

Project vs. Organizational Success

As I studied in the preceding section, the actual degree of project success is the domain of project success criteria, and project success criteria are measured against project objectives. And according to A. De Wit the most appropriate measurements for project success criteria are indeed project objectives. A project's success is determined by the degree to which these objectives are met. However, there are quite a few more objectives involved in a project than just cost, time, and quality, particularly when all stakeholders are considered. PMI defines a project as a temporary endeavor undertaken to create a unique result, of which the end is reached when the project's objectives have been achieved.[9]

---

[9] Basu, 2012; Beleiu, 2015; De Wit,1988; PMI, 2021

If project objectives are linked to project success by being its measurement (the project perspective), how is project success linked to organizational success (the organizational perspective)? Within the Theory of Constraints (TOC) production and process optimization methodology— introduced and developed by Eliyahu Goldratt, organizational success is captured by *productivity*, bringing a company closer to its goal.[10] L.A. Patah concludes in his paper that projects are the way to implement corporate strategies in an organizational environment.[11] Therefore, project objectives should be directly linked to strategic organizational objectives.

Collin adds these last additions in the upper right corner of the flip chart.

"Project objectives are linked to the organization and its organizational success by business benefits." (Figure 1-4)

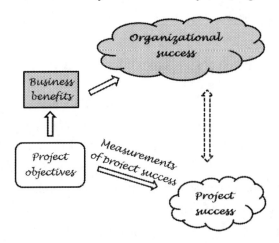

Figure 1-4. *Project, project management and project success*

---

[10] Kim, 2008; Simsit, 2014; Techt, 2015; Youngman, 2021
[11] Patah, 2010

"Note that benefits are currently addressed as 'business' bene-fits, which should be considered generic. However, it does have a commercial character, while organizations can be both commercial (a company) or non-commercial, for-profit (a company) or non-profit. We will later come back to this by transforming to a generic definition of benefits instead," Collin explains.

Figure 1-5 completes the diagram with all its components.

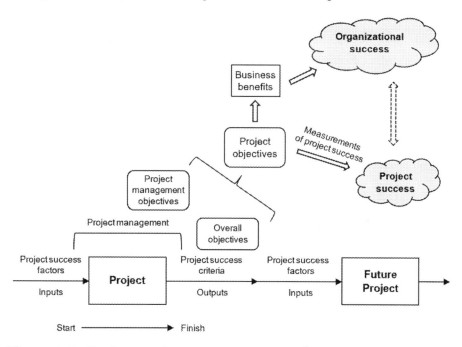

Figure 1-5. *Project, project management, and project vs. organizational success*

From the organizational perspective, project objectives are linked to the organization and its success by business benefits. However, although organizational success might be linked to project success by project objectives and its business benefits, it is not necessarily a direct or instant link in general. So, what does this link look like at organizations involved in the project?

Project Objectives

Various definitions of generic and project management-related project objectives have been introduced in the preceding section. Such as that they provide a measurement of the success of the project, that a project plan is executed to fulfill the project objectives, or that the end of a project is reached when the project's objectives have been achieved, or that a project is undertaken to meet unique goals and objectives; or that the secondary—and more ambitious—challenge of a project is to optimize the allocation of necessary inputs and apply them to meet predefined objectives. More definitions exist. One definition defines a project objective as a business benefit an organization expects to achieve due to spending time and exerting effort to complete a project; furthermore states that project objectives are often confused with project products. Another defines that a project objective describes the desired results of a project, which often includes a tangible item. An objective is specific and measurable and must meet time, budget, and quality constraints. And yet another defines that project objectives are specific and are considered lower-level statements. They describe results—specific, tangible deliverables that the project will produce.[12]

> *"So, we concluded that it is not easy to find commonly accepted views because a wide difference of opinions remains in the project management field on project success and project objectives," Collin explains to John while he walks up to the second flip chart in the other corner of the room.*

> *"A typical and exemplary version of a conventional definition of 'project objectives' formed the basis for developing our project objectives management method. It can be found on the website knowledgerush.com."[13]*

---

[12] Infolific, 2013; Smartsheet, 2021; Projectmanager.com, 2021

[13] Knowledgerush, 2012

In project management, a project objective is a business benefit that an organization expects to achieve due to injecting project product(s) into itself or its environment.

The term business benefits refers not only to strictly monetary gains, but to all kinds of changes in parameters describing the workings of any organization that bring it closer to its goal.

"Let's break this down into its core elements in a diagram for better understanding."

"I already started wondering why we had to buy that many flip charts." John Jr. grumbles.

Collin doesn't react but smiles while he starts drawing, writing, and explaining step by step. A house with the text 'organization' in the lower left corner, and then inside at the bottom a diamond with the text 'project product(s)', an arrow 'injection' coming into the house connected to the diamond, a rectangular 'business benefits' above with finally a circle 'goal' at the top, both connected by vertical upward arrows. (Figure 1-6)

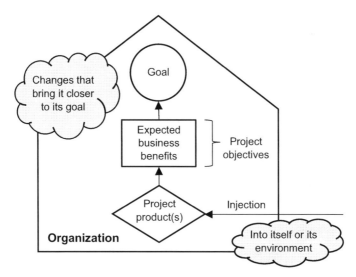

Figure 1-6. *Definition of project objectives of a project within an organization*

And Collin further explains.

"So, project products are injected into the organization itself—with the house as a metaphor—or its environment. The result of this injection achieves business benefits, and such expected business benefits are the project objectives. Furthermore."

"OK, I get that!" Julie interrupts.

"Our solar panels, the products of our solar project, are installed on the roof of the Yorkshire factory, that's the injection within our client KC Foods. And of course, they have a business benefit, that's why they have the panels installed, which is their production of electricity during day time, thereby lowering their energy bill immediately, and return on investment already after several years!"

"Yes, a business benefit, as a result of installing your panels. Which is a change that brings KC Foods closer to its or one of its goals." (Figure 1-7)

Project at KC Foods

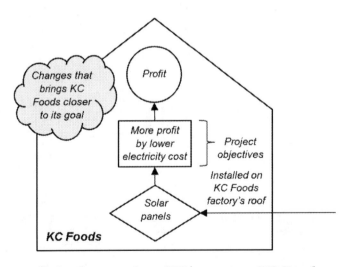

Figure 1-7. *Installed solar panels at SES' customer KC Foods*

Yes, more profit by lower cost!" Jr. agrees.

Next, we investigate two particulars of this conventional definition of project objectives: the perspectives of the definition in relation to the organizations involved in the project, and the conventional goal of a commercial company.

The Customer and Supplier Perspectives
The Customer and Absent Supplier Perspectives

"John, did you hear us say our solar panels and your solar panels earlier? KC Foods achieves a business benefit by installing your panels. Your panels, but where are you as the supplier in this diagram?" Collin continues while pointing at the flip chart.

"Uh, what do you mean?" John responds confused.

"Yes, where are we in this diagram!" Julie agrees, but Jr. still looks confused at the diagram. Collin proceeds.

"If this is the definition of project objectives and business benefits, where is the supplier in this definition, the project supplier, the organization that delivers the result through projects. Where is Smith Electrical Services in this definition?"

Julie thought she understood, however, now looks confused again at Collin and responds.

"But the definition says 'an organization.' Isn't that every organization, including SES?"

Let's take a closer look at the conventional definition of a project objective in Figure 1-6, specifically how this definition applies to the organization(s) involved in the project. Although the definition uses the generic term *organization,* it is evident from the fragment "injecting ... into itself or its environment," which refers to a receiving party in the project—that this organization is clearly the receiver of the project and, therefore, is the customer and user combined when injected within itself or the customer when injected within its environment and used by the customer's user. In both cases, however, the "generic organization" refers more specifically to the customer or user, as depicted in Figure 1-8.

> *"So, at KC Foods there is an instant business benefit, as a direct result of installing your panels. The organization is KC Foods, your customer, it's not just a generic organization." Collin concludes while deliberate striking through the word organization and writing the word customer above it.*

> *Now this bias to the customer or user is the customer perspective on project objectives." Collin says while drawing a big cloud in the upper right corner of the diagram. (Figure 1-8)*

Project at customer

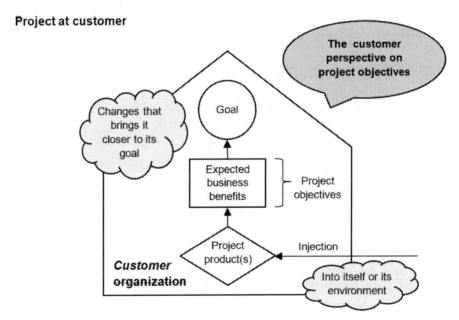

Figure 1-8. *Customer or user instead of a "generic" organization*

The customer or its user gains business benefits from injecting the project products into itself or its environment. Other definitions of project objectives in literature represent a similar bias on the customer or user of the project.[14] From here on, this existing bias to the customer or user of the project product will be referred to as the **customer perspective**.

The customer or its user gains business benefits; in fact, it gains *instant* business benefits. As a *direct* result of injecting the project products into itself or its environment (the customer perspective).

Project business, specifically a respective project, involves both a customer and a supplier of the project (results). Two parties are either linked by a contract or agreement between two separate organizations (supplier and customer) or an internal project delivery by an executing department to a using department (supplier and user) within an organization. From now on, they will be referred to as *customer* and *supplier* (or *project supplier*) and their organizations in relation to the respective project.

> *Collin turns around and looks at Julie.*
>
> *"Julie, if KC Foods is the customer, what are you then?"*
>
> *"Well, we are the supplier."*
>
> *"Yes, you are the supplier, the project supplier." Collin confirms and draws another house to the right of the customer's house and writes "supplier" in it.*
>
> *"And these products are your solar panels, so what do you do for KC Foods to be able to have those panels on their factory's roof?"*
>
> *"We deliver the panels to them and install them as well."*
>
> *"Correct." And Collin extends the arrow under "injection" into the supplier's house and marks it with "product delivery." (Figure 1-9)*

---

[14] Prince2, 2017; Infolific, 2013; PMI, 2021; IPMA, 2018

Project at supplier and customer

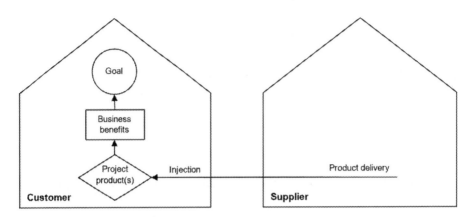

Figure 1-9. *Project objectives of a project for customers vs. suppliers*

"Furthermore, the supplier must also have business benefits and goals," And Collin includes them in the diagram. (Figure 1-10)

Project at supplier

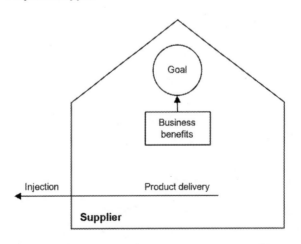

Figure 1-10. *Project objectives of a project at a supplier*

"But what is the connection between the product delivery and the business benefits for the supplier at Smith Electrical Services?" Collin asks while writing a question mark in between and punctuates it by thumping the dot hard on the flip chart. This is the problem with the conventional definition of a project objective. Where is this other party in the definition, the supplier of the project products? (Figure 1-11)

Project at supplier and customer

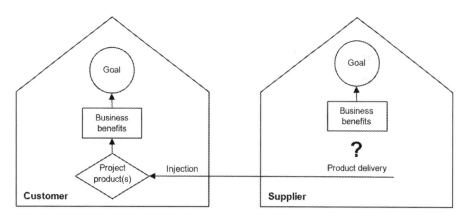

Figure 1-11. *Project objectives of a project for customers vs. suppliers*

This absent perspective, opposite to the customer perspective, will be referred to from here on as the **supplier perspective** on project objectives.

As opposed to the customer, the project supplier has no *direct* products to inject within its organization and, therefore, cannot gain *instant* business benefits from its product. It seems that the supplier can only gain business benefits indirectly by delivering the products to the customer (Figure 1-12).

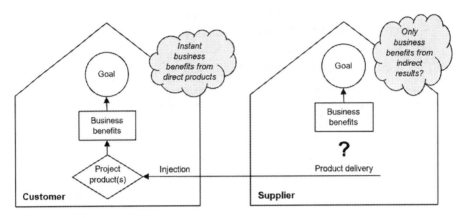

Figure 1-12. *Project objectives of a project for customers vs. suppliers*

Without a direct link between product delivery and business benefits for the supplier, project success might not directly lead to organizational success for the supplier.

"But we do have direct business benefits. We have a satisfied customer. We make a profit, right?" John Jr. steps in.

"Yes, you are right, but even these are not a direct result. There is no instant business benefit."

"What do you mean?" Jr. asks.

Collin stands up, walks over to one of the flip charts, and folds back a page to reveal a clean page.

"Let's take your KC Foods project with its solar panels as an example," Collin says while drawing a sun in the left upper corner and the roof of KC Foods' factory.

"We are not going into technical details, just to trigger your imagination." (Figure 1-13)

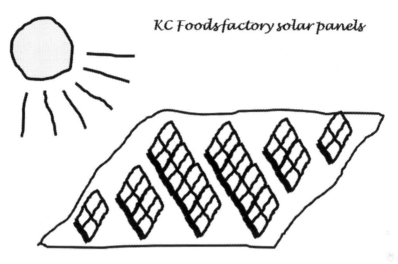

Figure 1-13. *Solar panels on KC Foods factory roof*

"Can it be," Collin continues, "that even with a successful installation of your solar panels, KC Foods might still not be satisfied or that you make limited or no profit?"

"Uh, well, we did have some friction between KC Foods and our project manager, but he was loaded with other work and had some issues at home. There were also some discussions on some defects and payment for extra work ... bottom line of this project was not much profit left anymore when everything was sorted out. But I guess we will get some future business at KC Foods with which we can make up."

Meanwhile, Collin has already started to update the diagram specifically to the solar panel project of SES at KC Foods and responds, "So, the delivery and installation of these solar panels provided an indirect result that at best could turn into achieved business benefits for SES, if other factors where supportive as well."

"And surely," Collin adds to complete his point. "there must be more business benefits. However, not evident from this conventional definition of project objectives. There must be additional benefits that your project can achieve that ares important for SES's future. And what are SES's goals?" (Figure 1-14)

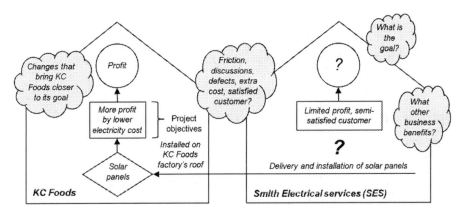

Figure 1-14. *Installed solar panels at SES' customer KC Foods*

This explicit focus on the organization (the customer or user) that implements the project product(s) within itself or its environment, and the absence of the other organization (the supplier) that delivers the project result and its absent direct benefits, is characteristic for this existing, conventional definition of project objectives: it represents a customer perspective and no supplier perspective on project objectives. To recapture, within organizations, project success might be linked to organizational success via project objectives and business benefits. For customers, project success is directly and instantly linked to organizational success (represented by the customer perspective on project objectives). However, for suppliers, there is no such direct or instant link. In line with this absence of a direct link between project actions and business benefits for the supplier, project success might not directly lead to organizational success for the project supplier.

Collin concludes today's session with a question.

"What about the supplier perspective on project success criteria and project objectives? Does it exist, and if so, what does it look like?"

And he draws another cloud next to the supplier's house: the supplier perspective on project objectives, with a question mark. (Figure 1-15)

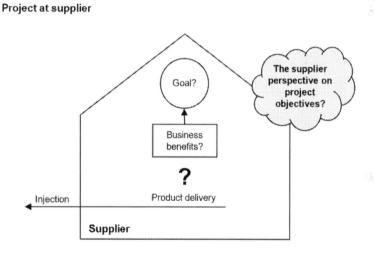

Figure 1-15. *What is the supplier perspective on project objectives?*

The Absent Supplier Perspective Further Explored

An important business and project management model is the iron triangle, also called the *triple constraint* or *project triangle* (Figure 1-16), initially contains the three constraints—time, quality, and cost—but later extended with other constraints, such as scope.

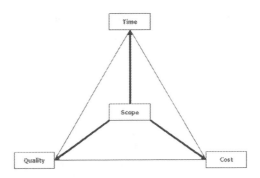

Figure 1-16. *Iron triangle of project management (Atkinson, 1999)*

While its origins are unclear, the iron triangle has been used since at least the 1950s, and in his paper, Robert Atkinson identifies the following.[15]

- The quality of work is constrained by the project's budget, deadlines, and scope.

- The project manager can trade between constraints.

- Changes in one constraint necessitate changes in others to compensate, or quality will suffer.

For example, a project can be completed faster by increasing the budget or cutting the scope. Similarly, increasing scope may require equivalent increases in budget and schedule. Cutting the budget without adjusting the schedule or scope will lead to lower quality. In practice, however, trading between constraints is not always possible. For example, spending money (and people) on a fully staffed project can slow it down.

Moreover, in poorly run projects, it is often impossible to improve budget, schedule, or scope without adversely affecting quality. The triangle is used to analyze projects. It is often misused to define success as delivering the required scope, at a reasonable quality, within the

---

[15] Atkinson, 1999

established budget and schedule. The triangle is therefore considered insufficient as a model of project success because it omits crucial dimensions of success, including impact on stakeholders, learning, and user satisfaction.

Atkinson, however, proposes a new framework by separating success criteria into one delivery stage, the iron triangle, and three post-delivery stages. The iron triangle has scope, cost, time, and quality as its criteria for the delivery stage. The post-delivery stages consist of the following.

- **information systems**: maintainability, reliability, validity, and information quality use

- **organizational benefits**: improved efficiency, improved effectiveness, increased profits, strategic goals, organizational learning and reduced waste

- **stakeholder benefits**: satisfied users, social and environmental impact, personal development, professional learning, contractors profits, capital suppliers, content project team and economic impact to surrounding community

The base iron triangle focuses on the customer perspective, concerned with direct aspects and instant results of the project itself. The three post-delivery stages however, although still project delivery from a customer perspective, identify various criteria that are involved in project execution and therefore applicable to the supplier perspective as well. For example, organizational benefits, such as improved efficiency, organizational learning and social impact; or stakeholder benefit, such as personal development and professional learning.

To further identify examples of a supplier perspective on project objectives, project success criteria (as introduced earlier) are now further investigated. One study identifies 13 separate success criteria: functional performance; meeting technical specifications; meeting schedule goal; meeting budget; fulfilling customer needs; solving a customer's problem; the extent to which the customer is using the product; customer satisfaction; commercial success; creating a larger market share; creating a new market, creating a new product line; and developing a new technology. Besides various direct project or customer related success criteria, creating a larger market share, a new market, or a new product line, and developing a new technology, are examples of indirect or supplier related success criteria. Another study divides project success criteria into four dimensions.[16]

- meeting design goals, which applies to a contract that the customer signs

- benefit to the end user, which refers to the benefit to the customers of the end products

- benefit to the developing organization

- benefit to the technological infrastructure of the country and firms involved in the development process

Benefit to the developing organization—the project supplier—consists of relatively high profit, opening a new market, creating a new product line, developing a new technological development, and increasing positive reputation.

Various other papers study project success criteria and define project success in five metrics (success criteria areas).[17]

- **Project efficiency** is a short-term metric concerned with whether the project was completed according to plan.

---

[16] Shenhar and Renier, 1996; Sadeh et al.,2000
[17] Sadeh et al, 2000; Chan, 2004; Agarwal, 2006; Turner, 2012; Siddique, 2016; Shenhar and Dvir,2007

- **Client impact** represents the main stakeholders and should clearly show how the project improved the client's business.

- **Impact on team** assesses the team's satisfaction and the indirect investment that the organization made in the team members, including further qualifications and professional and managerial skills development.

- **Commercial and direct success** is related to the project's commercial success and contribution to the organization's final results.

- **Preparing for the future** reflects how well the project helped the organization prepare its infrastructure for the future, and how it created new opportunities.

These five areas, although still defined from a customer perspective, identify various criteria involved in project execution and result delivery, and therefore applicable to the supplier perspective.

In one study (software development) project success and failure is considered from the supplier's perspective, concluding that in addition to project management success criteria (meeting time, cost, functionality and quality goals), there is an emphasis on meeting business goals, presented in terms of having short-term or long-term business success for the supplier. They extract three criteria for project success from the supplier's perspective: customer satisfaction, short-term business success for the supplier such as profit, and long-term business success for the supplier such as future business or long-term business benefits. Other studies identify that, while earlier research stresses the integration of suppliers and their diverse technological capabilities as a core capability of systems integrator firms, research on ways in which this integration is achieved in practice remains scant and rarely considers the suppliers' perspective to integration. And a study of suppliers of materials and components in construction projects and their relationships with contractors and designers concludes that suppliers are one of the most neglected research categories in the construction industry.[18]

New approaches have appeared to project management, leading to refocusing the goals of project management to make them customer and stakeholder-based; however, they fail to make the step to include the supplier as an important stakeholder as well. Where the views of three main stakeholders (project owners, administrators, and end users) are often identified as paramount to project success's judgment, the project supplier is often left out as an important stakeholder.[19] One paper studies the differences and the need to consider both the client and vendor (customer and supplier) perspective in evaluating success in internationally sourced information technology projects. It concludes that earlier studies primarily ignored the supplier perspective and that studies considering both the customer and the supplier perspectives are comparatively rare.[20]

One guide to risk management states that consideration of the objectives of key suppliers in seeking to become involved with a particular project is often overlooked, as is their assessment of what they see as the key project risks and how they intend to deal with them. The assumption is often made that they will be entirely motivated by profit. While this will remain an underlying motivation, the chances of successful collaboration are greatly enhanced where both client and key suppliers have mutually compatible objectives. Although this consideration demonstrates a perspective on the supplier, it still pursues alignment with the customer's project objectives. It does not demonstrate a focus on the project supplier's objectives. In general, most definitions of project failure or success do not

---

[18] Savolainen et al.,2012; Ahola et al, 2017; Sariola, 2018

[19] Velayudhan, 2016; Kerzner, 2009

[20] Haried and Ramamurthy, 2009

consider the supplier's point of view, and studies taking both the customer and the supplier into account are relatively rare.[21]

One study of publications on the subject concludes that two approaches to project success exist, namely the process approach and the product approach: according to the process approach, success relates to being on time, within budget, and conform specifications. These are usually the formal project goals and are declared to be complied with to be successful. According to the product approach, success relates to added value for the organization, benefits for the users, and satisfaction of users and line management. Despite the formal goals of the process approach, project managers are measured against these product goals.[22] Another extensive study conducted a systematic literature review on software development project success and failure from the customer's or supplier perspective, including an extensive table in which articles are classified in accordance with their perspective. They noticed that the number of articles that cover only the supplier perspective (4 articles) or both perspectives (6 articles) is very small compared to the number of articles that cover only the customer perspective (61 articles). However, it should be noted that most of the articles discuss in-house software development projects. Examples of topics in articles involving the supplier perspective consist, among others, of the impact of project risks on project success, the impact on vendor's performance by vendor's trust in the client and client's control over the vendor, supplier perspective to integration of their technological capabilities and the supplier perspective on the electricity industries' downstream capacity to recognize and assess the potential value of innovations.[23]

---

[21] Be CC, 2013; Haried, 2009

[22] Heemstra, 2011

[23] Ahonen and Savolainen, 2011; Levina and Ross, 2003; Heiskanen et al, 2008; Martinsuo and Ahola, 2010; Ahonen, 2011; Frödell, 2011; Kasse and Johansen, 2014; MacKerron et al, 2015; Hellström et al, 2016; Lehtimäki et al, 2018; Taylor, 2007; Mao et al, 2008; Ahola et al, 2017; Sköld et al, 2018

However, despite such examples of studies involving project success, project objectives, and project suppliers, explicit studies of a perspective from the supplier of the project-on-project success criteria and project objectives—as opposed to a perspective from the customer—remain rare in the project management field.

> *Collin finishes the session by drawing a simple sketch on the flip chart, with two people standing near the edge of two cliffs with a gap in between.*

> *"And this, this absent supplier perspective on project objectives, is what we simply refer to as the gap," Collin says while writing "THE GAP" in large capital letters above the sketch. He concludes, "The gap between project and organizational success for the project supplier." (Figure 1-17)*

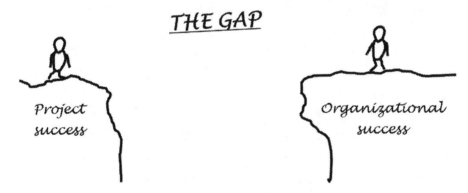

Figure 1-17. *The gap between project and organizational success for the project supplier*

The Conventional Goal of Making Money

Although not stated explicitly in the conventional definition of a project objective (Figure 1-6), it should be no surprise that for most commercial companies, the main goal is to make money. And, where non-commercial organizations likely have another main goal, managing their funding vs. cost remains important to their continuity.

> *"I have more homework for you," Collin says while he hands out a red colored book to Julie and Jr.*
>
> *"I promise you, once you start reading you will finish it in a couple of days. The book is not meant to be studied in detail. It is just to get you motivated to think differently about your company and how you manage it."*
>
> *"I heard about him and his system. What was it, constraints theory or something?"*
>
> *"Yes, this is Eliyahu Goldratt's first book, The Goal, and his Theory of Constraints method. You will hear more about him and his theory during the coming weeks."*

Eliyahu M. Goldratt was an influential Israeli business consultant and originator of various well known and successful process and production techniques, such as the TOC, the thinking processes, and Drum-Buffer-Rope. He wrote successful business novels, such as *The Goal, It's Not Luck,* and *Critical Chain.* Goldratt was born in 1947 in British Mandatory Palestine and obtained his bachelor's degree from Tel Aviv University and master's and PhD degrees from Bar-Ilan University in Ramat Gan, Israel. He left the academic world early in his career to join a private company that supplied software for production environments. After publishing his first books based on his experience working for this company, Goldratt finally left and created the Avraham Y. Goldratt Institute in 1985 to promote his TOC method and its worldwide implementation in business. After many further work and publications, Goldratt retired from the institute in 1997 and created the Goldratt Group in 2000.

As part of his theory, Goldratt defines the following in *The Goal*.[24]

There is only one goal, no matter what the company.

The goal is to make money.

Everything else is just a means to achieve the goal.

Supplier benefits are an important project success criterion for a long-term relationship between a supplier and a customer. A supplier needs to run a profitable business; therefore, the overall project portfolio of the supplier needs to make a profit in the long run. Generally, for-profit or non-profit organizations need to secure financial funding. All firms aim to achieve a competitive advantage in relation to their rivals. A competitive advantage enables a firm to earn profits higher than the average profit earned by competitors (excess profits).

Furthermore, extensive research identifies stock market value as a key indicator of company success.[25] Although these studies do not conclude that profit is the ultimate purpose or goal, it is one of the results of being great. However, a difference of opinion remains regarding the main goal of a company.

As I will show later, many companies, researchers, and authors in the field claim different ultimate purposes or goals of a commercial company, however, it is justified to conclude that money is at the forefront of day-to-day operations of any organization. Even non-profit organizations have money as an important constraint as well, to be able to run their organizations, but is it the ultimate goal? Making money seems the conventional goal of commercial companies, but should it be the ultimate goal? (Figure 1-18).

---

[24] Goldratt and Cox, 1984
[25] Pokorny, 2011; Stonehouse and Snowdon, 2007; Porter, 1985; Collins, 2001

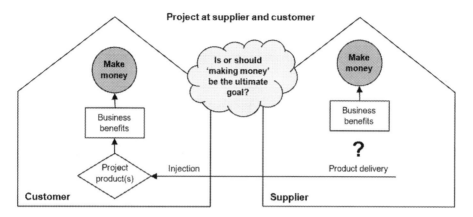

Figure 1-18. *Conventional goal of commercial companies to make money*

The Project Supplier's Problems

To further investigate and identify worst-case problems of a biased customer perspective and an absent supplier perspective on project objectives combined with a conventional main goal to make money at companies, I further focus on a typical project supplier most affected by such effects, characterized as follows.

- a for-profit (commercial) company

- delivering projects to an external customer (organization)

- a multi-project environment with limited resources (e.g., human resources) for all ongoing projects

- small to medium-sized

- without extensive and matured organizational project management procedures embedded within their organization to manage their projects

- or growing fast in size or revenue

- or operating in a turbulent, continuously changing business field

- or operating in a highly competitive business field

Collin elaborates.

"Examples of such typical project suppliers are a painting company doing all paintwork at an office construction project, or a steel fabrication company fabricating steelwork for another commercial company."

Providing Less Than Possible or Even Insufficient Benefit

The bias toward the customer perspective and absence of a specific supplier perspective on project objectives might lead to less awareness of the fact that with an absence of such a direct link between all potential project objectives and business benefits for the supplier, project success might not directly lead to complete organizational success for the project supplier. In other words, less awareness that something else might be required or available. This is the gap between project and organizational success for the project supplier. This lesser awareness might lead to circumstances with less focus on all available benefits for the supplier, and thereby, the project might not provide the best possible benefit for the supplier itself; thus, providing less than possible or even insufficient benefit from the project for the project supplier itself. A recent study researched the early concept of the iron triangle and its project success criteria or controls (cost, time, and quality) and how this has changed over the last 45 years. The question is raised about why project management remains reluctant to adopt other criteria besides the iron triangle, such as stakeholder benefits against which projects can be assessed. Such reluctance is still present today.[26]

Extending the iron triangle, the Prince2 project management method defines six control variables involved in any project; therefore, six aspects of project performance to be managed: cost, timescale, quality, scope, risk, and benefit. It places project objectives into the context of achieving goals for each of these six control variables. Furthermore, a project can bring three types of benefits to an organization.[27]

- **Direct savings** bring direct money savings.

- **Quantifiable benefits** do not bring direct money, but the benefit is nevertheless measurable.

- **Non-quantifiable benefits** do not bring direct money and are not quantifiable but lead indirectly to direct savings or quantifiable benefits.

Although benefits are a control variable, in practice, without an explicit focus on the supplier itself, a bias toward the customer perspective might keep the focus mainly on direct customer benefit instead of its benefit. This bias toward the customer perspective can also be found within most used project management methods. As you will see, a project management method is a system of practices, techniques, procedures, and rules to conduct project management in a structured way.

Usually, the project, the project manager, and the project team officially start from a project initiating document, sometimes called the *project initiation document*, or the *project brief* in Prince2, or the *project charter* in PMI. Such an initiation document gives the project manager the authority to apply resources to project activities. It formally authorizes a

---

[26] Pollack and Adler, 2018; Atkinson, 1999

[27] Prince2, 2017

project and documents the business needs, such as measurable project objectives and related success criteria. It also describes the business case, explaining how the project supports the business strategy, which is the business strategy of the user of the project result, the customer.[28]

This project initiation document, the way the project manager executes this and how the organization rewards this, usually tends to focus on customer-focused project objectives and project controls (such as cost, time, quality, organization, and information), which align with his day-to-day operations; and tend to focus less on its own supplier focused project objectives or benefits. Although benefits such as acquiring process assets, lessons learned, or training of employees might be a focus in many organizations, including project suppliers, it might still be ad hoc, incidental, or perhaps driven by certain personally motivated employees only, and usually such objectives are not included in the project initiation document.

"Julie, do you recognize this within SES?" Collin asks Julie.

She looks a bit caught on surprise but responds. "Well, we do indeed have a project initiation form. And yes, I guess it might be filled in a bit as a standard process from a template that our project managers take from their last project."

"Exactly, and what is the added value of that?" Collin asks.

"Yes, I guess everybody, management, and the project team, sort of want to get the process and forms done because it needs to be ticked off for our corporate procedures," Jr. adds.

"And," Collin continues while he looks at Jr. "could it sometimes happen, despite having a formal project initiation in place, that you, as a stakeholder John, communicate new expectations to your project team, which were not included in the initiation?"

---

[28] Prince2, 2017; PMI, 2021

In practice, despite having a formal project initiation in place, stakeholders tend to address new expectations or objectives, which were not included (yet) in the initiation document, to the project team whenever they arise during the project. Which is good in a way, better late than never if they are valid, however, it is not structured and therefore disruptive to the project, and the surprise part could be avoided.

I do not conclude that project initiation documents and project management methods are wrong. They do aim at the primary and important objective of the project to provide the project product(s) as per user or customer expectations and pursue the project controls, which is good. However, something is missing related to the project's benefits for the supplier organization. Even without a biased project initiation document, it is natural for the project manager or team to focus on their project alone and not immediately on the benefit of other projects within their organization.

> *"Sounds familiar, project managers that focus only on their own project? Collin checks again.*

> *"Yes," Jr. answers. "We often experience that our project managers prefer certain project team members, who obviously are the most experienced, or who they just prefer to work with."*

> *"So that is an example of the absence of the supplier perspective. However, the interesting thing is that it also offers an opportunity. You might be able to optimize efficient use of your employees if certain project managers are a good match with certain technical specialists or other team members, either experienced or less experienced."*

> *"Mm, I haven't looked at it that way," Jr. responds and starts thinking about it.*

> *"Let's hold that topic for later though," Collin says while he notices that John starts thinking about this alternative, and he steps back to the earlier question.*

"Coming back, I am sure you think differently about these project manager's preferences, don't you?"

"Yes, we often have discussions with some of our project managers explaining that we must divide our resources evenly over all projects or even have a new inexperienced resource being trained within his project team with experienced team members. Then a discussion starts because they say we also want them to get the best project result possible."

Then Julie jumps into the discussion and adds.

"I also see that some of our project managers look for quick fixes, some existing knowledge or a template they can use on their projects, however, are never caught spending much time to feed back lessons learned themselves to other teams."

"Yes, and might that be because he is not specifically recognized or rewarded for this or that he simply never gets the time for it?"

John and Julie look at each other and start seeing the point that Collin is trying to make.

Part-time Project Team Members

The number of hours per week that key team members are assigned to the project has a distinctive influence on project processes—project management and product-oriented processes—and team cooperation. Organizational planning, staff acquisition and team development can only work well when team members are assigned a certain minimum duration on the project. Performing these tasks well requires the opportunity to align the team member's main objective with the project's main objective.

A typical feature of small to medium-sized projects is that part of its project team members are only part-time assigned to the project and part-time work on other projects as well. When a team member is not full-time working on the project, commitment can never be fully for that respective project, which can significantly impact the project's success. Even when in consultation with the line manager, the respective project has been assigned as the main priority, there are still other projects to work on, or personal commitment might still not be prioritized on the respective project. Sooner or later, resource or priority conflicts will arise between the various projects that the team member is working on.

Furthermore, in case the team member is not working full-time on the project, he cannot be temporarily reassigned by the project manager to support with completing a certain other short-term or priority task that might be linked to change that could provide a significant benefit to the organization when completed (in time). Instead, if the team member is full-time assigned to the project, such an agreement could be made within the boundaries of the project (team) without required consultation with line management or other projects. Therefore, team and commitment building is also more challenging within the project team for part-time project team members.

> *"Hi, George. Can I have a worth with you? I need your help,"* *project manager Elena asks George, a procurement engineer working part-time on the KC Foods project, reporting to Naomi, head of procurement with SES.*
>
> *"How can I help you?" George asks in return.*
>
> *"Well, you heard about the scope of work document for the movable solar panels that we need to finish this Friday, which is already a week behind our postponed date."*
>
> *"Yeah ..." George answers slowly and reluctantly.*
>
> *"Well, I need all the help we can get to finish that scope of work. And a major part concerns the break down structure and description of the hardware components, while Christos and Daniel need all their time working on the automation and software requirements." Elena explains and continues.*

"To be honest, I see no other solution than that you assist with writing this section."

"I was already afraid you would go in that direction. You do know that writing the scope of work is not my job. That is the work for engineering and project management and is what I should normally receive, not prepare!"

"I know," Elena answers and now sighs reluctantly. "but that is also why you understand how it should be written, and I have no other options."

"But I do not have time for this, you know that I have to work on three other projects as well, with some priorities this week."

"Is there no way you can discuss this with Naomi to find a solution to support? It only takes one or two days, perhaps even less?" Elena tries.

"Yeah, well, remember last month when I needed some help from engineering with sorting out the specifications to source those long lead items? I didn't get help then either, did I? So why should I help them now if they don't help me when necessary?"

"Can I otherwise discuss this with Naomi myself?" Elena asks.

"Yes, of course, be my guest. But I really don't have time this week!"

Added Value

Even without structural and active management of project objectives during the project execution, the customer is usually provided with many possible business benefits after implementing the project result within its organization. However, the project supplier, instead, without active management, could be left with minor possible business benefits. On this basis, a professional project supplier without such active management of project objectives can still end up with a satisfied customer, an acceptable profit, a more experienced project manager, specialist, or new engineer who gained useful experience, and a report on lessons learned could be established; all clearly business benefits. So, even without active management, this could be achieved.

But what if the project supplier is less fortunate? What if the experienced project manager or specialist leaves the organization during or after the project, or what if he prevented the inexperienced engineer from joining the project team and gaining experience? What if the project manager or specialist does stay within the organization and is not motivated to transfer any of his gained knowledge and experience to the organization by lessons learned into new processes, guidelines, or tools? In that case, the project supplier does have the problem that less or minimum added value is being transferred from the project to the organization.

Misalignment Between Organization and Project Regarding Continuous Improvement

Within many organizations, there exists a misalignment between the organization and the project (team) regarding continuous improvement. Where the organization and sometimes its specific organizational department try to focus on continuous improvement through interaction with the project teams, usually by introducing (new) initiatives or procedures that the project teams must adhere to, the project teams are troubled by more urgent (other) challenges and objectives in their day-to-day activities. It has to do with the difference between importance and urgency.

Urgent topics and problems take most of their daily focus and time, while important topics and problems, such as continuous organization improvement, are left with little remaining focus and time.

Newly introduced initiatives or procedures by the organizational departments—through email, department meetings, or other means of communication such as intranet communication groups—get short-time attention; however, after that slowly fade away in the continuous follow-up of new instructions or messages. Such initiatives or procedures are revived now and then and face the same faith all over again. The new initiatives or procedures might get lost if they are not properly embedded in a strong, long-term, and daily observably structure within the organization and the daily work of the project team members and if they are not properly aligned with the management of tasks and rewards of the project team members.

A Core Quadrant Analysis of Innovations

"Today, we will explore examples from practice to get a better understanding of project supplier problems. For this, we will use the so-called core quadrant to investigate an example of a conflict between opposite objectives caused by the absent supplier perspective on project objectives." Collin starts.

"The core quadrant is based on the concept of The Core Quality by Daniel Ofman and three strongly related concepts: The Pitfall, The Challenge, and The Allergy." Collin introduces, while turning the flip chart, showing a prepared diagram of the core quadrant. He further explains the concept without going into too much detail, as the diagram is mostly self-explanatory." [29] *(Figure 1-19)*

---

[29] Ofman, 1995

Figure 1-19. *The core quadrant (Ofman, 1995)*

"We will use this method today to analyze innovations at SES."

Julie raises an eyebrow but is careful not to say anything. But John is looking at her with the same reluctance. They both know where this is going, a tough subject today, which they tried to avoid until now, but it had to come up sooner or later.

"Now, John," Collin starts and looks at him. "Let's take your sister's innovations as the core quality of SES. Put aside for the moment if you agree with that or not. What do you see as the biggest risk or concern?"

"It is too risky, too much investment without a guaranteed profitable product."

"OK, let's summarize that more exaggerated to get the point by reckless inventions. A result of innovations going too far."

"Yes, that is a nice one!" Jr. agrees, although Julie looks a bit reserved.

"What is the positive opposite of that, like what you might prefer?"

"More structured or planned development."

"Yes, let's call that careful development—the clear opposite of reckless."

"OK, we got something going here." Collin approves and turns to John. "Now, what happens if we take that too far?"

"Well, then nothing happens, no new things, no new business, and no happy future customers," Jr. responds.

"Yes, let's write that down as conservatism, no new technology. With that culture, innovation is experienced as difficult." With that, Collin completes the core quadrant on the flip chart, and he lets both think it over for a couple of minutes. (Figure 1-20)

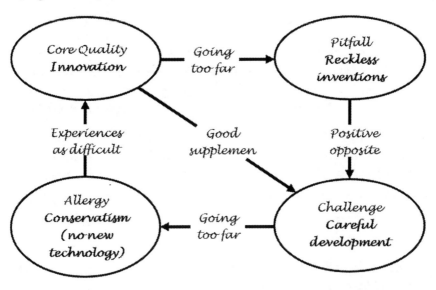

Figure 1-20. *Core quadrant example of Innovations at SES*

"Now, the diagonal arrow states that careful development is a good supplement to innovations. In other words, they can balance each other. Now, does this make any sense to you?"

"But before you answer," Collin continues immediately, "we will park this topic for now, so think about and later, we will come up with a solution for how to manage such type of conflict between objectives within SES."

A Current Reality Tree of Process Assets

"First of all, thank you all for joining this session today. John and Julie wanted you to participate as representatives of all departments within SES." Collin starts this morning and continues.

"You don't know yet what we are investigating and developing during these sessions. However, your input today is very important. You are the most important asset of SES, with all the knowledge and experience that SES possesses. And, you know about the various challenges that SES is facing, and" Collin looks at Julie and Jr. and continues "that John and Julie are struggling with this and currently do not know how to bring SES back on the right track toward a successful future."

After a 15-minute introduction and recap of what John and Julie learned during their first sessions, Collin stands up and walks to the flip chart in the corner.

"Now, let's start." He says, and he smiles without anybody noticing, hearing someone in the back softly smirking about the old-fashioned flip charts.

"Today, we will look at another example of providing less benefit from your projects to your organization. As explained, this is caused by a bias toward the customer perspective and absence of a specific supplier perspective on project objectives."

53

"Yes, which you call the gap." Jr. steps in.

"Yes, correct, John," Collin confirms with a satisfied smile.

When an organization has executed several projects during a certain period, some experience and lessons learned from those projects might lead to templates, procedures, or guidelines (also called *process assets*) that can be reused on a new project instead of starting from nothing. The degree to which such useful process assets become available can vary from nothing or limited to a very high quantity or quality. Worst case, there is no lessons learned process to learn from former projects, and no development and reuse of any process assets, an extreme case of "providing less than possible or even insufficient benefit from the project for the project supplier itself."

To study a worst-case reality of process assets within a project supplier, I will use one of Goldratt's thinking processes,[30] incorporated in Goldratt's TOC method, the current reality tree (CRT). The CRT is a type of cause-and-effect diagram leading to undesirable effect(s) (UDEs) in the reality of the studied subject. A CRT is constructed by taking one or more UDEs or one main UDE at the top of the diagram, with starting points, statements, and assumptions combined in AND or OR links, leading to or connecting these UDEs (a circle marks an AND link through the concerned arrows).

"For example," Collin says while drawing some rectangles and arrows and continues explaining. "The statement that 'some employees work too hard' AND the assumption that 'some employees who work too hard will get overstressed,' leads to the UDE that 'some employees might report sick with a burn-out.'" (Figure 1-21)

---

[30] Goldratt, 1994

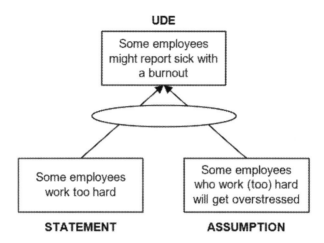

Figure 1-21. *Example of statement and assumption leading to UDE*

Statements and assumptions can be negative or positive or have no distinct classification. UDEs, however, are negative (undesired). Positive statements and assumptions can lead to (undesirable) UDEs. For example, if a positive assumption is linked with an opposite negative assumption by an "and" link, causing conflict. Also, without a clear distinction between positives and negatives, two opposite statements or assumptions can also lead to a UDE by causing conflict or confusion. The two opposite assumptions of (1) management putting pressure on employees to work hard and (2) management putting pressure on employees to take care of their health and take vacations can lead to the UDE of a frustrated or confused employee, which can lead to the following UDEs. And starting points describe activities as initiators for the CRT without any assumptions included (Figure 1-22).

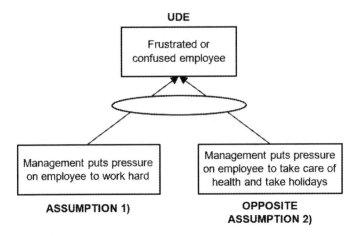

Figure 1-22. *Example of assumption and opposite assumption leading to UDE*

To better understand the result of providing less or limited benefits, I further analyze the worst-case possible (current) reality of process assets, mostly by identifying worst-case exaggerated statements, assumptions, and UDEs in the CRT diagram.

> *"So, as part of your homework, what main undesirable effect did you come up with for today?" Collin asks with a smile.*

> *"Well, a typical concern at SES is, although perhaps not the most critical, let's keep that one for later, is how to deal with lessons learned." John Jr. responds with a smile, taking the initiative to show that he is also into this process with Collin.*

> *"OK, let's work that one out in a current reality tree, and I propose to combine this one with process assets to make it even more explicit because lessons learned and process assets are highly interlinked, as we will see later," Collin responds and continues.*

"At the bottom of the CRT, we start with the main starting point—'Delivery of the project product(s),' linked to its result—'Injecting the project product(s) within the customer.' Furthermore, we have as a statement that 'Project supplier organizations usually lead in downsizing but lag in expansion requirements for staffing' and the assumption that 'Staffing requirements of project supplier organizations vary continuously'" (Figure 1-23)

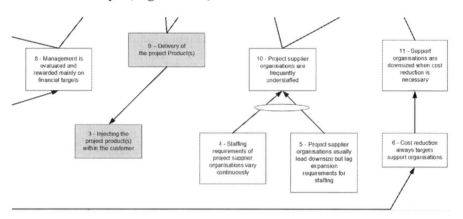

Figure 1-23.   The bottom of CRT of process assets, including the main starting point

"And in the center of the CRT, we have various elements, such as the starting point, assumptions, statements, and UDEs." (Figure 1-24)

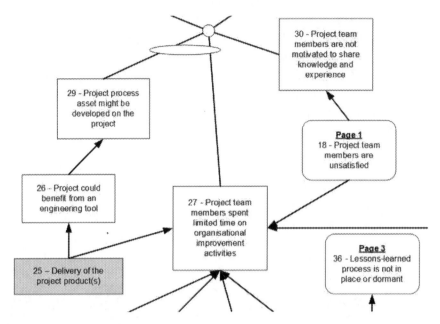

Figure 1-24. *Centre of CRT of process assets, including various elements*

"Finally, at the top of the CRT, we put the main UDE for process assets, 'The new project does not benefit from implementation of any organizational process assets.' A bold statement, but as I said, let's exaggerate today!"

And Collin draws another rectangle and arrow.

"This is caused by the UDE that 'Organizational process asset is not or unsuccessfully implemented in a new project.' This UDE will likely have several statements and assumptions as input, and it has, in this case, also as input the starting point of 'Delivery of the project product(s),' your main project activity as a project supplier, as we analyzed last week." (Figure 1-25)

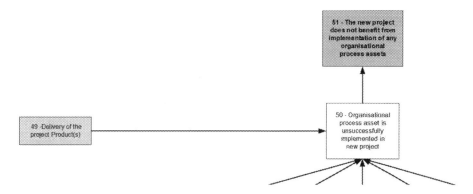

Figure 1-25. *Top of CRT of process assets, including the main UDE*

The complete current reality tree of process assets is split into four figures in Appendix I. In its totality, this might look like a rather complicated diagram. However, you can browse this CRT by following various paths from starting points, statements, and UDEs, from bottom to top. You start on page 1 of 4 and follow your way up to page 4 of 4, starting at the bottom of each page and ending at the top of each page. UDEs on the top reference one of the other pages, where the same UDE is repeated to enable us to follow the paths on that page from bottom to top again.

More Examples of Project Supplier Problems: SWOT Analysis

"Based on your last week's homework, today we are going to fill more flip charts with various problems or undesirable effects at SES." Collin starts the session. "However, we will also look at existing strengths or opportunities because I'm sure it's not all bad! These flip charts will be used as reference material in later sessions where we will work toward the solution."

"To help you focus on the pros and cons, we will divide each flip chart into the four SWOT quadrants. I guess that is familiar to you?" Collin asks.

"Well, we do now and then use a SWOT analysis. John intro-duced this a couple of years ago." Jr. answers proudly.

"Ha, ha, yes, we know something about improvement pro-cesses." Julie fills in and eagerly continues before Collin can respond.

"I guess we can start writing down last week's example of that lessons learned meeting for the KC Foods project," Julie says while she grabs a marker, then confesses.

"Well, to be honest, we do know how to wrap up lessons learned on our projects, but the real challenge is to get that information over to the following project teams and imple-ment those lessons in the new projects."

They all start writing furiously, and several flip charts are filled an hour later.

During one of his interview sessions with SES employees, Collin talks with Jenna.

"Jenna, you are working with Elena and Christos on the KC Foods project, correct?"

"Yes, I am an electrical engineer and work on the high voltage supply connection to the grid," Jenna answers Collin.

"I will throw you in the deep end and ask you some questions I need you to answer honestly. Are you aware of the main objectives of your project?" Collin asks.

"Well, not in detail, but," Jenna hesitates, thinks for a moment, and then continues. "Well, we have a deadline with penalties, and uh, we have a scope of work to fulfill and a budget."

"Yes, very well. Those are all examples of project controls, such as time, cost, and quality. Do you know any other objectives?"

"Uh, no, not really. What do you mean by other objectives? Jenna answers.

"Are you aware of any other objectives, like from internal stakeholders, such as the management team and the owners John Jr. and Julie?"

"No, not really, I guess?"

"Are you involved in any sessions to discuss targets and expectations from the organization?"

"No, not really," Jenna answers again, now looking a bit upset.

"What about lessons learned?"

"Ah, yes, of course, but are those objectives as well?" Jenna now answers a bit reassured but confused again as well.

But Collin does not answer and pushes on. "Or what about the calculation tools you use for calculating the power supply, do you sometimes make an update or improvement of that?"

Jenna thinks about this and remembers the recent updates she made but still did not send to Christos. In fact, she is not sure what to do with it to make sure that it does not get lost within SES?

Based on further sessions and talks, a final SWOT analysis of project business and management at SES is completed. (Figure 1-26, Figure 1-27)

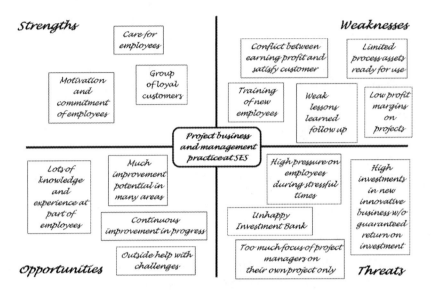

Figure 1-26. *SWOT analysis of project business and management at SES (1/2)*

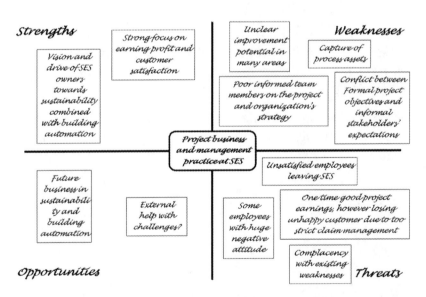

Figure 1-27. *SWOT analysis of project business and management at SES (2/2)*

Fewer Benefits Due to a Primary Focus on Commercial Objectives

Earlier, we explored the conventional goal of a commercial company to make money. Later, we will explore examples of introducing the collaborative importance of company owner concerns, employee concerns, and market concerns. Even in those examples, the practical measurements to judge the impact of local decisions on the global goal are defined by financial measurements only.

Dr. K.J. Youngman further elaborates on the theory that these three entities are important to the same degree. Making money, however, is much more tangible than the other two. It's the only one that can be measured. Goldratt and Fox refer to the *cost bridge* to bridge between the company's operational decisions and the company's success (Figure 1-28).[31]

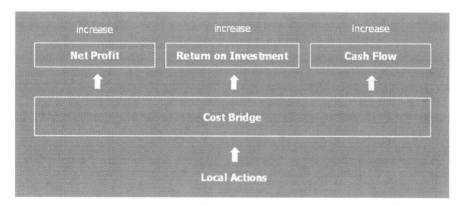

Figure 1-28. *Goldratt and Fox, cost bridge between operational decisions and success, with fundamental measurements net profit, return on investment and cash flow (Youngman, 2021)*

A check of (commercial) productivity toward the goal to secure a commercial company's future is conducted by measuring the following fundamental measurements.

---

[31] Youngman, 2021; Goldratt and Cox, 1984; Goldratt and Fox, 1986

- net profit

- return on investment (ROI)

- cash flow

Youngman continues his approach to measurements to judge the impact of local decisions on the global goal with financial measurements only: the fundamental operating measurements (future) throughput, inventory, and operating expense on the bottom-line results of net profit, return on investment, and cash flow. For a better understanding of the productivity way of thinking and a more strategic approach, he transfers the fundamental measurements of Goldratt and Fox into the following fundamental operating measurements, including the future condition (Figure 1-29).

- (future) throughput

- inventory

- operating expense

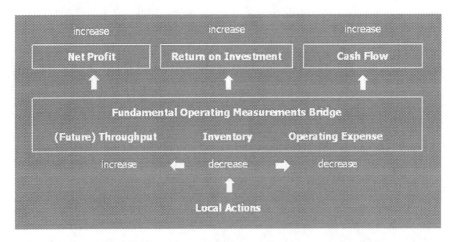

Figure 1-29. *Fundamental operating measurements (future) throughput, inventory, and operating expense (Youngman, 2021)*

As a result of the conventional goal of commercial companies to make money, in general, at commercial companies, fundamental measurements of success are financially based, which leads to a primary focus on commercial project objectives and thereby less on other important project objectives for the project supplier.

At non-profit organizations, focusing on securing sufficient funds vs. cost might distract from a primary focus on their organizational goals.

"Does this sound familiar?" Collin asks Julie and John.

"Yes. We are always focused on our finances because our cash flow is a monthly struggle, and our revenue is a challenge every year." John Jr. explains.

"Yes, our cash flow is definitely a challenge, it's even a question every month if we can timely pay our employee's salaries," Julie adds.

"But we also fight against many other challenges that hurt our future as well, although less immediate and therefore with less urgency in our day-to-day business, until some project is in imminent danger because we do not have the right resources for example." She says and sighs.

"So that distracts your attention from other important activities for your future," Collin asks.

"Definitely," Jr. confirms.

One study looked at the organizational challenges involved in managing two different objectives at the same time: purpose and profits. If you want to build a company that truly motivates its employees, it must have a sense of purpose. Purpose, they find, by its nature, transcends making money. It is about people coming together to do something they believe in and allowing profit to follow as a consequence of it rather than as an end in itself. But there is a paradox, they conclude; it is hard to fulfill a purpose without money, so purpose-driven organizations must rely on donations or benefactors to sustain themselves (as most charities and aid organizations do) or become self-funding through their profits. One of the main findings of their research is that it takes considerable effort for a company to maintain goals that involve working toward a common cause beyond just making money. And that if financial metrics are given too much prominence, they will typically displace a company's nonfinancial, purpose-related goals.[32]

Continuous Improvement

There is good news, however; although this potential is not fully utilized within project suppliers. It is important to emphasize that many organizations—if not all—including project suppliers continuously work on continuous improvement processes within their organizations. Of course, that importance is obvious and not a new revelation. Such continuous improvement touches upon many topics such as improvement of employee satisfaction, improvement of lessons learned processes and process assets, improvement of employee knowledge and experience, decrease of operating expenses by removing so-called *waste processes* or improving communication within the organization. However, in many cases, this is still not clearly linked to its projects and objectives by fully answering the question of how the project can benefit the organization most.

Usually, project team members have their direct project scope as the main priority of their project(s); however, they work on the side on one or more continuous improvement activities. The progress on their project scope is reported within the project progress reporting structure and their performance on their continuous improvement activity within a corporate improvement structure and their competence and appraisal process. However, in many cases, both work activities are not clearly linked or reported in an integrated structure, and priorities will conflict between both important activities.

---

[32] Birkenshaw et al., 2014

Summary

Why are changes to the project supplier's organization and its project execution practices needed?

Change is needed because the project might not provide the highest possible benefit, thus providing less than possible or even insufficient benefit for the project supplier itself due to a bias toward the customer perspective and the absence of a specific supplier perspective on project objectives for the project supplier, or a primary focus on commercial project objectives due to the conventional goal to make money, or because, although continuous improvement is part of many organizations, this is not linked to its projects.

CHAPTER 2

The Goal: Where to Change?

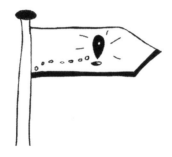

Where should a project supplier change its organization and its project execution practices to enable full utilization of all potential business benefits?

The previous chapter discussed the problems for the project supplier, among others, caused by a bias to the customer perspective, resulting in providing less than possible or even insufficient benefit from its projects for the project supplier itself. But how can we provide the highest possible benefit, or where can we make changes? Whereas several worst cases were analyzed in Chapter 1, this chapter looks at the other end of the spectrum, several best cases. Although extremes, both worst and best case together provide valuable insights in actual practice, usually positioned somewhere in between.

© Reitse van der Wekken 2024
R. van der Wekken, *Project Objectives Management*,
https://doi.org/10.1007/979-8-8688-0956-9_2

Provide the Best Possible Benefit for the Project Supplier

To provide the best possible benefit from projects to the organization of the project supplier requires that all possible and available factors that lead to such achievement are sufficiently present, now and in the future. If, instead, such factors are not sufficiently present or even absent, for example, due to a bias to the customer perspective, not all available business benefits will be achieved. What critical factors, if absent or present, have a critical negative or positive impact on the ability of the supplier to achieve all its available and, thereby, possible business benefits?

First, without sufficient focus on the importance of the future, project objectives connected to future business benefits will get limited attention. A strong focus instead on the future is required.

Next, without urgency within the supplier organization on such project objectives and business benefits from the supplier perspective (to provide added value from the project to the organization) and without criticality of such objectives for the project, the day-to-day attention of the project team might remain focused on project controls such as project cost, time, and quality only. Instead, such urgency is critical.

Without proactive action by the project team, limited additional project objectives might be achieved besides project objectives that lead to immediate business benefits from the project execution and delivery process, such as profit. Instead, proactive action by the project team is necessary.

Without proper follow-up by the organization, even achieved project objectives might remain within the project itself and not lead to actual benefits outside the project and within its organization. Therefore, proper follow-up by the organization is required.

And without sufficient focus on continuous progress, project objectives that might benefit the organization or the next project but with no direct benefit to the project itself, will also not get sufficient focus. A strong sense of urgency for continuous progress is also required within the organization. As explained by John Kotter in his book *A Sense of Urgency*,[1] what is missing and is needed in almost all organizations today is a real sense of urgency, a distinctive attitude, and gut-level feeling that lead people to grab opportunities and avoid hazards to make something important happen today, and constantly shed low-priority activities to move faster and smarter, now.

A Future Reality Tree of Process Assets

As an example of "providing less than possible or even insufficient benefit from the project for the project supplier itself," I studied the worst-case current reality of process assets. However, a study of the opposite, the best-case reality of process assets, provides an example of where to change with the organization to "provide the best possible benefit from the project for the project supplier itself." As concluded, when an organization has executed several projects during a certain period, some experience and lessons learned from those projects might lead to templates, procedures, or guidelines (also called *process assets*) that can be reused on the next project instead of starting from nothing. The degree, however to which such useful process assets become available can vary from nothing or limited to a very high quantity or quality. Best case, a successful lessons-learned process is in place to learn from former projects, and a high quantity and quality of process assets are developed from the project and reused on a new project.

---

[1] Kotter, 2008

To study a best-case reality of process assets within a project supplier, I will use another one of the Goldratt's thinking processes: the future reality tree (FRT)[2]. The FRT is a similar type of cause-and-effect diagram as the future reality tree (CRT), but leads to a desirable effect in the future of the studied subject. The FRT is constructed by taking one or more desirable effect(s) (DEs) or one main DE at the top of the diagram, with starting points, statements, and assumptions combined in "and" or "or" links leading to or connecting these DEs. A FRT can also be created from a CRT by implementing injections that invalidate all statements or assumptions that led to the UDEs. An injection is needed to transform all UDEs of the current reality tree into their opposites, the DEs of the strongly desired new reality.

Collin explains, "At the bottom of the FRT, we start with the main starting point 'Delivery of the project product(s),' linked to the assumption 'Process asset developed on project.'" (Figure 2-1)

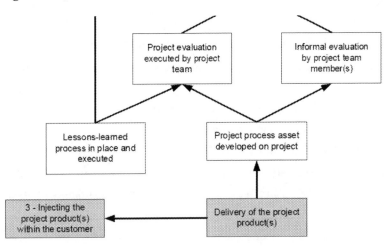

Figure 2-1. *Bottom of FRT of Process assets, including the main starting point*

---

[2] Goldratt, 1994

"With at the top of the FRT the main DE for process assets, 'Provide the highest benefit from the project for the project supplier itself,' with two DEs as input, 'Organizational process asset successfully implemented in project' and 'Project benefits from implemented organizational process asset.'" (Figure 2-2)

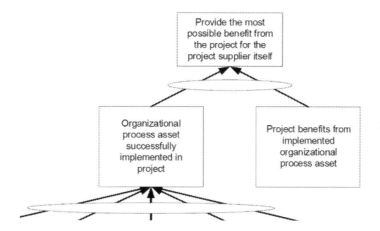

Figure 2-2. *Top of FRT of process assets, including the main DE*

"This is definitely an eye-opener, although perhaps obvious, but it really makes sense and provides insight into what is going on by comparing the current reality tree with the future reality tree of how to deal with process assets and lessons learned on a project and a new project," Julie concludes while taking notes.

The complete future reality tree of process assets is illustrated in Figure 2-3.

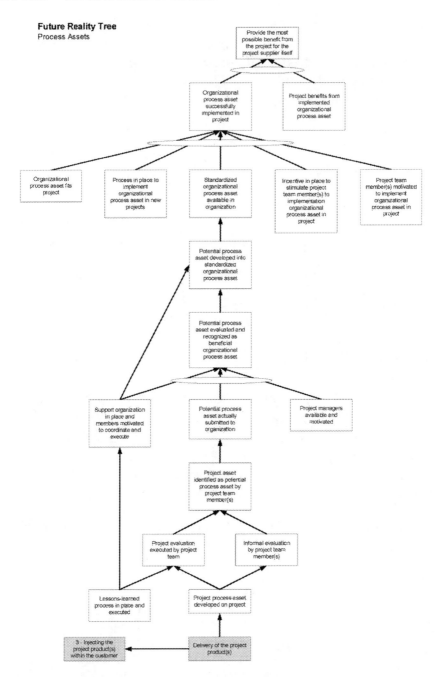

Figure 2-3. *Future reality tree of process assets*

Project and Organizational Culture

Paul Goyette explains that whether they know it or not, every company has a culture and many different types of corporate culture. Some evolve naturally, and some are intentional, but all fit the same definition. When we look at culture, we are looking at the total of the behaviors of all employees; culture is defined by what the organization's people do. Culture should not be confused with your company's mission, vision, and values. The company's mission sets the direction, whereas culture describes the environment around how the mission is achieved, and values define the culture. He next identifies six types of corporate or organizational culture, where an organization might show a mix of multiple cultures or a strong behavior of one culture.[3]

- **Empowered culture**: The embodiment of an empowered culture is when every individual in the organization feels fully engaged and actively participates in the business's success. People initiate new activities that benefit the organization, take ownership of their work, and are willingly responsible for the outcomes. People who prosper in an empowered corporate culture are not afraid to take initiative and exhibit confidence in their decisions. Some benefits of fostering this type of culture include: potential issues are identified and addressed before they become problems; employees feel comfortable coming to superiors with new ideas; individuals are engaged in improving the organization; people feel accountable for their actions and take ownership of their ideas.

---

[3] Goyette, 2016

- **Innovation culture**: In some industries, innovation is highly valued and necessary for the organization's ongoing success. A culture of innovation focuses on coming up with new ideas and following a rigorous process to bring those ideas to fruition. In a culture of innovation, diverse personalities enable ideas to percolate more readily. While some people may be better at the creative elements of innovation, others may be more adept at implementing the processes to bring them to life. The benefits of developing this type of culture in an organization include a unified commitment to innovation among all members, a competitive advantage in the marketplace through ongoing innovation, and an environment where everybody feels comfortable communicating their ideas.

- **Sales culture**: Creating a sales culture at your organization may signal an underlying motivation to support the activities that generate revenue for your company. For companies with a large sales force, undergoing a culture transformation to focus on sales within that group can make them better able to promote new products and services, approach new markets, develop a sales process that is in line with your company's values, and use the tools that will help them maximize sales. The individuals who prosper in a sales culture tend to be focused on delivering the product or service that best meets customers' needs. Implementing a sales culture at your organization can provide the following benefits: a salesforce that is fully informed about every product and service the company provides, a commitment from all teams to support the salesforce as needed, and accountability in committing to targets and trying to exceed those expectations.

- **Customer-centric culture**: A customer-centric culture is about the consumers who buy your company's products or services. This type of culture permeates your entire organization, including those without customer interactions. Employees in a culture of customer-centricity are empowered to see everything through the eyes of the customer and to make appropriate decisions based on their observations. The benefits of a customer-centric culture include company-wide accountability in all aspects of work, increased customer satisfaction, and a workforce committed to delivering an exceptional customer experience every time.

- **Leadership excellence culture**: In a culture of leadership excellence, individuals at every level have confidence that company leaders are committed to continuous improvement. Leaders demonstrate their commitment through ongoing training, leadership development programs, mentoring, and coaching. In this culture, individuals with natural leadership tendencies will readily rise to the top. Perhaps more importantly, those individuals with inherent leadership skills but unaware of them will be recognized and nurtured to fill their natural role. A culture of leadership excellence benefits from a robust leadership base, better employee retention through internal employee development, and strong leaders in every area of the organization.

77

- **Safety culture**: In industries that involve physical labor, heavy machinery, or hazardous materials, having a culture of safety means that you are committed to protecting the health and well-being of every individual. This includes having certain safety procedures in place, requiring specific behaviors, and ongoing training to ensure that everybody has all the necessary information to perform their job safely. In a culture of safety, employees inherently protect not just themselves but also their colleagues. The benefits of a culture of safety include fewer incidents and associated cost savings, a universal feeling that the organization values employee safety, and a proactive approach to safety and compliance.

For a project supplier to identify where to change its organization and project execution practices and how to secure its future, it needs to be aware of its current organizational culture, how the cultures of its projects relate to its organizational culture, and finally, what their desired culture is, if different from its current culture.

Secure the Future

The right organizational goal for the project supplier can address the two critical factors: the importance of the future and, a strong sense of urgency within the organization and a proper match between the project culture and the organizational culture. John Elkington[4] introduced an urgency for sustainability, which is strongly linked to the future, during the 1990s with a new framework to measure performance. This accounting framework, named the triple bottom line (TBL), elevated the traditional

---

[4] Elkington, 1994

measures of profit, return on investment, and shareholder value by including environmental and social dimensions. By focusing on the interlinked dimensions of profits, people, and the planet, TBL reporting can be an important tool to support sustainability goals. The interest in TBL accounting has grown across for-profit, non-profit, and government organizations, with many adopting the TBL sustainability framework to measure performance. The triple bottom line consists of the following.

- **Profit**: Addresses the traditional measure of financial performance. How responsible has the company been in terms of assuring its competitive prosperity?

- **People**: The measure of a company's social account. How socially responsible has the organization been in terms of its impact on the quality of life of the individuals it affects?

- **Planet**: The measure of the company's environmental account. How environmentally responsible has it been in terms of its impact on natural ecosystems?

I explored the conventional goal of a commercial company (to make money). However, E.M. Goldratt defines in his book *The Goal*[5] the goals of a company are

- **to make money** now as well as in the future, with the necessary conditions and boundaries within which the goal can be reached

- **to provide a secure and satisfying environment for employees** now as well as in the future

- **to provide satisfaction to the market** now as well as in the future

---

[5] Goldratt, 1984

However, he challenges this distinction between the goal to make money and these two necessary conditions by questioning whether these three entities are important to the same degree. Making money, however, is much more tangible than the other two. It's the only one that can be measured. With this statement, the collaborative importance of company owner concerns, as well as employee concerns as well as market concerns are introduced, the concluding statement that "making money is much more tangible than the other two—it's the only one that can be measured" confirms the focus on commercial objectives.

A common belief is that all firms aim to achieve a competitive advantage in relation to their rivals. A competitive advantage enables a firm to earn profits higher than the average profit earned by competitors (excess profits). In their book *In Search of Excellence,* T.J. Peters and R.H. Waterman Jr. see excellent companies along the lines of "a sound mind in a healthy body." They acknowledge the need for profit but consider it secondary to consumer orientation. As expounded by one executive they spoke to, "Profit is like health. You need it, and the more, the better. But it's not why you exist." In his books *Building to Last* and *Good to Great,* Jim Collins presents that "the stock market value is a key indicator of company success." But we should beware that he does not state that money is the ultimate purpose or goal. It is one of the results of being great and very satisfying for the shareholders.[6]

Youngman further elaborates on Goldratt's goal definition on his website, "A Guide to Implementing the Theory of Constraints," by highlighting the importance of the future, the social conscience, and the customers. Building on the three entities of Goldratt,[7] he elevates the goal definition of a public company traded on the open stock exchange to a full strategic level, to one goal: **secure the future of the company**, with three conditions that must at least be present (Figure 2-4).

---

[6] Porter, 1985; Peters and Waterman, 1982; Collins and Porras, 1994; Collins, 2001
[7] Goldratt, 1994

- Make money now and in the future.

- Provide employees with a secure and satisfying workplace now and in the future.

- Satisfy customers now and in the future.

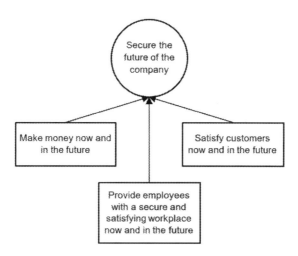

Figure 2-4. *Three necessary conditions to secure the future of the company (Youngman, 2021)*

For a non-profit organization, the goal definition consists of a similar employee condition. However, distinct conditions from the money and customers conditions result in the following: **secure the future of the organization** with the three conditions that must at least be present (Figure 2-5).

- Secure sufficient funding now and in the future.

- Provide employees with a secure and satisfying workplace now and in the future.

- Maximize the outcome now and in the future.

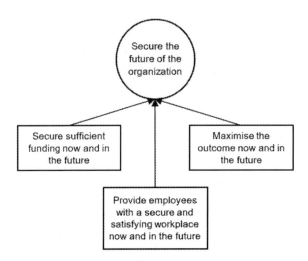

Figure 2-5. *Three necessary conditions to secure the future of the organization (Youngman, 2021)*

Another way he looks at this is that to make money, we must have an appropriate process (employees) and an appropriate product or service for an appropriate market (satisfied customers). Youngman refers to this definition as "Thinking about it further, this is really a succinct statement of the loyalty effect (investor, customer, and employee loyalty)."

As I reviewed, various studies looked at the organizational challenges involved in managing two different objectives at the same time: purpose and profits. To build a company that truly motivates its employees, it must have a sense of purpose. Purpose, they find, by its nature, transcends making money. It is about people coming together to do something they believe in and allowing profit to follow because of it rather than as an end in itself. One study highlights the importance of preparing organizational and infrastructure for the future, one of the four dimensions along which project success can be assessed. Focus on the future is an effective generic goal for the project supplier because it removes the short-term project focus (an ending undertaking) or the focus on just one specific goal, such as making a profit. Tom Peters and Nancy Austin wrote a second book on excellence in 1985 titled *A Passion for Excellence.* In this book, they implemented the findings from the first book into a simple model of excellence.[8]

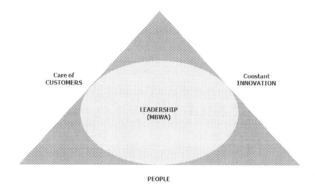

Figure 2-6. *A simple Model of Excellence (Peters and Austin, 1985)*

As indicated in Figure 2-6, Peters and Austin regarded excellence as the result of four critical success factors: **people** who practice, care of **customers**, constant **innovation**, and **leadership**, which binds together the first three factors through management at all levels of the organization.

> *Julie takes it all in and says to nobody in particular, "The other day, we talked about how our day-to-day focus is always on costs and our finances because of our monthly struggle with our cash flow and if we can pay our employees' salaries. So here we see the importance of our future, not only our finances but also our employees. Although paying the salaries in time is an important condition for satisfied employees, or employees without worries because they also have bills to pay at the end of the month."*

---

[8] Birkenshaw et al., 2014; Shenhar and Dvir, 2007; Peters and Austin, 1985

"I agree. Our focus should be on securing our future, which is not only about money, but other things, such as our employees." John adds.

Collin notices that Julie and John are talking with each other instead of via him. They are starting to go through this change process together as a team.

Project Management Objectives for the Project Supplier

The preceding chapter concluded that a bias to the customer perspective and the absence of a specific supplier perspective might not provide the highest benefit to the project supplier. Therefore, at project suppliers as opposed to customers, generic project (objectives) management practices based on such a biased perspective might not benefit its organization and, therefore might not be fully aligned with its organizational objectives. In the preceding section, various factors are explored in securing the future of the company or the organization based on the question of how to provide the highest benefit for the project supplier from its projects.

Securing the future of the project supplier requires specific project management objectives within the project supplier's organization that align project management practices with organizational objectives (supplier perspective) to benefit its organization (in addition to the customer). Furthermore, such project management objectives can and should address the critical factors to focus on the importance of the future and urgency for the project objectives and business benefits from the supplier perspective (to provide added value from the project to the organization) to ensure proactive action by the project team and proper follow-up by the organization as well, and to ensure sufficient focus on continuous progress, now and in the future.

A project supplier should fulfill the following generic project management objectives.

- Focus on overall project success and its criteria, not project management success and its criteria.

- Turn project success criteria back into project success factors for succeeding projects.

- Create a direct link between project success and organizational success.

- Elevate a supplier perspective above a customer perspective.

- Optimize for project suppliers and focus on their organization; however, do not impair the customer's interests.

- Incorporate an effective main goal for the project supplier.

- Stimulate an urgency-oriented culture.

- Implement continuous follow-up by the organization on project objectives that might lead to business benefits for its organization.

- Implement a proactive and continuous productive process, along with continuous improvement.

- Implement a permanent focus on long-term objectives and benefits (future) next to short-term objectives and benefits (now).

Project management objectives for the project supplier will benefit as well from incorporating organizational project management (OPM) principles[9] to **consistently and predictably deliver organizational strategy leading to better performance, results, and a sustainable competitive advantage**.

These OPM principles consist of the following.

- aligning project management practices with organizational objectives

- customizing and fitting these practices within the project supplier's context, situation, and structure

- providing the most benefit to the organization

Collin walks over to the flip chart sheet with a sketch of the gap and makes some changes as he explains.

"Supplier project objectives management closes the gap in project objectives management for the project supplier by eliminating or reducing that difference or imbalance between project and organizational success for the project supplier." *(Figure 2-7)*

---

[9] PMI, 2014

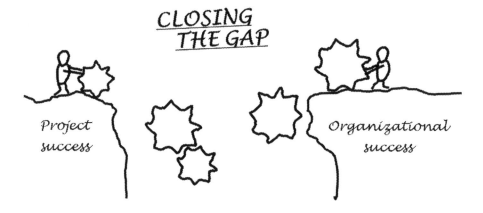

*Project objectives management
at the project supplier*

Figure 2-7. *Closing the gap between project and organizational success for the project supplier*

The Typical Project Supplier

The method focuses on a typical project supplier and its organization, characterized as follows.

- a for-profit (commercial) company or a non-profit (non-commercial) organization (e.g., institute, association)

- a project execution and delivery department delivering the project result to a receiving and using department (the internal customer or user) within one corporate organization; or a corporate organization delivering to another corporate organization (the external customer), or a corporate organization delivering to an (external) private person

- a multi-project environment with limited resources (e.g., human resources) for all ongoing projects

Furthermore, the method's focus is on any of the following.

- small to medium-sized organizations

- without extensive and matured organizational procedures embedded within their organization to manage their projects

- growing fast (e.g., size or revenue)

- in a turbulent or changing business field

- has many competitors

Examples of such typical project suppliers are an IT department developing and implementing new software in the procurement department of a commercial company, a painting company doing all paintwork at an office construction project, or a local house construction company building a new house for a private person; or a steel fabrication company fabricating steelwork for another commercial company.

I characterize the typical project supplier as an organization that mainly prepares and delivers its output using projects. With respect to one specific project, we can clearly define a supplier and a customer. However, in the totality of many respective projects, many project suppliers are also project customers, and vice versa.

"You can look at this from the perspective of a project supply chain, for example," Collin explains.

"You mean like when having a sub-supplier, supplier, and customer?" Julie asks.

"Yes, you can have a long product or project supply chain starting from a sub-supplier who delivers a product to a supplier, who delivers its assembled product incorporating the

product of his sub-supplier to their customer who delivers their project result to their customer, the end customer in the chain."

"Let's draw this up for SES," Collin says, walking to the flip chart.

"Yes, we have KC Foods at the top of the food chain, then us, SES, and, for example, our supplier for solar panels, Solar World." John fills in.

"So, you see, SES is both a project supplier for your project at KC Foods and a project customer for Solar Word's project for you." (Figure 2-8)

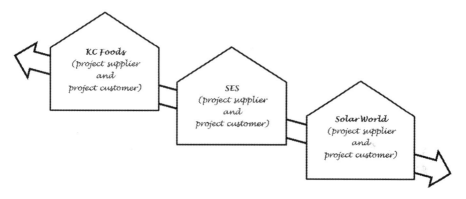

Figure 2-8. *SES project project supply chain*

Julie looks at the flip chart for a while and then asks, "But there is always another client in the chain, isn't it? Solar World is probably also a project customer in another of their projects, and KC Foods might also be a project supplier, in case of a project-based delivery."

Collin laughs and says, "Yes, you get the point. And even more, in the end, an end customer might deliver a service to a large transport company who transports goods to the sub-supplier, which closes a continuous chain." And he continues.

"So, it is important for you to realize that although you were perhaps thinking that SES is a project supplier, you are also a project customer. But still, when facing our challenges at SES, we will focus on you being a project supplier at your core. You are a supplier of results to your customer through temporary projects."

Summary

Where should a project supplier change its organization and its project execution practices to enable full utilization of all potential business benefits?

Change toward becoming an organization that is proactively and continuously productive toward the most effective goal for a project supplier: to secure its own future.

CHAPTER 3

Productive Aspects of Project Subjects: What to Change?

What should change in the project supplier's organization and its project execution practices to enable proactive and continuous productivity toward its goal of securing the future?

This chapter addresses this question and prepares you for the detailed *how* questions in Part II.

© Reitse van der Wekken 2024
R. van der Wekken, *Project Objectives Management,*
https://doi.org/10.1007/979-8-8688-0956-9_3

Productive Aspects of Project Subjects

There are two key items involved in a typical change process.[1]

- **subject**: a person or thing that is being discussed, described, or dealt with

- **aspects**: a subject's particular parts or features

However, not just change but *productive* change is critical for organizational success.[2] Therefore, with the question of what to change, we are not just considering aspects of subjects but also *productive* aspects of subjects. Within the project context, an example of a productive aspect of a project subject is, for example, the knowledge or experience of an employee working on the project.

This leads to the following definition of what to change in the project supplier's organization and its execution practices.

- **relevant project subjects**: persons or organizations (or any other living things) or things (tangible or intangible) related to the project

- **productive aspects**: particular parts or features of such persons or things that might benefit the project supplier when undergoing productive change

"So, first of all, we have project subjects involved in a project." *Collin starts, and he further explains.*

"Project subjects are any persons or organizations containing people or any other living things for that matter, such as animals or vegetation. Or they can be things; either material/tangible, real physical things, or immaterial/intangible things that you cannot physically touch."

---

[1] Oxford English Dictionary, 2020

[2] Goldratt, 1984

"Such as ideas?" John tries.

"Yes indeed, ideas or values," Collin responds.

"And in addition to that, we have productive aspects of such project subjects. Productive aspects are particular parts or features of such project subjects that lead to benefits when undergoing productive change."

"So, for example, when one of our employees is developing its skills." Julie steps in as well and says, "Yes and no. Yes, the employee is a project subject, and yes, a skill is a productive aspect of an employee. However, there we stop for now. Development of skills is, in fact, the next step, the productive change, which we will explore later. For our systematic, step-by-step familiarization, we will first explore examples of project subjects at SES, and later this morning, we will continue with their productive aspects."

"Understood." She confirms and eagerly starts writing yellow sticky notes for the flip chart with John. (Figure 3-1)

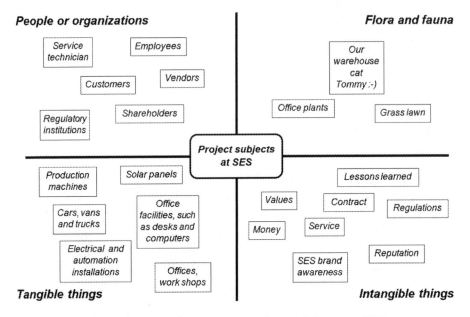

Figure 3-1. *Flip chart with various project subjects at SES*

"Let's have a look at this," Collin says while he theatrically grabs a red marker.

Julie looks worried at John, who raises his eyebrows while he returns a questioning look.

"I know that you really want to come up with at least something relevant in the upper right corner of 'Any other living things,' and I like the cat," Collin says with a smile and continues. "But these are not relevant to your typical project, just related to your organization. This is just how it is with your type of technical project. If your projects would involve, for example vegetation or livestock, this would be an important section, but not for SES. And that is okay. Not every section needs to be filled in."

And Collin crosses the items in the upper right corner.

"And a service technician is part of employees," Collin says while he crosses that one as well.

"Like this, he strikes through all our input," Jr. says disappointedly to Julie.

"No, you two are doing fine. This is a normal part of the process. Better have a lot of input to start with and separate the relevant input after that." Collin, however, reassures Jr.

"And furthermore, it is good to note that customers, employees, shareholders, and vendors all belong to the group 'stakeholders' of the project. Of which specifically customers and employees are of primary importance." Collin concludes. (Figure 3-2)

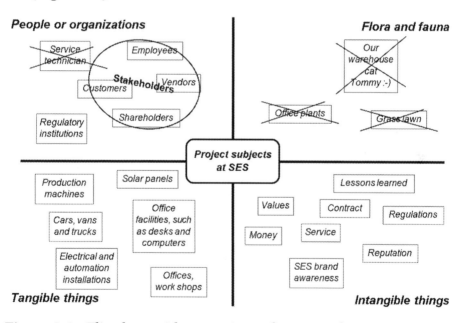

Figure 3-2. *Flip chart with corrections of project subjects at SES*

"Ah, okay, I understand," Julie responds.

"The rest is really quite good. For example, your production machines and the office facilities, although organizational resources, temporarily become project resources when used for your projects."

"And what about productive aspects of these project subjects?" Collin asks.

"But let's take a break and then continue with writing these down."

After the break Julie and John write down various productive aspects. (Figure 3-3)

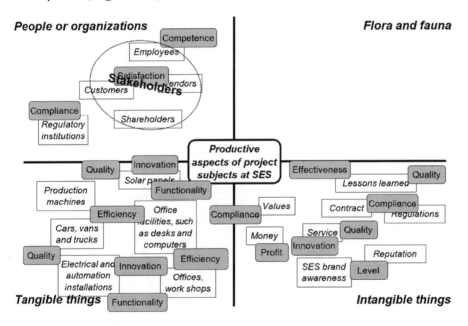

Figure 3-3. *Productive aspects of project subjects at SES*

"Great, I see many good points on the flip chart." Collin remarks after stepping back into the room. "Compliance, profit, quality, functionality, efficiency effectiveness."

Based on an extensive study of relevant literature, I have identified and summarized relevant generic project subjects and their productive aspects in Table 3-1.

Table 3-1. *Generic Project Subjects and Their Productive Aspects*

Project Subject Group	Project Subject	Productive Aspect
Stakeholders	Customers, Employees, Investors, Organizations, Suppliers, Society, Government	Competence (knowledge and experience), Satisfaction, Security, Values
Environment	Environment, City, Municipal	Satisfaction, Values
Rules	Contracts, Regulations, Standards, Values, Reputation	Compliance, Level
Finance	Investment, Cash, Credit, Debt	Money, Profit, Loss, Interest, Dividends
Project results	Products, Services, Other results	Functionality, Quality, Cost, Planning, Innovation
Process assets	Procedures, Knowledge bases, Processes, Tools, Lessons learned	Functionality, Scope, Quality
Resources	Materials, Tools, Facilities, IT, Employees	Effectivity, Efficiency
Assets	Offices, Facilities, Workshops, Factories, Warehouses, Brands	Quality, Performance, Durability, Maintenance, Efficiency, Reputation
Work	Activities, Actions	Quality, Satisfaction, Security

Summary

What should change in the project supplier's organization and its project execution practices to enable proactive and continuous productivity toward its goal of securing the future?

Change productive aspects of project subjects involved in project execution and its result delivery to the customer; project subjects such as customers, employees, money, process assets, regulations, resources, products and services, stakeholders, and values; and productive aspects such as satisfaction, lessons learned, productivity, effectivity, efficiency, and compliance.

PART II

How?

Part II of this book answers questions about changing a project supplier's organization and its project execution practices.

Chapter 4 further analyses the supplier perspective, addressing how to change. Chapter 5 looks at project objectives, addressing how to cause change. Chapter 6 develops the required process (the method) that integrates the supplier perspective with the generic project objectives, addressing how to implement change. Chapter 7 introduces appropriate management, addressing how to incorporate change. Chapter 8 examines the benefits (of the method), addressing how a project supplier can benefit from organizational changes and executing the practice.

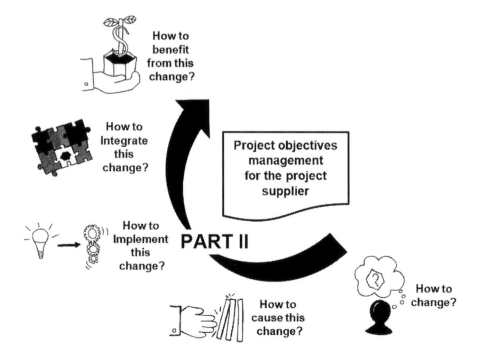

How to
benefit
from this
change?

How to
Integrate
this
change?

Project objectives
management
for the project
supplier

How to
Implement
this
change?

PART II

How to
cause this
change?

How to
change?

CHAPTER 4

The Supplier Perspective: How to Change?

How should the productive aspects of project subjects within the project supplier's organization and its project execution practices be changed?

Chapter 3 identified various generic productive aspects of project subjects to answer what to change in the project supplier's organization and its execution practices to enable proactive and continuous productivity toward its goal of securing the future. This first chapter of Part II takes a step back to further investigate the customer perspective on project objectives, leading to the supplier perspective on project objectives, to understand how productive aspects of project subjects

© Reitse van der Wekken 2024
R. van der Wekken, *Project Objectives Management*,
https://doi.org/10.1007/979-8-8688-0956-9_4

within the project supplier's organization and its execution practices can be changed. With this I prepare for the question of how to cause the change of productive aspects of project subjects in Chapter 5.

The Conventional Definition of Project Objectives

The conventional definition of a project objective introduced several relevant terms and their relationships, such as business benefit, project objective, project result, change, and goal. For the method, the typical definition of project objectives is now transformed into a more generic and suitable form by substituting the following terms.

- *business becomes organizational*

- *injecting becomes implementing*

- *product becomes project result* (being project product(s), service(s), other result(s), or a combination)

"This is important, especially the substitution of business with organization. Although the term business benefit is so commonly used, it is still more important to highlight the importance of the organizational or 'generic' aspect instead of the 'business' or commercial aspect only," Collin explains.

These substitutions result in the following new key definition.

The term *organizational benefits* refers not only to strictly monetary gains, but to all kinds of changes in parameters describing the workings of any organization that bring it closer to its goal.

In project management, project objectives are organizational benefits an organization expects to achieve as a result of implementing the project result—product(s), service(s), other result(s), or a combination—within itself or its environment.

Collin walks over to the flip chart and underlines part of the text.

"Let's focus on the second part of this definition, which states that 'the term organizational benefits refers not only to strictly monetary gains, but to all kinds of changes in parameters describing the workings of any organization that brings it closer to its goal.'"

Goldratt introduces in his book *The Goal* that "productivity is bringing a company closer to its goal. Every action that brings a company closer to its goal is productive. Every action that does not bring the company closer to its goal is not productive." This definition of productivity, actions, and the goal are redefined in the project context to the following.[1]

> **Any project action that moves the organization closer toward its goal is productive. Any project action that moves the organization away from its goal is not productive.**

Therefore, organizational benefits are any productive changes within an organization that take it closer to its goal (Figure 4-1).

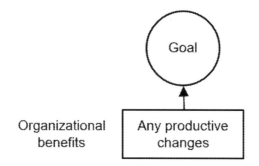

Figure 4-1. *Organizational benefits, changes, and goals*

A change is a process caused by an action; with as input the situation *before* the change and as output the situation *after* the change (Figure 4-2).

---

[1] Goldratt, 1984

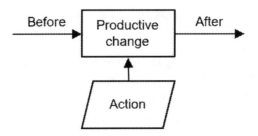

Figure 4-2. *Action causes change*

Project objectives (project changes) are a selection of organizational benefits achieved because of project implementation (project actions) as part of the total group of any productive changes within the organization (organizational changes) caused by any actions (Figure 4-3).

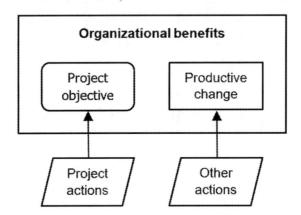

Figure 4-3. *Project objectives (changes) vs. any changes within the organization*

"Can you give me some examples of organizational benefits (changes) caused by a project and other actions at KC Foods?" Collin asks Julie while he points at the flip chart.

Julie looks at the flip chart in the corner and answers. "Well, obviously, the higher profit by lower electricity cost is an organizational benefit caused by the project action to install solar panels on the factory's roof."

"Correct, and you have an example of an organizational benefit caused by other actions?"

She thinks for a couple of seconds and then answers. "Well, I guess KC Foods stepped in at the right moment when getting that government subsidy for investment in green energy. And I heard that they made quite a good deal with selling that acquired plot next to the factory which they did not need anymore, after their major efficiency improvement program of the factory."

"Indeed, the simple point is, all project objectives (should) lead to organizational benefits, but not all benefits are project related," Collin concludes. (Figure 4-4)

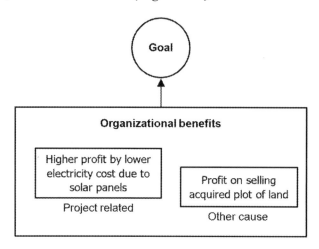

Figure 4-4. *Examples of different types of organizational benefits at KC Foods*

The project objective is an organizational benefit achieved as a direct result of implementing the project result—product(s), service(s), other result(s), or a combination—into itself or its environment, referred to as *project implementation* in the broad sense. Therefore, the word *implementing* is embedded within project actions to emphasize that actions cause changes. The project's resulting organizational benefit is the change that takes the organization closer to its goal (Figure 4-5).

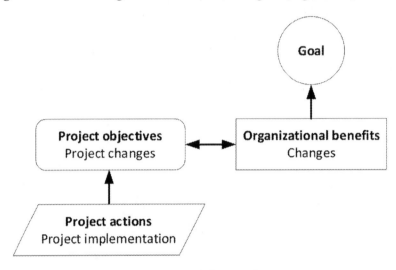

Figure 4-5. *Project actions toward the goal*

In project management, project objectives are organizational benefits an organization expects to achieve as a result of project actions, which implement the project result—product(s), service(s), other result(s), or a combination—within itself or its environment. Organizational benefits are changes within an organization that take it closer to its goal. (Figure 4-6)

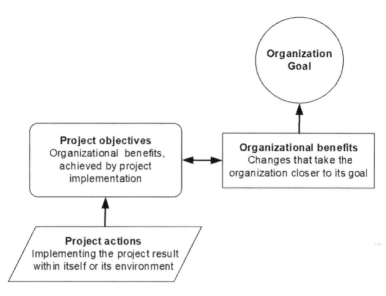

Figure 4-6. *Customer perspective on project objective*

It is clear from the definition and important to highlight that a project has no goal. A project has objectives, which are benefits that take the organization, not the project, closer to its goal. Therefore, there is no project goal, only an organizational goal.

Note that this definition is still conventional, defined from the customer perspective, to provide the highest possible benefit to the customer's organization.

The Customer vs. Supplier Perspective

The customer and supplier perspectives on project objectives are defined relative to the concerned project. Relative to different projects, an organization can be both a supplier to another customer and a customer to another supplier. However, in the case of a delivering department to a user department within an organization, the roles of customer and supplier are fixed; for example, an IT department (supplier) that executes the project and delivers the project result (new software feature) to the user (financial department), which implements the new feature within its existing software and process.

I concluded in the previous section that the general definition of a project objective, initiated by a project action leading via change within the organization toward its goal (Figure 4-6), is still defined from the customer perspective only and does not represent the supplier. And therefore, this general definition is clear from the customer perspective but still unclear from the supplier perspective. For the customer, project objectives become organizational benefits by implementing the project result into itself or its environment, taking the customer closer to its goal. However, the supplier has no result to implement within its organization to gain organizational benefits.

The main questions representing the supplier perspective are (Figure 4-7).

- What are project actions for a supplier?

- How do they achieve project objectives?

- What changes are there, and how do these turn into organizational benefits?

- How do these changes take the project supplier closer to its goal?

- What is the most effective goal of a project supplier?

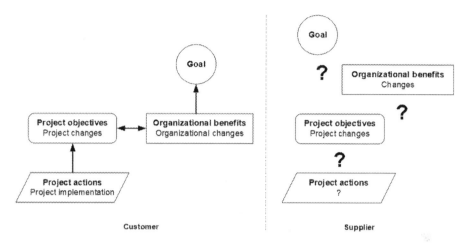

Figure 4-7. *Main questions representing the supplier perspective on project objectives*

The following four deductions, which lead to the customer and supplier perspectives via their differences, correlations, and relationships between the elements of their respective perspectives, are further explained.

- deviating project actions
- product vs. process focus
- deviating relationships between project objectives and organizational benefits
- customer and supplier goals

Deviating Project Actions

Figure 4-8 recaptures the link between the customer (perspective) and the supplier (perspective). It consists of the link between the injection of the project product(s) injection within the customer's organization (project result implementation) as a result of the product delivery by the supplier.

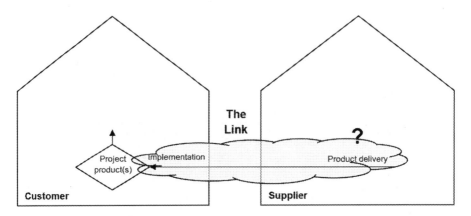

Figure 4-8. *Implementation linked to delivery*

With this clear link established, let's now further investigate the project actions of the supplier as opposed to the project actions of the customer in more detail, as question marked in Figure 4-7. The customer receives the project result from its supplier, implements it into itself or its environment (project implementation), and starts the project result life cycle. The project supplier can only gain organizational benefits from this project implementation for the customer as an indirect result of delivering the products to the customer, perhaps of something else. A specific study and analysis divides project success into four dimensions, with the third dimension being the benefit to the developing organization, which refers to the benefit gained by the developing organization as a result of executing the project, the developing organization being the project supplier (both can be part of one organization with both a user and a supplier department).[2]

Therefore, the clear distinction with the customer is that the supplier—the developing organization—both *delivers* the project result to the customer and (also) *executes* the project to accomplish this, together defined as *project execution* (Figure 4-9), as opposed to project implementation by the customer.

---

[2] Sadeh, 2000

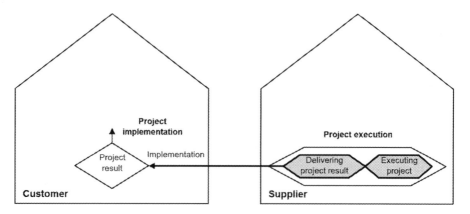

Figure 4-9. *The supplier's project action (project execution), consisting of executing the project and delivering the project result, vs. the customer's project action (project implementation)*

These are the deviating project actions (project execution) of the supplier, consisting of executing the project and delivering the project result, vs. the project action (project implementation) of the customer, implementing the project result.

> *"Now, let's look back at our earlier flip chart page of your installed solar panels at KC Foods." Collin remarks and turns over a few pages on one of the flip charts. (Figure 4-10)*

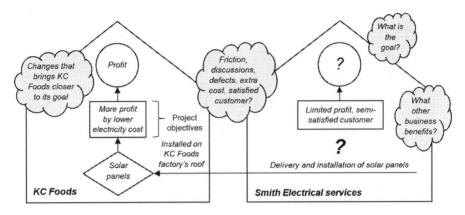

Figure 4-10. *Delivery and installation of solar panels at SES customer KC Foods*

"Let's compare both drawings."

They take a few moments and then Collin asks.

"Can you now modify your solar panel example in line with that newly defined "project execution" action? John and July grab a clean flip chart page and start working on it. When finished, Collin looks at the page and concludes.

"Perfect, you guys start to understand the philosophy. Your project execution indeed consists of executing the project, such as procurement and fabrication of your solar panels, and delivering your project result, including installation of your panels on the factory's roof and testing, which provides the link to KC Food's project actions of project implementation, installing your solar panels on their factory's roof." (Figure 4-11)

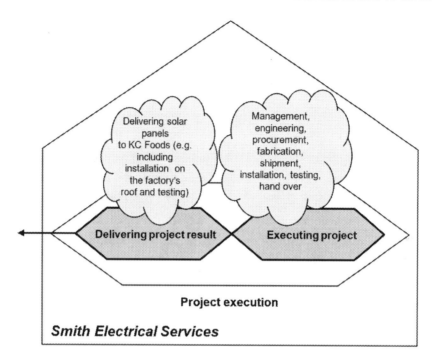

Figure 4-11. *Smith Electrical Services' project actions (project execution), consisting of executing the project and delivering the project result*

This project execution constitutes the project actions of the supplier instead of the customer's, as represented in Figure 4-12.

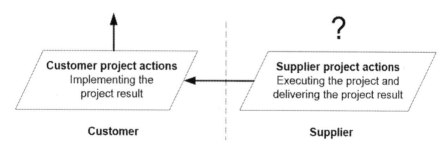

Figure 4-12. *Deviating project actions*

The organizational benefits for the customer are project objectives achieved directly from using the implemented project result. The organizational benefits for the supplier are not equal because the supplier delivers the project result to the customer and does not receive or use the result itself.

There are exceptions, such as a software supplier that develops modules on a project that can be reused in new products and projects. Therefore, because the supplier is not using the project result, its project objectives can only be achieved by this project execution, the combination of executing the project and delivering the project result to the customer.

However, although some execution and delivery actions might directly achieve project objectives, there is no guarantee that project objectives are achieved just by execution and delivery. No, to successfully achieve project objectives that lead to organizational benefits for the supplier, it is necessary to actively execute specific and different actions directed at the project objectives and the internal organization. These specific objective actions are the method's foundation and are defined as **supplier project objective actions.**

Such objective actions are executed through the project actions of executing the project and delivering the project result. This difference and relationship between the various actions is represented in Figure 4-13.

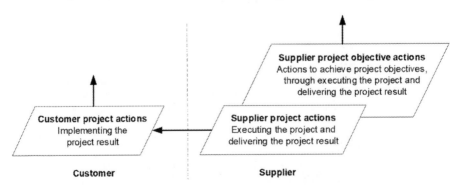

Figure 4-13. *Supplier project objective actions through project execution*

Note that the supplier project actions that execute the project and deliver the project result (external focus) act as a catalyst for these supplier project objective actions (internal focus) that achieve the supplier project objectives within the supplier's organization (Figure 4-14).

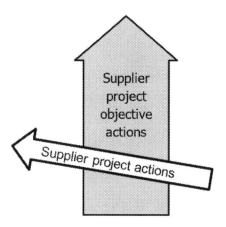

Figure 4-14. *Project objective actions through project actions*

A key principle within the method is to elevate the passive results of project actions by the active results of project objective actions. The passive result of supplier project actions, executing and delivering the project result, is enhanced by actively managed execution of supplier project objective actions to achieve specific supplier project objectives.

Product vs. Process Focus

F.J. Heemstra found two approaches to project success within an organization: the process approach (where success relates to on time, within budget, and conform specifications) and the product approach (where success relates to added value for the organization).[3] From this definition, you would identify the supplier perspective as the product

---

[3] Heemstra, 2011

approach, focusing on the added value for the organization from project execution. However, when separating the customer from the supplier perspective, we have two different organizations or departments (user and supplier) within an organization instead of the product/process approach within the same organization. In this case, the customer focus is on the project result, and the product focus and the supplier focus should be on the added value for the organization of the project execution (executing the project and delivering the project result delivery) within its organization. Therefore, within the customer and supplier perspectives, the supplier perspective is indicated as the process focus, and the customer perspective is the product focus (Figure 4-15).

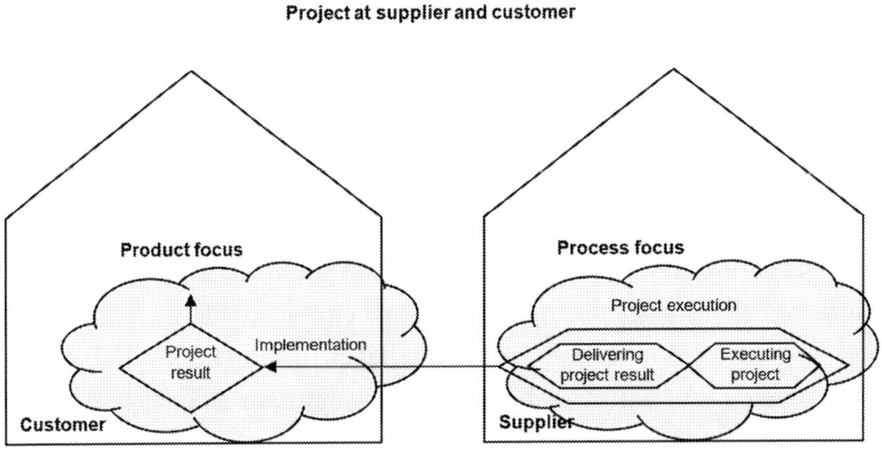

Figure 4-15. *Product focus on customer vs. process focus on supplier*

And Collin further explains.

"You can also think about this difference between the product and the process focus by the journey and destination metaphor."

Jr. thinks about this for a couple of seconds and then steps in.

"I understand! You mean that the project execution for the supplier, the process focus, is the journey to reach the destination. And the project result implementation for the customer, the product focus, is that destination."

"Exactly," Collin confirms, satisfied.

Deviating Relationships Between Project Objectives and Organizational Benefits

Another difference between the customer and supplier perspective is the link between the project objective and the organizational benefit. For the customer, the project objectives are instant organizational benefits directly resulting from the implemented project result. However, for the supplier, in general, there is no guaranteed or instant benefit of project objectives achieved by project execution and result delivery; although exceptions exist, such as immediate earned income and a satisfied customer. The achieved project objectives might still be only of benefit within the project, and still be only potential organizational benefits at best within the organization, that only turn into actual realized organizational benefits when they are actively embedded within the supplier's organization. These differences are represented in Figure 4-16, with distinct single vs. double-sided and horizontal vs. vertical-oriented arrows within the customer and the supplier perspectives.

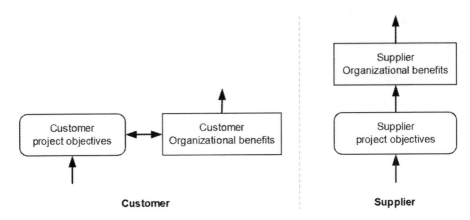

Figure 4-16. *Deviating links between objectives and organizational benefits*

In other words, direct organizational benefits to the customer and indirect organizational benefits to the supplier. Note that all supplier project objectives are potential organizational benefits for the supplier. However, not all organizational benefits for the supplier result from projects; various other sources exist for internal organizational benefits, not resulting from their main project business. Examples are internal organizational improvements, innovations not through an external project, or a charity initiative creating positive publicity.

Furthermore, although project objectives and organizational benefits are both types of changes—the organizational benefit being an achieved project objective—a subtle difference is made, specifically for the supplier. Project objectives are defined as actions and organizational benefits as their results. For example, a project objective is to make a profit on the project, the resulting potential organizational benefit, once the project objective is achieved, is the anticipated profit (more revenue than cost), and the actual realized benefit for the organization, when embedded by the organization through fulfilling the payment conditions, submitting the formal invoice, and receiving the actual payment, actual cash received.

Customer and Supplier Goals

The goal of the customer and supplier might be equal, for instance, when they are both suppliers and customers in the project chain of sub-supplier to supplier to customer to end-customer. Or the goals might deviate in case of a fixed relationship of supplier and user within a single organization. The goal of for-profit companies (supplier and customer) might be equal, for example, making money. The main question is

> **What is the goal of the customer or supplier, both
> project-based organizations, profit or non-profit,
> with internal or external project deliveries,
> operating in a multi-project environment?**

In Chapter 2, the unique goal and most effective goal within the customer and supplier perspective and the method of both project customers and suppliers is redefined to the generic definition for both for-profit and non-profit organizations to **secure the future of the organization**.

However, for some non-profit organizations, such as a human aid organization, the goal to provide human aid might be their highest goal. However, for this organization to be able to provide such aid on a long-term basis, now and in the future, it should still ensure that its future is secured in the long term. Providing human aid without sufficient focus on securing its future might actually risk its continued existence, thereby not being able to provide that human aid in the future.

The Customer vs. Supplier Perspectives

The preceding deductions are summarized in Table 4-1 and depicted in the customer and supplier perspectives diagram (Figure 4-17), structuring the differences, correlations, and relationships between their various elements.

Table 4-1. *Deviating and correlating elements of the customer and supplier perspectives*

Perspective element	Customer	Supplier
Goal	Secure the future of the organization	Secure the future of the organization
Organizational benefit	Change within its organization that takes the customer closer to its goal	Productive change, only when embedded as actual realized organizational benefits within itself, takes the supplier closer to its goal
Project objective	Organizational benefit achieved by project action (project implementation)	Potential organizational benefit achieved by project objective action
Project objective action	None	Action to achieve project objective through project actions (project execution)
Project action	Project implementation (implementing the project result—products, services, other results, or a combination—within itself or its environment)	Project execution (executing the project and delivering the project result to the customer)

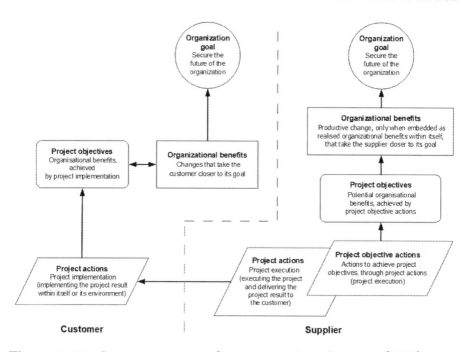

Figure 4-17. *Customer vs. supplier perspectives diagram (CSP)*

It is important again to highlight the link—a partnership—between the supplier and the customer established through part of the supplier project actions, namely through the project result delivery part of the project execution, linked with the customer's project actions of implementing the project result. PMI[4] defines the project charter as a document formally authorizing a project or a phase and documenting initial requirements that satisfy the stakeholders' needs and expectations. It establishes this partnership between the performing organization and the requesting organization (or customer, in the case of external projects). The project charter documents the business needs, current understanding of the customer's needs, and the new product, service, or result intended to satisfy, such as measurable project objectives and related success criteria.

---

[4] PMI, 2017

The Supplier Perspective on Project Objectives

The project supplier, also known as the *supplier* or *supplier organization*, is characterized by the following.

- a for-profit (commercial) company or a non-profit (non-commercial) organization (e.g., institute, association)

- an executing and delivering department delivering to a receiving and using department (the internal customer or user) within a corporate organization or a corporate organization delivering to another corporate organization (the external customer)

- a multi-project environment with limited resources (e.g., human resources) for all ongoing projects

The preceding deviations between the customer and supplier perspectives result in the following distinct definition of a project objective from the supplier perspective, as opposed to the customer perspective Figure 4-18).

In project objectives management at a project supplier, supplier project objectives are potential supplier organizational benefits, achieved by actively fulfilling supplier project objective actions, along with and through supplier project actions (which execute the project and deliver the project result – product(s), service(s), other result(s) or a combination – to the customer).

These potential supplier organizational benefits turn into productive changes; however, only when embedded by the organization as actual realized supplier organizational benefits within itself, which take the project supplier closer to its goal to secure its own future.

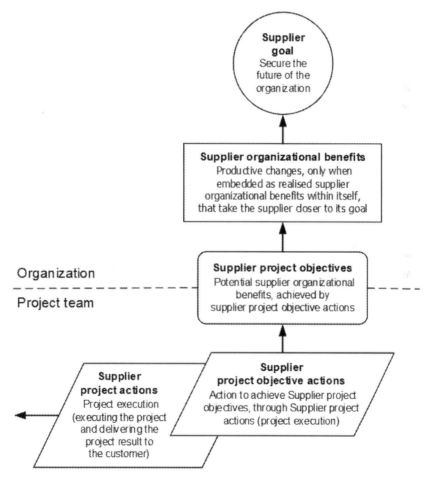

Figure 4-18. *Supplier perspective on project objectives*

This perspective on project objectives for the project supplier, the supplier perspective, forms the core philosophy of the method; it provides the means to close the gap between project and organizational success for the project supplier. Although also valid from the customer perspective, it is highlighted that supplier project objective actions act on the project level, project objectives act on both the project and organization levels, and organizational benefits and the goal act on the organization level.

Furthermore, it is of primary importance within the supplier perspective of the method to realize and accept the following.

- the project has no primary goal of its own

- there is only one goal: the organization's goal

Therefore, the project (team) should subordinate to the organization and, ultimately, the organization's goal by **implementing supplier project objective actions**.

Active subordination (alignment) of the project (team) to its organization and its organization's goal is a governing principle and part of the core philosophy, and an essential requisite for success for the supplier that distinguishes the supplier from the customer perspective on project objectives. The project subordinates to its organization's goal and not its own goal. A project's goal does not exist within the method to emphasize the importance of this principle. It is important for the project objectives and their definitions to highlight the link between the project and the organization and its subordination to the organization.

There must be a clear link between the outputs created by the projects and the requirements of the organization's business strategy for an organization to create optimal value from its investment in projects. This means organizations need a structure to align the project deliverables with organizational goals. The benefit map, as introduced by Rodney Turner in his book The handbook of project-based management, is an effective tool to align such project objectives with organizational objectives.[5] Although apparent to the customer, such subordination is less apparent for the supplier, where the project usually has the highest priority. For example, within a project team there might be a high and logical incentive to keep the best resources within their team without sharing with other projects.

Although apparent for the customer, where projects directly achieve organizational benefits that take the customer closer to its goal, such alignment or subordination is less apparent for the supplier, where projects themselves usually have the highest priority, at least for the project team, for example, incentives to keep good resources on their project without sharing with other projects. One study developed a universal framework for assessing project success: project success is seen as a strategic management concept where project efforts must be aligned with the strategic long-term goals of the organization. Another study introduces the term *balancing act* related to precedent-breaking management innovation as a critical trade-off where one side always seems to prevail at the expense of the other.[6]

Within the project supplier, this balancing act is the trade-off between the project's and the organization's interests or goal, a potential for friction when not actively managed. This balancing act must be actively managed by subordinating the project to its organization, by implementing aligned supplier project objective actions.

Supplier project actions are possible without supplier project objective actions; however, contrary, supplier project objective actions are not possible without supplier project actions. Supplier project actions still provide the highest possible benefit to the customer, along with which supplier project objective actions aim to provide the most benefit to the supplier. Furthermore, note that supplier project objective actions act on the project level, project objectives on both organizational and project levels, and organizational benefits and goals on the organizational level.

---

[5] Too and Weaver, 2014; Turner, 2009
[6] Shenhar et al., 1995; Hamel and Breen, 2007

Summary

How should the productive aspects of project subjects within the project supplier's organization and its project execution practices be changed?

Change by fully subordinating the project to the supplier's goal to secure the future through a change from the customer to the supplier perspective. First, specific project objectives are achieved by fulfilling supplier project objective actions by the project team through executing the project and delivering its result to the customer. These achieved objectives are potential organizational benefits, which turn into productive changes only when embedded by the organization as actual realized organizational benefits within itself. These changes finally take the supplier closer to its goal, to secure its future.

CHAPTER 5

Project Objectives: How to Cause Change?

How do you cause productive changes of the project supplier's organization and its project execution practices?

Chapter 4 isolated the supplier perspective on project objectives from the combined customer and supplier perspectives on project objectives, including its supplier project objective, to address how to change productive aspects of project subjects within the project supplier's organization and its project execution practices. In preparation for the complete model and process of the method introduced in Chapter 6, this chapter develops the generic supplier project objectives from relevant, productive aspects of project subjects (Chapter 3) to answer the question of how to cause this change.

© Reitse van der Wekken 2024
R. van der Wekken, *Project Objectives Management*,
https://doi.org/10.1007/979-8-8688-0956-9_5

First Steps Toward Generic Project Objectives

The Initial Three

Youngman elevated Goldratt's goal of a company to "make money now as well as in the future" to the full strategic level to "secure the future." More specifically, he defined "secure the future of the company" for both a commercial company and a non-profit organization, with their deviating necessary conditions, as illustrated in Figure 2-4 and Figure 2-5.

Within the method, these three goal conditions are combined and rephrased.

- generic form for an organization (for-profit or non-profit)

- *project execution* context from the supplier perspective (instead of a generic organizational perspective)

This leads to the first three generic supplier project objectives.

- Generate *project* profit or secure funds now and in the future.

- Satisfy *project* customers now and in the future.

- Provide *project* employees with secure and satisfying work.

Applicable Productive Aspects of Project Subjects

With the initial three generic supplier project objectives as a basis and guidance, a set of supporting principles is followed to identify the method's remaining generic supplier project objectives based on the relevant, productive aspects of project subjects, as discussed in Chapter 3. However, it is noted that not all productive aspects of project subjects, as identified in Table 3-1, are applicable and involved in the method's generic supplier project objectives. The productive aspects of project subjects directly related to project cost, time (planning), and scope (quality) of the project result—product(s), service(s), other result(s), or a combination—remain the domain of the (traditional) project controls, such as cost, time, *quality*, organization, and information control.

These project controls control the "project actions" of the supplier, consisting of "executing the project and delivering the project result to its customer" (project execution). The link between these traditional project controls and the generic supplier project objectives is the supplier project objective actions. The supplier project actions are controlled by the project controls and act as a catalyst for the supplier project objective actions that achieve the supplier project objectives (Figure 5-1).

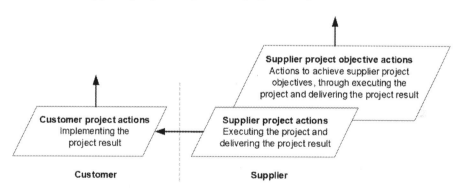

Figure 5-1. *Supplier project actions*

Collin grabs a red marker and gives it to John Jr. while he points at the earlier made flip chart page hanging on the wall.

"Now, John, can you cross out any productive aspects of proj-ect subjects that are already covered (controlled) by your tra-ditional project controls? You know cost, time, quality, organization, and information control, and therefore not applicable for the generic project objectives of the method."

"Yes, I can," Jr. answers, striking through several items.

"Very good. Productive aspects of project subjects related to the project controls, such as scope, quality, time, and cost control, are therefore not applicable to the generic project objectives within the method. For example, the functionality of your solar panels, which is really the domain of the project controls' scope and quality."

Collin continues, "One productive aspect remains applicable—innovation of project results."

"Okay, so I should not cross out this one," John answers and points to innovation on the flip chart.

"Yes, although we do look at it from a generic point of view."

Collin looks at the flip chart and continues.

"Furthermore, specific project results, such as your solar panels or electrical installations, will be replaced by the generic description of project results, being products, services, other results, or a combination," Collin confirms.

"It's good to group these items here, employees and vendors, as stakeholders." Collin points at the upper-left corner of the flip chart, and then he draws circles around them and writes 'stakeholders' over it.

"In summary, we don't want an overlap between both methods, the project controls vs. the new method; however, their interaction and alignment are covered in the new method, which we will later see." (Figure 5-2)

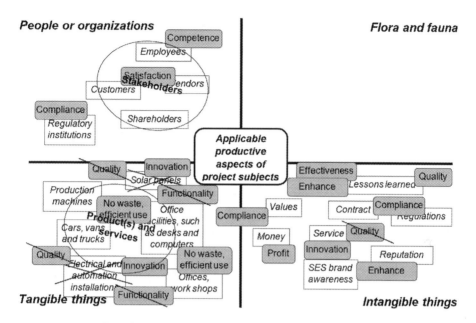

Figure 5-2. *Flip chart indicating applicable productive aspects of project subjects at SES*

Although productive aspects of project subjects related to the project controls of the project results do not apply to the generic supplier project objectives, the project controls are aligned with the new method, which will provide the proper objectives for the project controls. So, these productive aspects, functionality, quality, planning, and cost, are not applicable; however, innovation of project results remains applicable (Table 5-1).

Table 5-1. *Applicable Generic Project Subjects and Their Productive Aspects*

Project Subject Group	Project Subject	Productive Aspect
Stakeholders	Customers, Employees, Investors, Organizations, Suppliers, Society, Government,	Competence (knowledge and experience), Satisfaction, Security, Values
Environment	Environment, City, Municipal	Satisfaction, Values
Rules	Contracts, Regulations, Standards, Values, Reputation	Compliance
Finance	Investment, Cash, Credit, Debt	Money, Profit, Loss, Interest, Dividend
Project results	Products, Services, Other results	~~Functionality, Quality, Cost, Planning~~, Innovation
Process assets	Procedures, knowledge bases, Processes, tools, Lessons learned	Functionality, Scope, ~~Quality~~
Resources	Materials, Tools, Facilities, IT, Employees	Effectivity, Efficiency
Assets	Offices, office facilities, Workshops, Factories, Warehouses, Brand	~~Quality~~, Performance, Durability, Maintenance, Efficiency, Reputation
Work	Activities, Actions	~~Quality~~, Satisfaction, Security

Supporting Principles

Six supporting principles enable the systematic deduction of the method's remaining generic supplier project objectives.

The **first principle** emphasizes that the objectives are project objectives, not organizational objectives, which lead to organizational success via organizational benefits. It is important for the project objectives and their definitions to highlight the link between the project and the organization and its subordination to the organization.

The **second principle** is added value. What is the project's added value for the organization? As we know, where for the customer, the added value is obvious, the organizational benefits of the project implementation, for the project supplier however, this is not always that obvious. Therefore, the continuous question is what the project's added value can be for the organization? Such questions, followed by rigorous (active) management of objective actions to achieve that added value, is an important principle.

The **third principle** is "now and in the future," which emphasizes that the project should not have a short-term goal of its own but instead subordinate to the organization and its long-term goal to secure its future. Covey[1] explains that effectiveness lies in the balance between producing desired results and production capability, the ability or asset that produces the result. There are three kinds of assets: physical, financial, and human. Balance means proper investment in the asset instead of short-term production maximization, ensuring long-term (future) returns.

The **fourth principle** is leadership vs. management. Peter F. Drucker was a famous and influential business philosopher, writer, and consultant, sometimes called "the father of modern management," analyzing economics and society for over 60 years. His famous dogma stated that management is doing things right; leadership is doing the right things.[2] Leadership relates to effectiveness, and management relates to efficiency. The standard supplier project objectives emphasize leadership, management, or a combination.

---

[1] Covey, 2004
[2] Drucker, 2001

The **fifth principle** is qualitative vs. quantitative. The generic supplier project objectives can be categorized as qualitative, quantitative, or a combination. Note that quantitative and qualitative are connected to the second principle's productive changes increase and improve.

The final and most dominant **sixth principle** emphasizes the importance of *productive* change, not just change. As further studied by S. Waddock and S.B. Graves,[3] in their book *Built to Last*, J.C. Collins and J.I. Porras separate the single most successful habit of visionary companies as core ideology in a visionary company working hand in hand with a relentless drive to stimulate progress that impels change and forward movement in all that is not part of the core ideology.[4] Continuous productive change is a continuous improvement process based on continuous awareness that every small productive change takes the supplier closer to its goal. Or in other words, to generate "added value" from the project for the organization during and after project completion, by each productive aspect of the project subjects. Productive change of productive aspects, being (pro)active actions such as to increase, improve, satisfy, provide, secure, innovate, evaluate, feed back, utilize, or enhance. Productive change is also directly captured in four supplier project objectives related to competence, innovation, lessons learned, and process assets, all involved in the continuous improvement of project subjects such as the project result, resources, process assets, and employees.

Other considerations supporting the deduction of the generic supplier project objectives of the method consist of various supporting questions such as the following.

- Are organizational resources unlimited, or could a project benefit the organization by deploying certain resources efficiently?

---

[3] Waddock and Graves, 2002
[4] Collins and Porras, 1994

- What improvements, potentially beneficial for the organization, could a project establish by project execution?

- What improvements, potentially beneficial for the organization, could a project manager establish by project execution?

- Are project results one-time developments or could the project develop project results in such a way that it benefits the organization beyond this one project?

- What added value could be left in place after the project is completed?

- What added value could be left in place after a project manager has left for another organization?

- Are there certain rules that the project needs to comply with, such as certain preconditions, or can the degree of compliance with certain rules benefit or disadvantage the organization?

Introduction to Generic Project Objectives

This section further explains generic supplier project objectives.

Competence

Competence

Human resources, or employees, are widely considered the most important asset of an organization, with a major impact on its organization. Studies confirm that continuous improvement of employee competence is a major success factor in performing the next project better and staying ahead of the competition. In his book *Good to Great*, J.C. Collins found that in a good-to-great transformation within a good-to-great company, people are not your most important asset. The "right" people are.[5] And the right people are people with various levels of competence, character, and attitude. Most projects create two outputs: deliverables (tangible outputs such as content, software, and guidelines) and competence (non-tangible outputs that should be documented and shared). Competence combines knowledge (specialized or generic) related to theory and experience (hard and soft skills) related to practice.[6] D.P. Slevin and J.K. Pinto developed the ten-factor model of project implementation.[7] The fifth and sixth factors for successful project implementation consist of personnel: recruitment, selection, and training of the necessary personnel for the project team; and technical tasks: availability of the required technology and expertise to accomplish the specific technical steps. They explain that personnel as a factor, is concerned with developing a project team with the requisite skills to perform their function. However, A.J. Shenhar and J.J. Renier raised whether the project contributed additional capabilities or competencies to the organization under their principal success criteria of "future opportunity."[8]

---

[5] Collins, 2001

[6] Blindenbach-Driessen, 2006

[7] Slevin and Pinto, 1986

[8] Shenhar and Renier, 1996

While Collin further explains the competence objective, Julie thinks back about her recent discussion with Mike, one of their senior and most experienced but sometimes very stubborn project managers.

"Mike, why do you never support our training of new engineers on your projects? You always find a way of not having them on your projects! I have had enough of this. You should know that this is important." Julie says somewhat desperately to Mike.

"Why should I? It is not mentioned in my project assignment, is it?" Mike responds in defense and further sums up.

"Our standard project assignments only mention making money, satisfying our customers, meeting the deadline, delivering the right quality, and so forth. There is nothing on training in there at all, so why is this so important for you?"

All projects can benefit their organization by increasing and improving competence as a secondary output or result next to the primary project result.[9] This introduces the incentive of the project to add value to the organization (success criteria) instead of only benefiting from the organization (success factors). An extensive field survey into the effects of project management efforts on project success under the parameters of scheduling, cost, and margins found that efforts in training and capabilities development have a significant and positive relationship with the schedule parameter.[10]

Within the method, this objective is captured in the "competence" generic supplier project objective to **increase and improve project employee knowledge and experience.**

---

[9] JISC, 2013
[10] Carvalho et al, 2015

"Julie, in your standard project assignment, is there a section on training or resource competence?" Collin asks him.

"Well, no, not in our project assignment, but we have something on that in our competence and appraisal process of our employees, but they're only related to that employee," Julie responds, already on the defensive, suspecting trouble, however thinks for a couple of seconds and then answers.

"Well, to be honest, I had this discussion recently as well with Mike, one of my senior project managers. A discussion I lost, although I am convinced that I am right. He complains that he and his projects always get the new ones, the beginners. Of course, he knows it is important to train new employees, he has been one himself, but it takes time, holds up progress, and might frustrate the customer, and what does it bring him? It's not that the project assignment instructs him to do this or that he gets rewarded for it! But why does everything need to be fixed in procedures? Why can't I expect, demand, from my seniors that they act to take our organization closer to its goal, independent from any document or procedure!"

"You are right. You can and should. However, for clarity and transparency and to avoid lengthy discussions, it's a must to capture it. Both in your project assignment and personnel targets in the appraisal of your seniors Collin answers."

Customers

Customers

Numerous literature sources consider customer satisfaction a project's most important objective and success criteria. To many, the most important stakeholder is the customer since the project is being created for the customer. To others, project supplier internal stakeholders, such as programmers, overwhelmingly consider meeting the scope of software projects, which comprises the functionality and quality of the project outcome (customer's requirements), as the highest determinant of success.[11] Customers are a subgroup of stakeholders, however, that important that it justifies its dedicated objective.

Within the method, this objective is captured in one of the three initial generic supplier project objectives—"customers," based on the three goal conditions of the Theory of Constraints (TOC) to **satisfy project customers now and in the future.**

It is important to note that customers are a subgroup of stakeholders, however, that important that it justifies its dedicated objective. Also, customers are intentionally defined as plural; a project might have multiple customers, such as a direct customer and its end customer, the user in whose organization the project result is implemented; both the customer and end customer require specific stakeholder management.

---

[11] Williams, 2015; Agarwal, 2006

Note a non-profit organization does not have a customer-oriented goal condition and, therefore, not a primary customer-oriented generic objective—although certain non-profit organizations do supply products to paying customers, even if it is against cost price—however, they do have a primary process to maximize their outcome, which is covered by the generic objective to satisfy, not their customers, but their stakeholders.

Certain organizations, non-profit or for-profit, put their customers or end users at the highest priority within their organization, per their organizational vision and values. Although "customers" are also covered in the project controls through scope or quality control, customers can be given the appropriate attention and prioritization within the organization in relation to the other generic objectives via this generic objective. It can also describe and clarify the link between the project and the organization through the customer.

Employees

The competence objective defines people and the right people as the most important asset. The first step is to get or develop these right people (competence objective), and the next step is to keep these right people. Means of satisfying the employee involve—besides the organization—the employee itself as well, by motivation and commitment; this can be reached by (e.g., career development, training, challenges, and autonomy). Anne M. Mulcahy, former CEO of the Xerox Corporation, stated, "Employees are a company's greatest asset—they're your competitive advantage. You want to attract and retain the best; provide them with encouragement and stimulus, and make them feel that they are an integral part of the company's mission." "Employees who believe that management is concerned about them as a whole person—not just an employee— are more productive, satisfied, and fulfilled. Satisfied employees mean satisfied customers, which leads to profitability."

Within the method, this objective is captured in one of the three initial generic supplier project objectives—"employees," based on the three goal conditions of the TOC to **provide project employees with secure and satisfying project work**.

Jim Highsmith explains in his book *Agile Project Management: Creating Innovative Products* that the essence of the agile movement or principles, whether in new product development, new service offerings, software applications, or project management, rests on two foundational goals: delivering valuable products to customers and creating working environments in which people look forward to coming to work each day.

Innovation

Innovation

A.J. Shenhar and D. Dvir ask if the project created a new market or product potential or assisted in developing a new technology.[12] Organizational benefits are directly linked to innovative project results for the project customer. However, the project supplier, specifically pushing innovation objectives directed to future benefits, can potentially result in substantial (future) organizational benefits for itself. In *Built to Last*, Collins and

---

[12] Shenhar and Dvir, 2007

Porras separate visionary companies' single most successful habit as core ideology, working hand in hand with a relentless drive for progress that impels change and forward movement in all that is not part of the core ideology.[13] One thesis increases our understanding of improving the position of non-central actors, such as suppliers in project networks, because suppliers are regarded as key sources of construction project innovations. An exploratory case study of a long-term co-innovation relationship between a project supplier and customer recognized its high benefits value for both parties.[14] Steve Jobs, former co-founder and CEO of Apple Inc., said, "Innovation distinguishes between a leader and a follower."

Can innovation on the project (supporting the execution of a pilot project within the project) be a productive internal project objective leading to new products or applications, which can secure future project profit or funds? Yes, it can and does in many instances on projects, sometimes developing on the project just by coincidence or along the way, however not proactively pushed by the organization. By innovating the project, an end product (or more generic project result) life cycle can be succeeded by a new project result life cycle, potentially generating future money for the organization.

> *"But your project team members or project manager might be reluctant to conduct such an innovative pilot on their project. Or they might be reluctant to introduce new products or systems within their project that might still have start-up issues. Do you recognize that? Collin asks.*

> *"Yes, we experience that a lot actually. They tell us to let another project take that risk. We have already enough challenges of our own!"'John Jr. agrees.*

---

[13] Collins and Porras, 1994
[14] Lehtimäki et al, 2018; Sariola, 2018

"What can we do? I mean, if they don't want it, the pilots are never going to be a success?" Julie adds in desperation.

Within the method, this objective is captured in the "innovation" generic supplier project objective to **innovate project products, services, or other results.**

Lessons Learned

Lessons learned are one of the most important and value-added aspects of the project management lifecycle to the organization; however often also the most ignored part of finishing a project. A study with 32 field interviews concludes that by creating a learning organization attuned to complexity and its management, companies are more likely to have the knowledge and skills to respond competently to the complexity frequently encountered in new product development projects. To provide clearer guidance on fulfilling project success criteria, another study identified underlying factors that affect performance and, thus project success in construction processes, finding that the top five most important process factors related to knowledge and communication sharing.[15] In their standard *Guidance on Project Management*, the International Organization for Standardization defines, besides the project charter, lessons learned from previous projects as a primary input to develop the project plans.[16]

---

[15] Walker, 2008; Kim and Wilemon, 2007; Lindhard and Larsen, 2016
[16] ISO, 2021

Within the method, this objective is captured in the "lessons learned" generic supplier project objective to **identify and "feed back" project lessons learned.**

> *Collin explains, "'Feed back' is deliberately phrased as a verb with a space in between 'feed' and 'back,' and not as a noun. It means to actively 'feed' 'back,' feeding lessons learned back into the organization because the method recognizes the importance that it will only be successful with such active action. And even then, lessons learned are among the most challenging processes within many organizations.*

Although lessons learned are usually considered a means to achieve process assets, the "process assets" objective might not capture all lessons learned potential. Lessons learned can contribute to achieving various other project objectives if also actively pursued. Because such contribution to achieve other objectives—and the actual improvement of that achievement—is so important, it justifies its dedicated objective.

> *"Actually, lessons learned is a topic that I gained quite some knowledge on during the past years because it is always a topic of interest when discussing what value the project can add to other projects, so to the organization," Collin explains and continues.*

> *"A common statement when reviewing lessons learned is to say that 'we should never make this mistake again and always do this or that in future!.' However that is easy to say in hindsight when having this extra knowledge of what actually happened. The question is, would you make or not make the same decision again when having the same information?*

> *"Well, it's a lesson learned, isn't it? So you would make sure not to make that same mistake again, would you?" Julie answers.*

"Yes, you would think so. However, you do not know for sure that some problems will occur again. So would you spend resources or money upfront to prevent the same risk from happening, not sure that it will happen again? No, in reality, there will be a discussion within the organization all over again, questioning why to spend money upfront to mitigate a certain risk, not knowing if it will materialize again. So, it might be that nothing is done with the earlier concluded, at that time obvious, lessons learned!"

Money

Within the method, this objective is captured in one of the three initial generic supplier project objectives—"money," based on the three goal conditions of the TOC to **generate project profit or secure funds now and in the future**.

Project subjects or objectives directly related to project cost, time, and scope remain the domain of the (traditional) project controls such as cost, time, and quality control. These project controls control the "project actions" of the supplier, consisting of "executing the project and delivering the project result to its customer" (project execution). However, the "money" objective is yet created as a primary generic project objective within the method, despite this traditional (cost) project control. However, the "money" objective is broader than just direct cost control on the project. It covers all cost related organizational benefits for the organization linked to supplier project objectives.

"Can you think of a good example of the difference between now and in the future related to money?" Collin asks John.

"Well, I guess the difference between a healthy cash flow now vs. a net profit at the end of the project," Jr. answers.

"Yes, or a projected profit now, and on a monthly basis vs. an actual net profit at the end of the project," Julie adds.

"And what about the longer-term future or after the project?" Collin digs deeper.

"What do you mean after the project? Ah, okay, you mean like getting a new contract and thereby future profits."

"Yes, and that one is specifically important within the method because such longer-term benefits might get less attention or urgency."

"But we take on a project with a minor or even no projected profit when we at least cover our fixed cost," she says.

"Yes indeed. So, all such things should and can be part of the method's process related to the generic project objective 'money,' as we will see later," Collin concludes.

Although money, or cost, is already covered in the project controls as well, including money in the generic objectives ensures that the generic objectives are complete and cover all possible objectives relevant to the method. Furthermore, it enables them to give money the highest priority within their organization per their vision and values, for example, within a for-profit organization that puts money first.

Process Assets

Process assets

Projects can benefit by reusing useful templates, procedures, and guidelines, developed from experience and lessons learned from former projects within the organization. According to the *PMBOK Guide*, organizational process assets include any or all process-related assets from any or all the organizations involved in the project that can be used to influence the project's success.[17] These process assets include formal and informal plans, policies, procedures, and guidelines. The process assets include the organization's knowledge bases, such as lessons learned and historical information. Organizational process assets may include completed schedules, risk data, and earned value data. Updating and adding to the organizational process assets as necessary throughout the project are generally the responsibility of the project team members. Within the capability maturity model implementation (CMMI) for development, the process management process areas feed the organization's standard processes, work environment standards, and supporting assets within the advanced project management process areas based on received lessons learned and planning and performance data.[18] The integrated project management process area establishes and maintains the project's defined process tailored to the organization's standard processes. The project uses and contributes to the organization's process assets.

---

[17] PMI, 2021
[18] CMMI, 2007

Within the method, this objective is captured in the "process assets" generic supplier project objective to **increase, improve, and innovate project process assets**.

Note that *increase* refers to the quantity within process assets, *improve* refers to quality, and *innovate* refers to change. Process assets are closely linked to lessons learned; lessons learned being the process, process assets one of its specific results.

Some organizations, for example, an applied engineering-driven company in a market with very small profit margins, can only remain on the same pace with or ahead of its competitors by full optimization and continuous improvement of its engineering and logistic processes. For such a company, unconditional use of its process assets, but also continuous improvement of its process assets (such as standard processes, calculation sheets, and checklists) by its project teams is of primary importance. For such a company, the specific generic objective "process assets" can provide the proper focus within the method.

Resources

Resources

Organizational resources are defined as means the project uses to accomplish the project result, consisting of employees, facilities, money, organization, process assets, and tools. Can the project utilize resources with minimal impact on its organization or even positively impact it? According to the *project excellence model*, resources must be utilized effectively and efficiently to maximize benefit to the stakeholders involved.[19] CMMI for development defines that the management of the project ensures that the relevant stakeholders associated with the project coordinate their efforts in a timely manner. It does this by providing for the management of stakeholder involvement; identifying, negotiating, and tracking critical dependencies; and the resolution of coordination issues within the project and with relevant stakeholders.[20]

Multiple projects often need to be planned together; strategic resources and critical chains are important. A scheduling approach for multiple projects with several advantages is the strategic resource approach, in which resource contention is resolved between projects for the strategic resource only. The advantage of resource contention for all resources is that projects can remain scheduled in isolation, which is much more practical and feasible, except for the strategic resources. One study on managing multiple projects concludes that despite having sufficient and sustainable resources leads to effectiveness, resource sufficiency and sustainability are uncommon. Strongly related to organizational resources, R. Atkinson defines two prime success criteria within the post-delivery stage related to organizational benefits: improved efficiency and improved effectiveness. A.J. Shenhar identifies project efficiency as one of their four dimensions to assess project success.[21]

Within the method, this objective is captured in the "resources" generic supplier project objective to **utilize project resources effectively and efficiently**.

To provide the most benefit to the organization, it is important for "organizational" resources, which temporarily become project resources, to be used effectively and efficiently on and by the project. This is important to acknowledge. The generic objective describes

---

[19] Westerveld, 2003

[20] CMMI, 2007

[21] Newbold, 1998; Patanakul and Milosevic, 2009; Atkinson, 1999; Shenhar et al., 1997

project resources; however, it concerns organizational resources that are temporarily available and, where applicable, returned to the organization after project completion.

Furthermore, note that "effectively" relates to doing the right thing (leadership) and "efficiently" to doing the thing right (management). However, resources such as employees and process assets are defined as *dedicated objectives* due to their importance.

Is one of a project's objectives to utilize the organization's resources efficiently? That cannot be a goal. At most, this is one of the prerequisites for the project. Or not?

> *"I come across them in most organizations, because it is understandable. They focus on their project only and what they need from the organization. They are reluctant to resolve a resource conflict with their colleague project managers, and mostly escalate to management." And Collin continues, impersonating a fictitious person.*

> *"It's already hard enough to take care of my project, with all our challenges and your requirements and expectations. I just need Henry on my project for a quick finish. Let Dave train that new guy on his project!"*

> *Both Jr. and Julie are smiling, each having someone in their mind within SES.*

The senior project manager philosophy is an important principle within the method, whereby resource conflicts between different projects are expected to be resolved between involved senior project managers within the best overall interest of the organization instead of the independent projects. This philosophy will be explored later in more detail.

Rules and Values

In researching for *Built to Last*, Collins and Porras, contrary to business school doctrine, did not find "maximizing shareholder wealth" or "profit maximization" as the dominant driving force or primary objective through the history of most visionary companies.[22] They tend to pursue a cluster of objectives, of which making a profit is only one and not necessarily the primary one. Visionary companies do not see it as a choice between living to their values or being pragmatic; they see it as challenging to find pragmatic solutions and behave consistent with their core values. Furthermore, the organization's reputation is strongly linked to its core values and external influences, such as public opinion from society (e.g., regarding the environment).

Det Norske Veritas states, "The overall objective with this Recommended Practice is to establish guidelines and recommendations for the process required to reach an acceptable and controlled exposure to risk during marine operations, for personnel, environment, assets, and reputation."[23] Reputation relates to the rules and values of the organization. A study defines enhancing a company's reputation as an important project success criterion because the loss of reputation caused by a project reflects the customer's attitude toward the company rather than its individual project.[24] On many occasions, regulations,

---

[22] Collins and Porras, 1994

[23] DNV, 2003

[24] Al-Tmeemy et al., 2010

standards, and values are considered conditions that are complied with or not, without any positive or negative contribution to the organization. However, they should and can be treated as opportunities for positive contribution, depending on the degree of compliance.

Within the method, this objective is captured in the "rules and values" generic supplier project objective to **enhance project compliance with legislation, regulation, and societal and organizational values.**

Collins[25] found that the most successful habit of visionary companies is that "Core ideology in a visionary company works hand in hand with a relentless drive for progress that impels change and forward movement in all that is not part of the core ideology." Preserving the core of the company while stimulating progress in all other areas. Such preserving of the company's core relates to the objective rules and values.

Stakeholders

Stakeholders

New approaches to project success have led to refocusing project management goals to stakeholder-based, thereby stressing the importance of stakeholder opinions and satisfaction to project success.[26] As E.M. Goldratt and Dr. K.J. Youngman concluded, customers and employees are the two most important stakeholders of a supplier and

---

[25] Collins, 1994

[26] Turner and Zolin, 2012; Davis, 2014; Gemunden, 2015; Velayudhan, 2016

its project, therefore defined as dedicated project objectives.[27] Other key stakeholders include subcontractors, sub-suppliers, executive management, shareholders, and non-governmental organizations. Their satisfaction will also benefit the organization and take it closer to its goal.

Within the method, this objective is captured in the "stakeholders" generic supplier project objective to **satisfy project stakeholders now and in the future**.

All supplier project objectives are directly related to or indirectly driven by stakeholders. In a business context, a stakeholder is a person or organization with a legitimate interest in a project or entity. Stakeholders of a project or the executing organization vary from employees, project team members and management team, suppliers, customers, and shareholders. Although the objective "satisfy project stakeholders now and in the future" is already linked to shareholders in general, due to their importance and influence, within the method, four generic supplier objectives are directly linked to two key stakeholders of a project: one to customers and three to employees. The objective "satisfy project customers now and in the future" is obviously linked to customers, and the three objectives "provide project employees with secure and satisfying work," "utilize project resources effectively and efficiently," and "increase and improve project employee knowledge and experience" is linked to employees.

Through the "stakeholders" objective, the method provides a framework for transparent management of the objectives of the project's various specific or special stakeholders.

> *"For example," Collin explains. "it might be of key importance, and thereby of benefit, for the organization to give proper attention to an important supplier. For example, a supplier with key market knowledge and experience has a special relationship with the customer or is a preferred supplier.*

---

[27] Goldratt, 1994 ;Youngman, 2021

While most contact with such a supplier is through the projects, such relationship is often managed unofficially and uncoordinated at best."

"Which does not benefit the organization most," Julie concludes.

"Indeed!" Collin agrees.

Stakeholder management is sometimes defined as a separate process from the management of project objectives, but usually, it overlaps or conflicts. At first sight, stakeholders" targets and expectations might seem less demanding than actual contractual requirements for the project; however, in reality, they are conceived as more demanding. One of the reasons that sometimes certain stakeholders greatly influence the project is because contractual requirements are not always that clear or strict in practice. Compromises, more or less far-reaching, are therefore many times inevitable. For example, a contractual delivery date penalized by a weekly penalty seems 100 percent fixed. But what about discussions with, for example, the customer on who caused the delay, an internal discussion about whether a limited delay could be acceptable for the customer at a certain stage within the project, or an assessment of how successful the customer can claim a penalty?

Synergies Between the Generic Project Objectives

All conceivable project objectives can now be classified as one of the generic supplier project objectives developed in Chapter 4.

- **Competence**: Increase and improve project employee knowledge and experience.

- **Customers**: Satisfy project customers now and in the future.

- **Employees**: Provide project employees with secure and satisfying project work.

- **Innovation**: Innovate project products, services, or other results.

- **Lessons learned**: Identify and "feed back" project lessons learned.

- **Money**: Generate project profit or secure funds now and in the future.

- **Process assets**: Increase, improve, and innovate project process assets.

- **Resources**: Utilize project resources effectively and efficiently.

- **Rules and values**: Enhance project compliance with legislation, regulation, and society and organizational values.

- **Stakeholders**: Satisfy project stakeholders now and in the future.

"Although most generic supplier project objectives are inter-connected and create various synergies, even stronger connections exist between specific generic supplier project objectives," Collin explains while he points at the flip chart.

"For example, rules and values are connected to employees, stakeholders, and customers." And Collin points at the various arrows in between.

Jr. agrees and says, "And employees are connected to competence, and stakeholder and rules and values." (Figure 5-3)

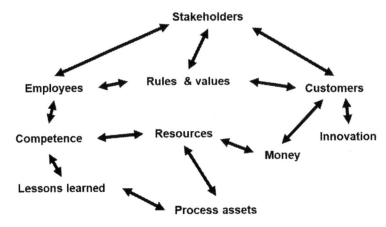

Figure 5-3. *Interconnections between the generic supplier project objectives*

And Collin continues. "And if you recall the earlier introduced metaphor of 'project objection actions through project actions, with the supplier project actions acting as catalysts for the supplier project objective actions," Collin explains. (Figure 5-4)

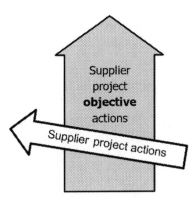

Figure 5-4. *Project objective actions through project actions*

"This provides a nice symbolic representation of the generic supplier project objectives and their links. A house representing the supplier project objective actions to achieve the generic supplier project objectives seen through the windows of the house. And the house also an arrow pointing upward toward the organization's goal via the supplier organizational benefits." Collin explains while pointing at a figure in the book. *(Figure 5-5)*

Figure 5-5. *The generic supplier project objectives*

I have defined the generic supplier project objectives because of a certain classification of objectives based on productive aspects of project subjects, which best supports the method. The generic objectives do not have an order of priority. In fact, priority assessment between objectives for the specific organization and the specific project, is an important step in the method's process (Chapter 6).

Thinking back on Goldratt's goal definition in his Theory of Constraints and Youngman's elaboration for a "public company traded on the open stock exchange," it might be straightforward to suggest that the most important objective is money, followed by customers and employees, and other objectives. However, within the method—a generic method for either non-profit or for-profit organizations—all generic supplier project objectives have equal importance until they are prioritized for the organization via the method's implementation process (Chapter 6). Therefore, the method does not include any priority and lists generic supplier project objectives without prioritization in alphabetic order.

In principle, each conceivable project objective should fit within one of these generic supplier project objectives, with the non-specific "stakeholders" objective being a collective group for (special) objectives linked to the project's stakeholders, which are less well captured by one of the other more specific generic objectives.

Objectives vs. Constraints?

Are all supplier project objectives clear, or do some act more like a constraint or partially as a constraint? Before answering this question, we must understand the difference between objectives and constraints. An achieved objective or target that results in added value, the organizational benefit, is an actual objective. However, an objective or target that must be complied with does not bring any added value and seems more like a constraint instead and not an objective. A constraint can be thought of as a catalyst as well, necessary for a process but not directly used or involved in the output of a process. Some project objectives look more like constraints at first glance instead of objectives, however, they can still be used as objectives, just like any other objective.

> *"For example, a project's compliance with the main applicable electrical standard. You might think you can either comply or not comply with such a standard. But I guess you realize in*

practice that it is not that black and white. In fact, it is more likely that your project complies up to a certain (high) degree instead of not or fully. Doesn't it?"

"Yes, definitely!" Julie confirms.

"And such an objective that looks like a constraint at first glance might create added value instead." Collin continuous.

"Like acceptance or recognition from society by compliance with certain values of society, such as renewable energies. That is an added value. So, an objective might indeed be to comply with a certain standard or a society value as much as practically possible, balanced with other objectives, thereby resulting in the added value that the organization benefits from."

Table 5-2 indicates various supporting principles to identify the method's remaining generic supplier project objectives, such as leadership vs. management, qualitative vs. quantitative, and productive change. The standard generic supplier project objectives can, therefore, also be categorized as typical leadership (customers, innovation, rules, values, and stakeholders), management (competence, employees, lessons learned, process assets, and money), or both leadership and management (resources). Or categorized as typical qualitative (such as customers, employees, innovation, rules, values, and stakeholders), quantitative (such as money), or a combination of both (such as competence, lessons learned, process assets, and resources).

But why is quality itself, not a generic supplier project objective? Because quality is already integrated with other project objectives, such as customers (the customer is only satisfied when it receives the expected quality of the project result), stakeholders (certain stakeholders might demand a minimum quality as well), or rules and values (the organization might have a certain quality level as a core value). Furthermore, project quality is also controlled by the (standard) project control "quality" controlling the project actions (project execution). Finally, the generic supplier project objectives can be categorized by their primary productive change driver: to increase, improve, satisfy, provide, or secure.

Table 5-2. *Leadership vs. Management, Qualitative vs. Quantitative, and Productive Change*

Generic Supplier Project Objective	Leadership vs. Management	Qualitative vs. Quantitative	Productive Change
Competence	management	quantitative, qualitative	increase, improve
Customers	leadership	qualitative	satisfy
Employees	management	qualitative	provide
Innovation	leadership	qualitative	innovate
Lessons learned	management	quantitative, qualitative	identify, feed back
Money	management	quantitative	generate, secure
Process assets	management	quantitative, qualitative	increase, improve, innovate
Resources	leadership, management	quantitative, qualitative	effective, efficient
Rules and values	leadership	qualitative	enhance, compliance
Stakeholders	leadership	qualitative	satisfy

Part of the generic supplier project objectives are success criteria (outputs) and success factors (inputs) on the next project, such as competence, innovation, lessons learned, process assets, and resources. Each generic project objective is further introduced in the next section.

Supplier Project Objectives by Actions Through Project Execution

The supplier project actions that execute the project and deliver the project result act as a *catalyst* for the supplier project objective actions, which achieve the supplier project objectives within the supplier's organization (Figure 4-13). From this it is important to note that supplier project objectives are potential supplier organizational benefits achieved by supplier project objective actions *through project execution*: through executing the project or delivering the project result (Table 5-3).

Table 5-3. *Actions Through Project Execution*

Generic Supplier	Project Objective	Execution or Delivery Characteristic
Competence	Increase and improve project employee knowledge and experience	through executing the project
Customers	Satisfy project customers now and in the future	through executing the project and delivering the project result
Employees	Provide project employees with secure and satisfying project work	through executing the project
Innovation	Innovate project products, services, or other results	through delivering the project result
Lessons learned	Identify and "feed back" project lessons learned	through executing the project

(continued)

Table 5-3. (*continued*)

Generic Supplier	Project Objective	Execution or Delivery Characteristic
Money	Generate project profit or secure funds now and in the future	through executing the project and by delivering the project result
Process assets	Improve and innovate project process assets	through executing the project
Resources	Utilize project resources effectively and efficiently	through executing the project
Rules and values	Enhance project compliance with legislation, regulation, and society and organizational values	through executing the project and delivering the project result
Stakeholders	Satisfy project stakeholders now and in the future	through executing the project and delivering the project result

Summary

How do you cause productive changes of the project supplier's organization and its project execution practices?

This can be done by achieving specific project objectives from the supplier perspective, such as to make, improve, increase, innovate, utilize, secure, comply, satisfy, or "feed back" productive aspects of project subjects. The supplier project objectives are, in addition to customers and money, competence, employees, innovation, lessons learned, process assets, resources, rules and values, and stakeholders.

CHAPTER 6

Process: How to Implement Change?

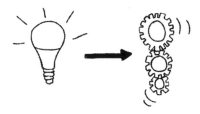

How can the required change be implemented within the project supplier's organization and its project execution practices?

The previous chapter focused on how to cause change by introducing generic project objectives. This chapter introduces the process of the method and addresses how to implement change within the project supplier's organization and its project execution practices.

The Model and Process

As the first part of the final step toward a project objectives management method for the project supplier—called *supplier project objectives management*, or SPOM-I merge the generic supplier project objectives (Figure 5-5) with the supplier perspective on project objectives

© Reitse van der Wekken 2024
R. van der Wekken, *Project Objectives Management*,
https://doi.org/10.1007/979-8-8688-0956-9_6

(Figure 4-18). The resulting SPOM model structures its key elements (supplier project objective actions, supplier project objectives, supplier organizational benefits, and supplier goal) alongside the execution of the project and delivering the project result to the customer (the supplier project actions) and defines the generic supplier project objectives, the primary interface between the project (team) and the organization, as illustrated in Figure 6-1.

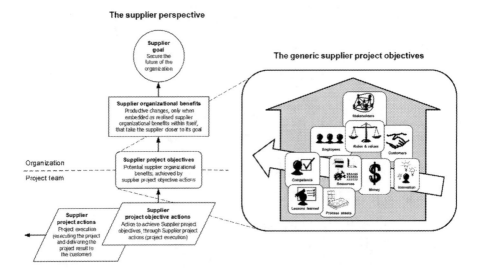

Figure 6-1. *SPOM model*

For these supplier project objective actions, I stress the importance of the following.

- the *active* action to actively change potential supplier organizational benefits into actual realized supplier organizational benefits by embedding them within the organization

- the responsible party (project team or organization) for these actions

According to T.J. Cooke-Davies, benefits are not delivered or realized by the project manager and project team. They require the actions of operations management.[1] This calls for close cooperation between the project team on the one hand and the *sponsor* or *customer* on the other. This fact is elevated to his ninth critical factor for project success: the existence of an effective benefits delivery and management process that involves the cooperation of project management and line management functions.

The SPOM Process

As the second part of the final step toward a project objectives management method for the project supplier, I capture the elements of the method's model in an implementation and execution process within the organization.

The following are the main principles of effective project objectives management for project suppliers.

- Create incentives to subordinate the project to its organization and its goal.

- Transform passive results of supplier project actions into proactively managed supplier project objective actions to achieve specific supplier project objectives (passive supplier project actions act as catalysts for active supplier project objective actions).

- Proactively embed potential supplier organizational benefits as actual realized supplier organizational benefits within the organization.

---

[1] Cooke-Davies, 2002

Note that the project objectives connect and align the activities of the project team with those of the organization, acting on the interface between the project and the organization. According to Cooke-Davies,[2] business or organizational benefits, as opposed to project objectives, are not delivered or realized by the project manager and project team. They require the actions of operations management. This is elevated to his ninth critical factor for project success: an effective benefits delivery and management process involving the cooperation of project management and line management functions. A major challenge is that certain objectives contradict or compete for available sources, which must be managed (balanced), always with the organization's goal to secure its future as guidance.

SPOM is implemented within the supplier's organization by six repetitive organizational and project team process activities.

- organizational definition of organizational objectives

- project definition of specific objectives

- planning of objective actions

- execution of objective actions

- measurement and control of objective actions

- embedding organizational benefits

---

[2] Cooke-Davies, 2002

These process activities are interlinked by a process flow from one project to the next via its organization, managed by the project team and the organization (management and staff departments) (Figure 6-2).

Oxford Dictionaries defines strategy as "a plan of action designed to achieve a long-term or overall aim." The organizational definition is the strategic level of the method executed by the organization.[3] Planning, implementation, measurement and control, and embedding are the succeeding execution levels of the method. Within the execution level, planning, implementation, measurement, and control are executed by each project; the organization again executes embedding and finally feeds back to the organization's organizational definition.

---

[3] Oxford, 2012

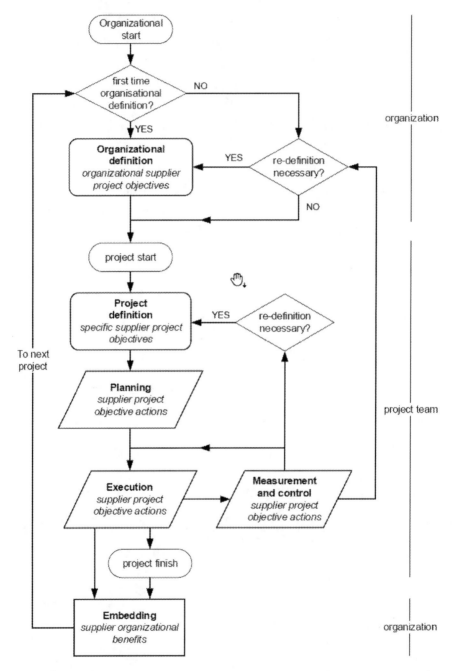

Figure 6-2. The SPOM process

The process consists of the following activities.

- **Organizational start**: The process starts with the implementation of SPOM within the organization, onwards to the first choice within the process.

- **First-time organizational definition?** Flowing from the project start or back from a completed organizational and project cycle, the first choice checks if this is the first time for the organization to conduct the organizational process activity of *organizational definition* or not. If yes, the process flows directly to that first organizational activity. If not, the process initially bypasses this first activity; however, it flows via another choice—*is redefinition necessary?*

- **Organizational definition**: This first and organizational process activity of the method allows for tailoring (definition) *generic* into *organizational* supplier project objectives specific for its organization, executed by the organization (management and staff departments). In addition, the organizational objectives are prioritized based on the organization's core philosophy and vision. These organizational supplier project objectives form the basis and the input for the remainder of the method's process by the project team and the organization.

- **Is redefinition of organizational objectives necessary?** This choice checks if the redefinition of the organizational supplier project objectives is necessary or not, flowing from the choice if it concerns a *first-time organizational definition*. If yes, the process does flow back to this first organizational process activity. If not, the process finally bypasses this first activity and flows onto the *project start*.

- **Project start**: From the organizational definition, the process flows on to the start of the project, where the project team starts the project-related process activities of the method based on the input from the *organizational definition* process activity. The process flows on to the first the first project team process activity of the method, *project definition*.

- **Project definition**: The first project team process activity of the method consists again of tailoring (definition), but now of *organizational* into *project-specific* supplier project objectives relevant or suitable for the project, executed by the project team and approved by the organization (management), based on the organizational supplier project objectives defined by the organization. From *Project definition*, the process flows on to *planning*.

- **Planning**: The next project team process activity consists of planning supplier project objective actions to achieve the project-specific supplier project objectives, executed by the project team, and approved by the organization (management). From *planning* and the control loop from the process activity measurement and control, the process flows to *execution*.

- **Execution**: The main project team process activity during the project execution phase is the execution of supplier project objective actions to achieve the project-specific supplier project objectives executed by the project team. From the *execution* process activity, the process can flow in different directions; back into the control loop via the "measurement and control" process activity; to the finish of the project, after having flowed through various control loops of *execution* and *measurement and control*; or directly to the next and organizational process activity, during the project execution (intermediate) prior to project finish.

- **Measurement and control**: The control loop of *execution* is conducted by measuring and controlling the supplier project objective actions, executed by the project team, and reported to the organization (management). This control loop flows various cycles until the finish of the project.

- **Is redefinition of project-specific objectives necessary?** Another process flows into this project team process activity of project definition flows from a choice which checks if redefinition of project-specific supplier project objectives is necessary or not, flowing from the *measurement and control* process activity.

- **Project finish**: From *execution*, the process flows to *embedding* directly, or via *project finish*.

- **Embedding**: Directly from the project following execution or after the project finishes, the process flows to the organizational process activity *embedding*, where supplier organizational benefits are embedded (made available by turning potential into actual realized organizational benefits) within the organization, executed by the organization (management and staff departments). After *embedding*, the process flows back

to the first choice, which checks if this is the first time
for the organization to conduct the organizational
process activity of *organizational definition* or not?

Each process activity and redefinition choice are further introduced in
the next section.

Supplier project objectives management (SPOM) is the management
of the active elements of the SPOM model (actions, objectives, and
organizational benefits) by the management of the six repetitive
organizational and project team process activities of the SPOM process
(definition, planning, implementation, measurement and control, and
embedding). The method revolves around the supplier project objectives,
to be achieved by implementing planned objective actions through
execution (executing the project and delivering the project result). The
achieved supplier project objectives are potential supplier organizational
benefits that turn into actual realized supplier organizational benefits by
embedding changes within the supplier's organization that take it closer to
its goal of securing the future of the organization.

The Process Activities

In this section, the six process activities and two redefinition choices of the
method are further introduced: organizational definition of organizational
objectives; redefinition of organizational supplier project objectives;
project definition of specific objectives; redefinition of project-specific
supplier project objectives; planning of objective actions; execution of
objective actions; measurement and control of objective actions; and
finally embedding of organizational benefits.

Organizational Definition of Generic Objectives

This first process activity consists of two steps. Step one tailors generic supplier project objectives to organizational supplier project objectives specific to its organization at the organizational level by the organization (management and staff departments), which should at least be achieved on its projects or be selected from its projects. It is important to note that this process activity *allows for* tailoring of the generic supplier project objectives; however, it does not explicitly *require* tailoring all generic objectives. Some generic objectives might already be sufficient or appropriate to be adopted as organizational objectives.

Applicable generic supplier project objectives are identified based on the project supplier's rules and values, core ideology, business type, and strengths and weaknesses. The project supplier selects applicable and removes non-applicable generic supplier project objectives; develops objectives applicable to their specific situation within each applicable group; assigns existing objectives within one of these groups; and, if applicable, assigns any uncommon objective connected to a specific stakeholder within the generic stakeholders objective. For this purpose, the generic stakeholders group is reserved for all other stakeholders besides customers and employees.

Next, the tailored organizational objectives are prioritized based on the organization's core philosophy and vision. In this activity, it should be kept in mind that these organizational objectives should match with the strengths, weaknesses, opportunities, and threats of the organization and its projects, and how the organization and its projects with its organizational objectives can create productive change within the organization to secure the future of the organization.

This process activity might be (partly) repeated when a redefinition is required, for example, based on an evaluation of the success of embedded actual realized supplier organizational benefits of a preceding project within its organization.

> *"So, let's work out the next generic supplier project objective into an organizational supplier project objective at SES, the competence objective of which you both expressed its importance at SES," Collin kicks off the morning session with John and Julie.*

> *"John," Collin continues while looking at Jr. "what does the generic supplier project objective of competence consist of?"*

> *"The competence objective is to increase and improve employee knowledge and experience," John answers confidently.*

> *"Correct, and I can see that you take this seriously and that you studied your homework. I appreciate that," Collin says and continues. "Now, what is so special about this objective at SES, and how do you want to tailor this to an organizational objective at SES?"*

> *"Well, we are working in a field of business with a high pace of new technology. We depend highly on our specialists that keep track of these developments, and we need to train less experienced employees quickly on these new technologies," Julie explains.*

> *"Yes, this is of critical importance now. This pace of development is already different from when I started working here. I hope our team of specialists will be able to grasp all these new technologies indeed," Jr. adds.*

"It's good that you make that point, and important to notice that you say 'hope,' because that is exactly what we need to and are going to change. Instead of hoping, we will work actively toward securing SES' future by implementing change.

"Now talking about change," Collin continues with a smile and asks nobody in particular.

"Is there anything you would like to change in the definition or wording of the generic competence objective to tailor it to SES' culture, for example, to make your organizational competence objective?"

"Well, in general, I would not change the essence of the generic competence objective. However, it would be good to align it with our names and definitions to highlight the SES culture," Julie answers and further explains. *"A term like fit for purpose, we use a lot, and competence as well. Everybody at SES knows that it consists of both knowledge and experience, as clarified in our competence and appraisal management process.*

"Something like to 'create fit for purpose project team members'?" Jr. steps in.

"That's a good start, I like that," Collin says encouragingly and writes it down on the flip chart under the underlined wording *organizational project objective.*

"Can I suggest changing 'create project team members' into 'create competences of project team members.' Rephrasing this to 'create fit for purpose competences of SES' project team members.'"

"Yes, I can live with that," Jr. confirms smiling.

Collin takes a couple of small sips of his coffee, and both Julie and John notice that he is thinking again. After some more time, Collin says.

"But I am still not sure about the word 'create.' That implies that you can just create a fit for purpose competence of a project team member."

"I don't see a problem with that. It's all about catching the essence and the feel of the wording, and it's not an exact science you told us yourself," Julie responds.

"Touché!" Collin answers with a big smile.

"I agree with Julie, but let's change 'SES' to 'our,' which gives it a more intimate tone that fits with SES,' with our culture," Jr. confirms.

"So that gives us to 'create fit for purpose competences of our project team members.'" Collin concludes.

"Well, now we are at it anyway, then I want to change the description to a 'SES supplier project objective.'" John Jr. steps in again.

"I like that, it shows that you really take ownership of the method's implementation, of tailoring it to SES," Collin says. (Figure 6-3)

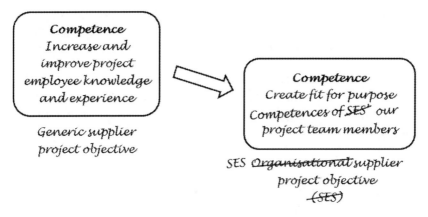

Figure 6-3. *Competence objective at SES*

"And of course, of high importance at SES is innovation," John Jr. says, which causes a big smile on Jr.'s face.

"Okay, I see that you get the hang of it now, but let's work that one further out in our next session," Collin replies while looking at his watch.

In this process activity, it is very important to tailor the generic supplier project objectives to relevant project objectives aligned with the organization's core philosophy and values. For the competence objective, it is important to define which vital competencies are highly important for the project supplier and its portfolio of project results and how these competences could be increased and improved on its project.

"Actually, I had a thought last night about your remark during our last session, about the importance of innovation," Collin says while walking to the flip chart with the last page of the last session.

"Why not combine these two, competence and innovation! Yes, innovation can be a stand-alone objective. However, apparently you are looking for personnel, all personnel, not only your engineers, with the same innovative mentality, with the same creativity, as you, or am I wrong?"

John and Julie look at each other, both thinking this over for a moment, and then Julie answers.

"Yes, definitely, I want Dad and our personnel to have the same vision on innovation, I know that it is of key importance for the future of SES!"

"So, let's see how that looks if we incorporate that to make the competence objective more to the point for SES," Collin says and walks over to the flip chart. (Figure 6-4)

Competence
Create innovative and creative project team members

SES 'Competence' project objective

Figure 6-4. *Updated competence objective at SES*

"Yes, I like that!" Jr. says, but Julie pushes on and says, "Yes, it's good, but why not make it even more specific?"

"I see where you're going," Collin answers with a smile. He is very satisfied with the initiative that is now changing toward John and Julie.

"I would like to add that we want our employees to develop creativity toward the building of the future, with a focus on automation, sustainability, and environmental impact."

Finally, after some more work they come up with a satisfying result. (Figure 6-5)

Competence
Have SES project team members develop creativity in environmentally friendly, sustainable and automated building technology

SES 'Competence' project objective

Figure 6-5. *Final competence objective at SES*

"And as we concluded earlier that within SES the combination of competence and innovation is a key part of your core philosophy and vision, so let's now define the SES innovation objective, which we can always further fine-tune later. This combination will strengthen both objectives!" Collin says, and they continue to formulate the innovation project objective for SES. (Figure 6-6)

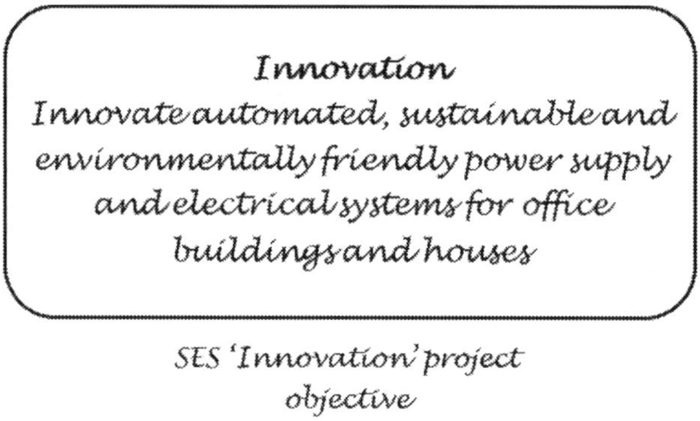

Innovation
Innovate automated, sustainable and environmentally friendly power supply and electrical systems for office buildings and houses

SES 'Innovation' project objective

Figure 6-6. *Innovation objective at SES*

For identifying and tailoring all organizational project objectives applicable to the organization, a good basis is provided by establishing various overviews—developed based on various methods, such as brain storing—of productive aspects of the relevant project subjects specific to the organization itself or a SWOT analysis of the organization.

"Now, after the last session's polishing of your competence objective and defining the innovation objective along with it, let's work the coming period on the other organizational project objectives of SES," Collin introduces the session.

"I thought about it, but I don't know where to start?" Julie says while sounding overwhelmed.

"That is a good question, but you already did a lot of the hard work during our earlier sessions," Collin responds while flipping over a page from one of the earlier flip charts. (Figure 6-7)

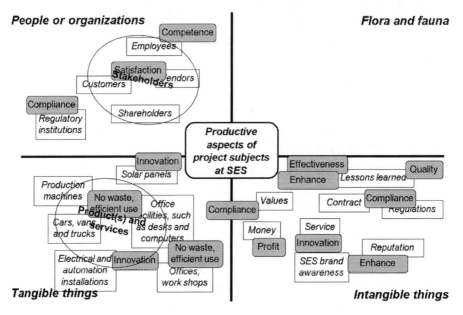

Figure 6-7. *Productive aspects of project subjects at SES*

"Ah, the productive aspects of our project subjects that we prepared earlier!" John Jr. says excitedly, and Collin responds.

"Yes, this page introduced the topic of productive aspects of project subjects. But this page showed the subjects before we made them generic to identify the generic project objectives. So, because these are tailored to SES, they are the perfect starting point now for the definition of your organizational project objectives of SES."

"And in addition, we have the SWOT analyses that we pre-pared as well," Collin adds while flipping over pages on the other flip charts. (Figure 6-8)

"I already know another important objective for SES," John says and continues.

"As an engineering driven company with fierce competition and tight profit margins, the use and improvement of our set of engineering tools is of primary importance. That is all about process assets."

And Julie adds. "Yes, we need unconditional use of those tools instead of sometimes having older personnel still using their own calculations, which they sometimes do not share with their colleagues as well."

"Indeed, unconditional use, a continuous process of actually improving the tools where required," Jr. steps in again.

"That is indeed an important principle for successful change management as well when you have people resisting the change. You need to convince them that they will be involved in further change or improvement. But first start with the first proposal, then use and review it, and then work on further improvements," Collin says, getting enthusiastic as well.

They summarize this together on the flip chart as "Unconditional use, improvement and innovation of SES' engineering tools by our project teams (process assets)."

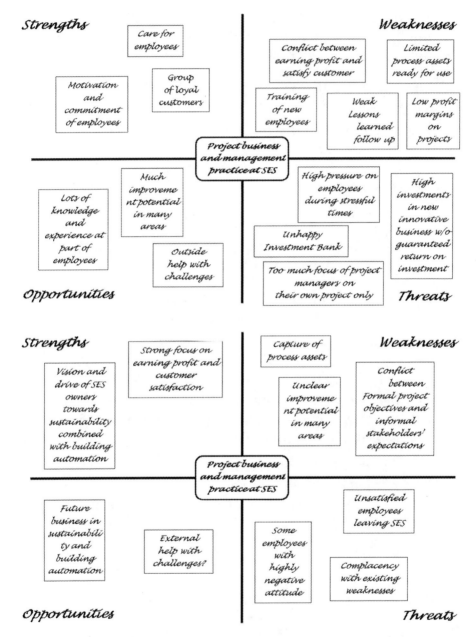

Figure 6-8. *SWOT analysis of project business and management at SES (flip charts 1 and 2)*

"You know how important satisfied customers are for me. I always want to solve our customers' challenges, and it is important for me that they know they can trust SES to put their interests as the top priority. However, I would like to combine this with your vision and drive to provide state-of-the-art solutions," Jr. says to Julie.

"Okay, then let's define our customer objective as 'provide state-of-the-art building solutions to solve SES' project customers' challenges, now and in the future.'" Julie concludes happily.

"I like this, Julie! It all comes together now."

"Yes, this is getting a good foundation to clearly share our vision and values and how we want to integrate this within our day-to-day operations with our management team and employees."

"Let's call it SES project objectives management 1.0. And now we can deeper involve our management team and employees to build version 2.0," John concludes.

Collin has nothing to add to this anymore. John and Julie are now unconsciously talking to each other and not to Collin anymore. He oversees it all, satisfied with a big smile. His work at SES with John Jr. and Julie is almost done and coming to an end. He will miss the lively discussions with Julie and John, and he learned a lot from this consulting job himself as well again.

Then, having another thought about it, Collin suggests, "Now, understanding how important competence, innovation, and customers are to you and to SES, I suggest the following 'rules and values' objective to further strengthen this within the DNA of SES. To 'Enhance project commitment to SES' vision and values to innovate and provide state-of-the-art building solutions for SES' customers.'"

And Collin has another thought and asks Jr. and Julie.

"Do you sometimes come across a project that has a new idea for a good innovation during the project execution?"

"Yes, we do," Jr. answers.

"And do these always generate additional revenue on the project in the end?"

"No, sometimes it only costs extra on the project in the end. But sometimes, even if we expect this, we still have them complete it on the project. But then the usual discussions start about having the cost transferred to a corporate cost position," Julie answers.

"But that's not what we want. We want to keep it simple without too many costs being transferred to cost accounts without any revenue. And, we think that there is more motivation and connection to a business case if we keep it on the project.

"I thought so," Collin says and then asks. "Then why not make this explicit in your SES objective for money?"

"You mean like defining in our corporate SES money project objective?" She asks.

"Yes, why not?" Collin asks in return. "You can still review and decide on such an innovation proposal case by case. However, you do make it explicit that such unplanned developments are stimulated."

After some further discussion John and Julie agree and end up with the SES money project objective to 'generate project profit now and in the future, however, stimulate unplanned project investment in innovations.' (Figure 6-9)

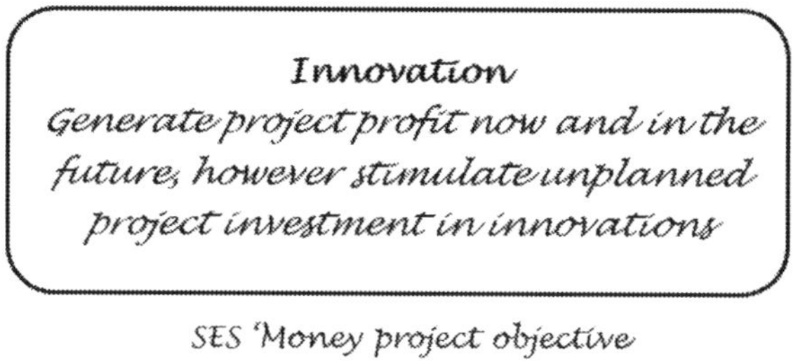

Innovation
Generate project profit now and in the future, however stimulate unplanned project investment in innovations

SES 'Money project objective

Figure 6-9. *Money objective at SES*

After more hard work during multiple follow-up sessions, John, Julie, and Collin came up with a complete set of applicable organizational project objectives for SES. The organizational definition activity does not require all generic objectives to be tailored; some remain as is, appropriate for SES; some are partly adapted, such as to generate project profit with SES being a for-profit company, and some have 'SES' included in the definition to make them easier to be identified with. (Table 6-1)

Table 6-1. *Tailored Organizational Supplier Project Objectives for SES*

Generic Supplier Project Objective		Organizational Supplier Project Objectives for SES
Competence	Increase and improve employee knowledge and experience	**Have SES project team members develop creativity in environmentally friendly, sustainable, and automated building technology**
Customers	Satisfy customers now and in the future	**Provide state-of-the-art building solutions to solve SES' project customers' challenges, now and in the future**

(*continued*)

Table 6-1. (*continued*)

Generic Supplier Project Objective		Organizational Supplier Project Objectives for SES
Employees	Provide employees with secure and satisfying project work	**Provide SES' project employees with secure and satisfying work**
Innovation	Innovate products, services, or other results	**Create at least one unplanned innovation per project, in automated, sustainable and environmentally friendly building technology**
Lessons learned	Identify and feed back lessons learned	**Relentlessly identify and feed back project lessons learned into the SES organization**
Money	Generate profit or secure funds now and in the future	**Generate project profit now and in the future, however, stimulate unplanned project investment in innovations**
Process assets	Improve and innovate process assets	**Unconditional use, improvement, and innovation of SES' engineering tools by our project teams (process assets)**
Resources	Utilize resources effectively and efficiently	**Utilize SES' project resources effectively and efficiently**
Rules and values	Enhance compliance with legislation, regulation, and society and organizational values	**Enhance project commitment to SES' vision and values to innovate and provide state-of-the-art automated, sustainable, and environmentally friendly building solutions for SES' customers**
Stakeholders	Satisfy stakeholders now and in the future	**Satisfy project and SES' stakeholders now and in the future**

"You know," Jr. says while looking at the two flip charts with the complete set of SES objectives. "The good thing is, thinking about the challenge of a change process within our organization, that this is not completely new stuff at all! These SES project objectives connect the vision and values of Julie and me of SES with our projects. However, these are mostly existing values and ideas."

"Yes, existing, but up to now not clearly written down and communicated with our employees and stakeholders," Julie responds.

"Well noted. Many times, setting up and implementing this method is not about a complete set of new things. Usually, it is mostly all already existing within organizations. However, now project success is clearly linked to organizational success. Like at SES, now project success at SES is clearly linked to SES' (organizational) success based on SES' vision and values," Collin summarizes.

In the next step of this process activity, the identified applicable organizational objectives are prioritized based on the organization's core philosophy and vision. Surely, some organizations and some for-profit companies will have money as the main priority. However, others might balance this with another core value of the company or even put another objective as the main priority. Some organizations will put their customers on a high priority as well. Non-profit organizations might altogether have other objectives, although these organizations also have financial objectives, if not profit at least to ensure future sufficient funding. Similarities will exist between many similar types of organizations. However, in the end, each organization will have its unique set of organizational objectives and its unique priority of these objectives based on its core philosophy and values.

"Now, today we have more hard work ahead of us. You thought that identifying the applicable organizational project objectives for SES was challenging, now we are going to put them in order of priority," Collin starts the morning session.

"What?" Julie replies. "But they are all important. We worked so hard to get all these important objectives on the table, and you want us to choose!?"

"Yes, I know that is difficult, but it is more important to give direction to your project teams. They should know which objective is more important than another in case of conflicts. And I assure you, conflicts will remain! But now you have a system, a method to deal with such conflict in a structured and proactive way. It will not make it A LOT easier, but it will make it easier," Collin answers and assures her.

"But relax, you might give one or more objectives the same priority, as long as you provide the priority which is in line with SES' core philosophy and values."

Finally, after hard work during another long evening session, they come up with an updated set of prioritized organizational project objectives for SES. (Table 6-2)

Table 6-2. *Prioritized Organizational Supplier Project Objectives for SES*

Priority	SES Supplier Project Objectives		
1	Innovation	Employees	Money
2	Customers	Competence	
3	Rules and values	Stakeholders	
4	Process assets	Lessons learned	
5	Resources		

"It is good to see how you have prioritized the first three objectives. It is crystal clear how important innovation and employees are, however, by putting money also at priority number one, you have a clear signal that bottom-line earnings remain critical for the SES as well," Collin concludes and looks at Julie.

"And in case of a conflict between one of these objectives, it does help that we have clearly defined in the money objective that some unplanned innovation cost is actually accepted, even stimulated," Jr. steps in and looks at her as well.

"I guess we agree that it was difficult to make such a prioritization, so now you also understand how difficult it is for your project teams to manage all targets and expectations thrown at them by all stakeholders of their projects. This list will help them greatly because now they know how SES wants them to prioritize. And as said, if you are not comfortable with the current prioritization or if it creates unwanted responses on your projects, you can always change it and send a new instruction to your project teams. However, make sure that you do explain why you made the change," Collin explains.

"Yes, we know, transparency and clarity are of primary importance for success," Both Jr. and Julie respond in unison.

Furthermore, in the organizational definition activity, relevant key performance indicators (KPIs) need to be defined by the organization for the defined organizational supplier project objectives—against which the project and its team members, management, and staff departments can be evaluated—in the measurement and control process activity. The priority of the defined organizational supplier project objectives can be managed by assigning weight factors to the KPIs to stimulate the focus and priority accordingly.

Redefinition of Organizational Supplier Project Objectives Necessary?

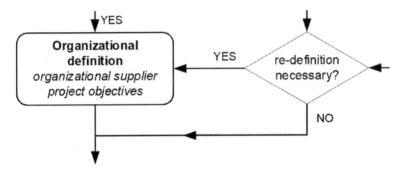

This first redefinition choice checks if redefinition of the organizational supplier project objectives is necessary because even if it is not a first-time definition of the organizational supplier project objectives, a redefinition might be required. Various reasons might cause such a choice to redefine all or part of the organizational supplier project objectives of the organization. They can be caused by internal or external changes in the organization, such as a change of the core values (internal), changing market circumstances (external), or a change in the job market for personnel (external). A redefinition can consist of a partial adjustment of an organizational supplier project objective or perhaps even the complete removal or addition of an objective.

> *Collin explains. "In the future, in SES' future, it might be necessary to adjust your competence objective, for example, if more specific objective actions need to be fulfilled on the next projects to be able to increase and improve a specific new competence of your project team members required within SES."*

Project Definition of Specific Objectives

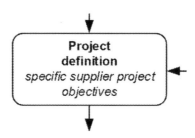

The defined organizational objectives are tailored again, or a selection is made from them. Next, they create project-specific objectives linked to the project's potential within the project by the project team and approved by the organization (management). In this activity, it should be kept in mind that these specific objectives should match with the project's strengths, weaknesses, opportunities, and risks and how the project and its specific objectives can create productive change within the organization to secure the future of the organization.

In practice, defining a specific supplier project objective often goes hand in hand or in parallel with an idea for a concrete supplier project objective action. First, the objective action is thought of and then, within the process captured under the relevant project objective. However, in other cases, no concrete objective action is thought of yet, and the specific objective is fixed as a potential target for the project. Reviewing the preliminary risk and opportunity matrix or a SWOT analysis of the project can provide further input for specific project objectives.

> *"So, I guess we will select the organizational 'competence' objective for the KC Foods project because during our last session, we already worked out a concrete project competence objective action with Elena and Christos on the KC Foods project. But let's see if we can tailor the organizational competence objective more specifically for the KC Foods project,"* Collin says.

"But if not, that is also fine. Sometimes you can or want to tailor it to a more project-specific definition, but sometimes it is good as it is."

"We defined to 'Have SES project team members develop creativity in environmentally friendly, sustainable and automated building technology" Julie summarizes.

"So, we can make it specific by tailoring it to creative and automation, if we only define that specific objective action with Christos, where we focused on his experience in creativity and automation," Jr. says.

"Yes, it is always good to make the specific project objectives for the project at hand as specific as possible," Collin concludes and writes this down on the flip chart. (Figure 6-10)

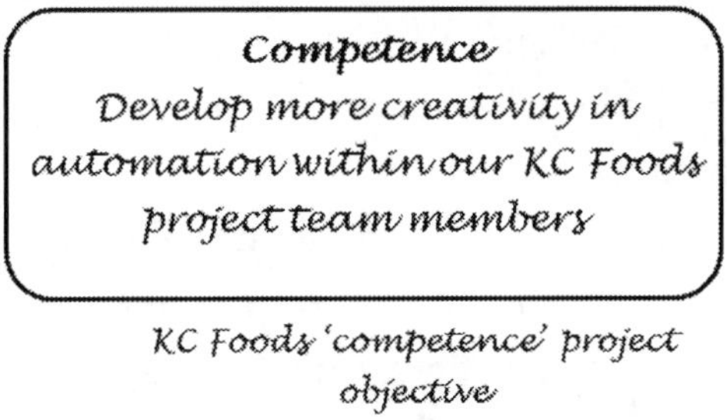

Competence
Develop more creativity in automation within our KC Foods project team members

KC Foods 'competence' project objective

Figure 6-10. *Competence project objective on the KC Foods project*

After defining all specific project objectives for the project, a prioritization is established; however, this could also result in multiple objectives with the same priority if no clear priority distinction can be made. Ultimately, the method should be an added value toward securing the future of the organization not a difficult or theoretical exercise.

"First, some background on the creation of specific project objectives for a project," Collin starts today's session, which is also joined by some of SES' project managers, such as Elena, who manages the KC Foods project. And Collin continues.

"If you have a project that starts off with a tight forecasted profit margin but limited other identified risks, that project might offer opportunities to achieve potential supplier organizational benefits toward productive change within SES. Perhaps further developing some new process assets such as an engineering tool, training of a new employee, or something else. A pitfall could be that a negative atmosphere develops around the project and during the progress meetings with management because of the tight profit margin.

"Yes, I understand what you mean," Elena steps in, thinking about some past projects.

"However, it would be an opportunity lost, if that negative atmosphere would prevent other potential organizational benefits to be pursuit. So instead, accept the situation with the tight profit margin that perhaps cannot be significantly improved, accept that the project objective 'money' will not provide significant productive change, however, instead focus on the opportunity to achieve various other potential for organizational benefits related to other specific supplier project objectives."

"That sounds like the principle to focus more on positives instead of negatives, which in practice unfortunately seems difficult for people, for us," Elena says.

"Correct, but it should still be depending on the circumstances," Collin says.

"What do you mean?" Julie asks.

"Well, in some cases you should focus on the negatives in case of a real threat to the project or organization. If you do have a project with a major risk or threat you should put some significant effort or muscle on it to mitigate. In that case the best decision might be to fully focus on that risk. Perhaps a full focus on the 'money' supplier project objective to prevent a major financial loss on the project, and not get distracted by

dividing the focus over other supplier project objectives as well," Collin explains.

"Ah, okay, so according to the method it is not required that we always and unconditionally focus on the full set of generic supplier project objectives?" Elena asks.

"Indeed. But on the other hand, if you do have a project in a good position with no challenges on the project controls such as time, cost, quality, organization or information, a major effort should be made to maximize the opportunity to achieve as much supplier organizational benefits as possible on that project."

Planning Objective Actions

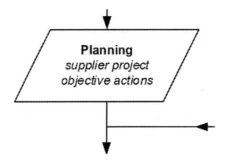

Specific supplier project objective actions are then planned by the project team and approved by the organization (management) that need to be fulfilled to achieve the defined specific project objectives. Again, in this activity, it is important to keep in mind that these objective actions should match with the strengths, weaknesses, opportunities, and threats of the project and how the project, with its objective actions, can create productive change within the organization to secure the future of the organization.

"Let's look at your organizational objective to create innovative and creative project team members, with an organizational focus on automation, sustainability and environmentally friendly," Collin says to start today's session, and he continues.

"As an organization, you can organize, and as a project team allow valuable time of a project team member for a creativity training of an inexperienced but motivated employee, but let's take this a step further to a real and concrete project objective action."

"What are you thinking about?" John Jr. asks Collin, suspecting that Collin has an idea and getting interested.

"The other day you told me about that Daniel, that young guy that just started as trainee," Collin says.

"Yes, we hired Daniel on a hunch because we do see potential in him. Obviously, he is not experienced yet, but now he is also struggling with bringing in added value to the Seaside Industrial Area project.

"And lately he also shows signs of less self-confidence. He doesn't dare to speak up anymore while actually we want him to speak up and come up with ideas, creativity, anything!" Julie adds.

"But you also told me about Christos," Collin answers.

Jr. and Julie look at each other, and then Julie says.

"I think I know where you are going with this. Christos is indeed an experienced engineer and very creative, always coming up with creative ideas that frequently get realized within his projects. His specialty is automation."

"And Christos is good with people, but he is working on the KC Foods project, and we actually need all his focus on that project, as we do have some massive challenges there," John says.

"Well, a productive and concrete objective action for 'compe-tence' could be to have Daniel join Christos on the KC Foods project and see if he can coach Daniel. That might perhaps be better than just sending Daniel to another training."

Collin notices that Jr. and Julie are a bit reserved to this idea but pushes on.

"In that case the KC Foods project team with Christos can potentially contribute a productive change on 'competence' to SES. But it should not be without obligations. It should be fixed as a well-defined project objective action for them to take ownership and accountability."

"You know what," Jr. says. "Let's get Christos and Elena into the meeting, if they are available, to further discuss the details." (Figure 6-11)

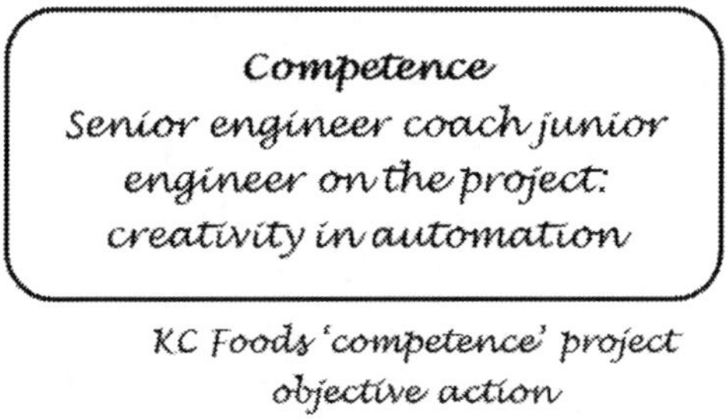

Competence
Senior engineer coach junior
engineer on the project:
creativity in automation

KC Foods 'competence' project
objective action

Figure 6-11. *Competence project objective action*

Of course, not all competence-related personal targets for each project team member must be or should be defined as project objective action for the concerned project. Only when the execution of that objective action has a (significant) impact on the concerned projects does it make sense to incorporate; otherwise, it can just be defined only as a personal target in the employee's personal competence and appraisal form.

Planning of objective actions can be done on various levels of detail. Depending on the organization and its size, or in the case of some larger objective actions or actions linked to a high-priority organizational project objective, they might require a detailed planning activity, including the definition of applicable measurements to conduct the measurement and control activity against. In other cases, or with less critical objective actions it is just a matter of simple definition and reporting the status and progress periodically in the progress report.

In case of such an objective action that requires more detail, the action should be described as detailed and specific as possible to allow for proper measurement as well. In that case, for example, a definition according to the SMART criteria could be adopted, in which case the action should be defined.

- (S)pecific
- (M)easurable
- (A)ttainable
- (R)elevant
- (T)imely

To fulfill the criteria of *measurable*, useful KPI might be defined if required, against which the measurement and control activity can be conducted in more detail by the project team, reporting to the management.

"We have an idea for an innovation that we could develop and implement as a pilot on our KC Foods project this year," Christos tells Julie, then looks to his side and says to Daniel.

"Daniel, why don't you run us through the proposal with your presentation."

"As you know, a traditional setup of solar panels on a flat roof consists of long rows of fixed solar panels, installed as close to each other as possible in a fixed orientation to the sun, to optimize the solar energy generation and maximize the number of panels per square meter," Daniel explains and continuous. (Figure 6-12)

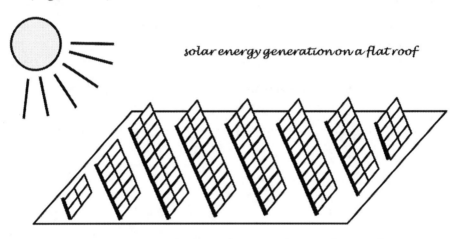

Figure 6-12. *Traditional design solar panels on a flat roof*

"We have run extensive calculations resulting in a solid estimate that, by installing our solar panels on a two-axes rotating base that automatically and continuously aligns each panel perpendicular to the sun, despite having fewer panels per square meter, we should be able to increase our total solar energy generation significantly." (Figure 6-13)

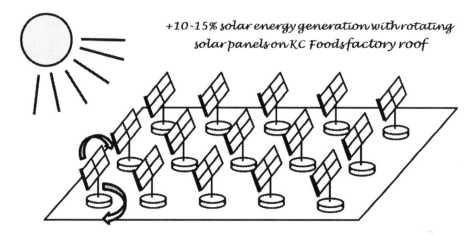

Figure 6-13. *Concept design automated rotating solar panels on KC Foods factory roof*

"Yes, we discussed this idea before. However, I was not aware that the increase was that significant. By how much do you estimate?" Julie asks Daniel.

Daniel looks at Christos, who nods to him in response.

"We now estimate by as much as 10 percent to 15 percent, based on the current concept design of the rotating base and based on a new experimental optimization and control algorithm," Daniel answers Julie.

Julie whistles softly and is seriously impressed.

After more discussions with key stakeholders, including SES' customer KC Foods management, they make the final decision and formally capture this innovation in a redefinition of the 'innovation' specific project objective and objective action on the KC Foods project. KC Foods accepts the pilot project to be implemented on their project, with a cost split arrangement based on positive results. Despite the significant estimate of 10 percent to 15 percent, they agree to a conservative SMART measure target of 10 percent. (Figure 6-14)

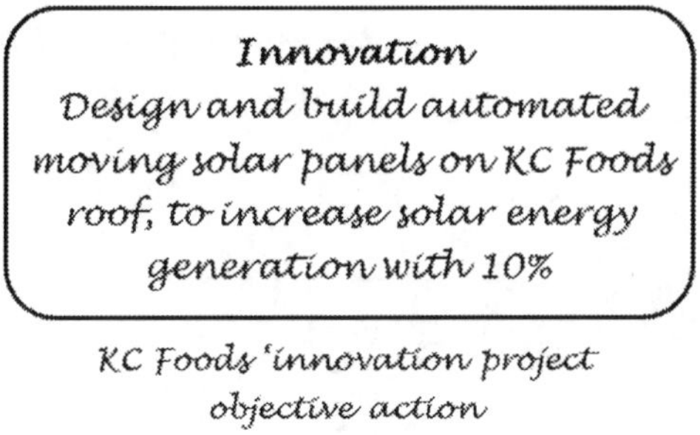

Innovation
Design and build automated
moving solar panels on KC Foods
roof, to increase solar energy
generation with 10%

KC Foods 'innovation project
objective action

Figure 6-14. *Innovation project objective action*

"Is there any specific objective action that we can do on your KC Foods project for the SES project objective to provide state-of-the art building solutions to SES' project customers' challenges, now and in the future?" Collin asks the large group in the meeting room, consisting of SES' management team, line managers and the KC Foods project team.

After another productive but intense brainstorm session, they agree on the bold objective to involve the customer KC Foods actively in the detailed specifications of the automated solar roof, where they normally involve the customer only in the requirements for customer specified scope.

"Let's look at your 'customers' project objective, which is already a bold objective," Collin says, and he continues.

"How can we make a specific action out of your objective to involve KC Foods actively in detailed specifications of the automated solar roof?" Collin now pushes on, while feeling the potential for a productive action with some many stakeholders present.

It is quite for a while, however, then out of nowhere, Daniel leans forward and says, "Why not invite an engineer of KC Foods temporary at our office and join our engineering team, to work out the specifications for the automated system?"

"We can't do that! We never want our clients looking over our shoulder, even worse, looking right at our computer screens!" Elena responds excitedly.

"Actually, I think this is not a bad idea at all! What have we got to hide about our specifications? And this will surely gain us significant goodwill from KC Foods," John Jr. says and continues.

"You know what, we can talk about it for a long time, but I will use my veto this time and decide here and now that we are just going to do this. Good idea Daniel!"

Julie looks at her brother with a big smile again. She is really happy with how things are going these last couple of months as SES. She really feels at her place now and confident in SES' bright future.

They decide to redefine the KC Foods customers project objective to involve KC Foods actively in detailed specifications of the automated solar roof, and as KC Foods customers project objective action to locate a KC Foods engineer temporarily within the engineering team involved in the design of the automated solar roof. (Figure 6-15)

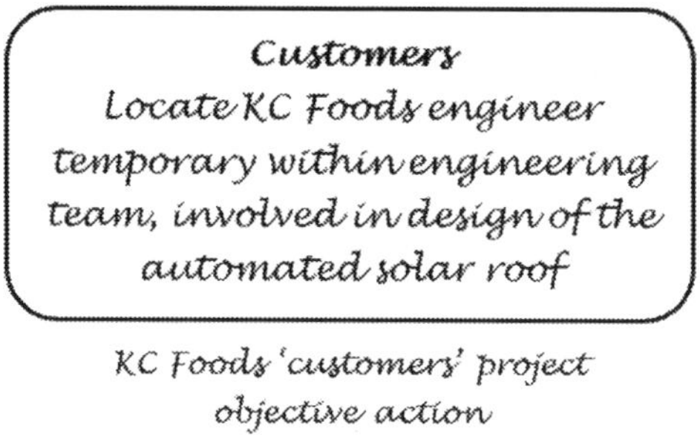

Customers
Locate KC Foods engineer
temporary within engineering
team, involved in design of the
automated solar roof

KC Foods 'customers' project
objective action

Figure 6-15. *Customers project objective action*

Note that within the method, it is not mandatory to develop new and detailed specific project objectives and linked project objective actions for each organizational project objective. There must be a balance between the number of objective actions vs. the project actions or the day-to-day project work.

> *"Now that we are so intensively working on the development and definition of various projective objective actions on the KC Foods project I do, however, want you all to clearly understand that we do not have to, it is not mandatory, to come up with new specific objectives and objective actions for each generic project objective of the method. There should remain a reasonable and manageable balance with your day-to-day work on the project," Collins explains.*

Even without the method, an organization and project team might have devised a certain action anyway, even without SPOM. The real benefit of the method is that the action is integrated within an overall system, becoming part of a structured and planned process, not just incidental, and being transparent, rewarded by the organization, and noted by other project teams.

> *"But if you have planned some specific continuous improvement anyway on a certain project, just make sure to describe it and incorporate it to ensure all is captured and can be managed and controlled during the execution of the actions."*

> *"Yes, we can incorporate two more actions that we had already defined as objectives and objective actions. One for generic objective 'employees' by planning two project team-building sessions, one of them including our customer KC Foods if the team agrees. And another one for an already planned initiative of our continuous improvement department, to actively interview project team members to fill the expertise database, what expertise the project team members have gained, instead of filling lessons learned databases," Elena explains.*

After a couple more review sessions they conclude on the sup-plier project objectives for the KC Foods project. Collin has all participants from SES gathered in the meeting room.

"We are there, don't you think?" Collin says while pointing at the various flip charts."

"Yes, I agree we do," John answers.

"And remember, it doesn't have to be perfect from the start. You just need a good starting point and be prepared for opti-mizations and changes along the way," Collin answers and adds with a smile.

"I see a nice job for a volunteer to gather all this in a nice PowerPoint presentation." (Table 6-3)

Table 6-3. *Organizational Objectives, Specific Objectives, and Objective Actions for the KC Foods Project*

SES Supplier Project Objectives	KC Foods Project Objectives	KC Foods Project Objective Actions
Competence		
Have SES project team members develop creativity in environmentally friendly, sustainable, and automated building technology	Develop creativity of KC Foods project team members in automation	Senior engineer coach junior engineer on the project: creativity in automation
Customers		
Provide state-of-the-art building solutions to solve SES' project customers' challenges, now and in the future	Involve KC Foods actively in detailed specifications of the automated solar roof innovation	Locate KC Foods engineer temporarily within engineering team, involved in the design of the automated solar roof

(continued)

Table 6-3. (*continued*)

SES Supplier Project Objectives	KC Foods Project Objectives	KC Foods Project Objective Actions
Employees		
Provide SES' project employees with secure and satisfying work	Create a secure and satisfying work environment for the KC Foods project team	Organize two project team-building sessions during the project, one including our customer KC Foods
Innovation		
Create at least one unplanned innovation per project in automated, sustainable, and environmentally friendly building technology	Develop and implement an automated solar roof on the KC Foods project to maximize solar energy generation	Design and build automated moving solar panels on the KC Foods factory roof to increase solar energy generation by 10 percent
Lessons learned		
Relentlessly identify and feed back project lessons learned into the SES organization	Maintain a special focus on feedback on lessons learned during the KC Foods project	Have all KC Foods project team members interviewed by continuous improvement to update the expertise database
Money		
Generate project profit now and in the future, however, stimulate unplanned project investment in innovations	Generate a profit on the KC Foods project, however, invest in the design of automated solar roof	Book and accept (generic) design cost of potential new product (automated solar roof) on KC Foods project

(*continued*)

Table 6-3. (*continued*)

SES Supplier Project Objectives	KC Foods Project Objectives	KC Foods Project Objective Actions
Process assets		
Unconditional use, improvement, and innovation of SES' engineering tools by our project teams (process assets)	Create at least one calculation tool on the project that can be reused as process asset on the next project	Have junior engineer develop a generic solar energy optimization tool for moving solar panels
Resources		
Utilize project and thereby SES' resources effectively and efficiently	Utilize engineer team efficiently on the KC Foods project	Rearrange responsibilities within project team to allow senior engineer to coach junior engineer without adding additional experienced engineer
Rules and values		
Enhance project commitment to SES' vision and values to innovate and provide state-of-the-art automated, sustainable, and environmentally friendly building solutions for SES' customers	Actively promote SES' vision of automated, sustainable, and environmentally friendly building solutions on the KC Foods project	Have senior and junior engineer together present the new automated solar roof development during the next municipal/industry environmental conference
Stakeholders		
Satisfy project and SES' stakeholders now and in the future	Keep key stakeholders, SES management team, and customers informed and involved in key decisions	Organize quarterly steering group meetings with management and customers

Executing Objective Actions

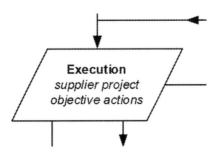

Next, the planned supplier project objective actions are executed, along with and through the supplier project actions (that execute the project and deliver the project result to the customer) by the project team. Yet again, it remains important to keep in mind that these objective actions should match with the strengths, weaknesses, opportunities, and threats of the project and how the project, with its objective actions, can create productive change within the organization to secure the future of the organization.

A couple of weeks after the transfer of Daniel to the KC Foods project, but several weeks before he and Christos bring in the idea for the pilot project with the automated solar roof, Collin asks John Jr.

"And how is Daniel doing with Christos on the KC Foods project?"

"Well, I think it's going all right. No big change. However, they have started the process. They arranged for Daniel to sit and work in the same room as Christos, and I think they are getting along, having some discussions now and then."

"Yes, I talked to Christos the other day and he said that Daniel is opening up a bit and that he has good conversations with him on technology and ideas," Julie adds.

Measurement and Control of Objective Actions

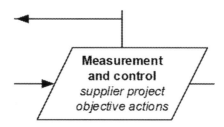

The execution of the planned supplier project objective actions is periodically measured and controlled by the project team and reported to the organization (management).

Measurement and control of objective actions can be done on various levels of detail. Depending on the organization and its size, or in the case of some larger objective actions or actions linked to a high-priority organizational project objective, they might require a detailed measurement and control activity against defined KPIs. In other circumstances or smaller objective actions, it is just a matter of reporting the status and progress periodically in the progress report, discussing the status and progress during the periodic progress meeting, and defining or discussing changes (control) if required.

Furthermore, measurements of objective actions can be done at the level of the objective actions or the project objectives.

Actions can be defined according to the SMART criteria (specific, measurable, attainable, relevant, and timely). These SMART criteria seem logical and easy; however, they might prove more challenging in practice than expected. Therefore, it is not a must, a mandatory requirement; in the end, a clearly defined objective action is better than no objective action. For example, if it proves difficult to agree on a target measurement (such as a fixed value), an estimate is as good as well because just having a target value and measuring actual values already helps awareness, focus, and understanding of the subject matter.

Simple Reporting

The simplest and suggested first step of implementing the method is to report the progress and planning of the defined objectives and actions within the existing project progress reporting to management (Table 7-1). Just list the objectives and their actions, progress, and planning (e.g., on track or mitigations necessary). This way, the measurement and control are conducted on the project level, however, involving management who are aware of all projects running within the organization.

Simple Measurements

The following is a simple measurement of a project and overall summary for all projects and the whole organization (e.g., yearly).

1) Count the number of defined project objective actions on the project.

2) Count the number of fulfilled (yes/no) objective actions on the project.

3) Calculate the percentage of defined project objective actions compared to ten (10) generic project objectives (number of defined objective actions divided by ten (10)).

4) Calculate the percentage of fulfilled actions (number of fulfilled objective actions divided by number of defined objective actions).

"For example. In case you have defined seven specific objective actions for a project, of which four are completed. Can you write down the simple measurements for me?" Collin asks Elena.

Elena walks over to the flip chart and writes down the numbers.

"Yes, and for reference, you can add on top that we have ten generic supplier project objectives." (Figure 6-16)

# Specific project objectives	= 10
Project objective actions	
# Defined	= 7
# Fulfilled	= 4
% Defined	= 70%
% Fulfilled (of defined)	= 57%

Figure 6-16. *Simple measurements (statistics) on a SES project*

"It looks too simple, but even such basic measurements are very helpful as a basis for your project statistics Collin concludes.

"And you can simply add up all projects for the whole organization as SES organizational statistics, A SES organizational dashboard." (Figure 6-17)

SES project objectives management Dashboard

Baseline	
# SES project objectives	= 10
# Total projects	= 23
# Minimum total potential	= 230
project objective actions	
Project objective actions	
# Defined	= 134
# Fulfilled	= 87
% Defined	= 58%
% Fulfilled (of defined)	= 65%

Figure 6-17. *Simple organizational measurements (statistics), a SES organizational dashboard*

Key Performance Indicators (KPIs)

More complex measurements are conducted within the method by assigning *key performance indicators* (KPIs) for the defined organizational project objectives or project objective actions, against which the project and its team members, management, and staff departments will be evaluated. Weight factors can be incorporated to manage the priority of the organizational project objectives, as defined in the organizational definition process activity. A higher weight factor for one objective or objective action coupled with a higher priority organizational objective will stimulate a higher focus.

> *"The target of a 10 percent increase in solar energy generation by automated moving solar panels on KC Foods roof is a clear example of a key performance indicator for your innovation project objective action on the KC Foods project," Collin explains.*

> *"Yes, and we will start measuring and reporting the actual percentage of increase during all stages of the innovation project," Elena confirms.*

> *"Do you have examples?" Collin asks.*

> *Yes, we have the results of our initial high-level estimates and the more detailed calculation estimates. And we will continue with the calculations during our detailed engineering, followed by detailed simulations and a test scale model system," Elena answers and continues.*

> *"And finally, we will measure the solar energy generation increase during the various phases of the actual installed system, such as during commissioning, testing, handover, and during the first period after handover." (Figure 6-18)*

KC Foods project
'Innovation' project objective action:
"Design and build automated moving solar panels on KC Foods roof,
to increase solar energy generation with 10%"

KPI
Target increase %	≈ 10%

Engineering measurements
Initial estimates	≈ 10-15%
Detailed calculation	≈ 12,7%
Detailed engineering estimate	≈ 11,9%
Detailed simulations	≈ 12,1%
Test scale model	≈ 11,7%

Implementation measurements
Commissioning	≈ 11,7%
Testing	≈ 11,2%
Handover	≈ 12,1%
After handover (3 month period)	≈ 12,8%

Figure 6-18. *Simple measurements (statistics) of project*

Fundamental operating measurements and the productivity check

E.M. Goldratt introduced the productivity check toward the goal. Productivity is the act of bringing a company closer to its goal. Every action that brings a company closer to its goal is productive. Every action that does not bring the company closer to its goal is unproductive.[4] Within SPOM, this is rephrased for project management at a supplier as any action that moves the project toward securing the company's future is productive. Any action that moves the project away from securing the company's future is not productive. Here, actions are the planned supplier project objective actions. The process is an active implementation of objective actions instead of a passive result of supplier project actions: executing and delivering the project result.

---

[4] Goldratt, 1984

At a for-profit organization or company, and with modified measurements at a non-profit organization, the financial part of the productivity check toward the goal can be done with the following measurements.[5]

- net profit

- return on investment (ROI)

- cash flow

Which, for better applicability in the productivity way of thinking and a more strategic approach, can be transferred into the fundamental operating measurements (Figure 6-19).

- (future) throughput

- inventory

- operating expenses

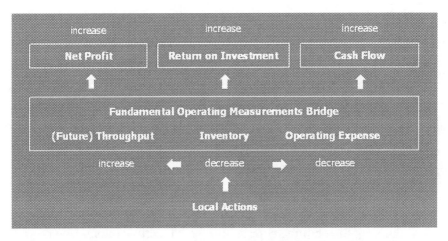

Figure 6-19. *Fundamental operating measurements (future) throughput, inventory, and operating expense (Youngman, 2021)*

---

[5] Youngman, 2021

Note that throughput is replaced by the more fundamental (future) throughput. Although theoretical accounting tells us that when inventory increases, net profit also increases, and yet nowadays, it is understood that increasing inventory in the long run is harmful to profit[6]. Therefore, a decrease in inventory results in an increase in future throughput.

> *"Where, as you know, throughput is sales minus total variable cost, and return on investment is your net profit divided by your investment," Collin writes down on the flip chart.*

> *"And from there, they derive the most important fundamental measurement, that productivity is throughput divided by operating expense. This is important within productivity thinking because it decouples cost from sales, thereby putting less focus on the less productive method of increasing profit in the longer term by decreasing cost. Instead, productivity should be increased by increasing throughput while holding operating expenses constant or with minimum increase. Furthermore, as explained, we consider the more fundamental measurement of future throughput instead of just throughput." (Figure 6-20)*

---

[6] Goldratt and Fox, 1986

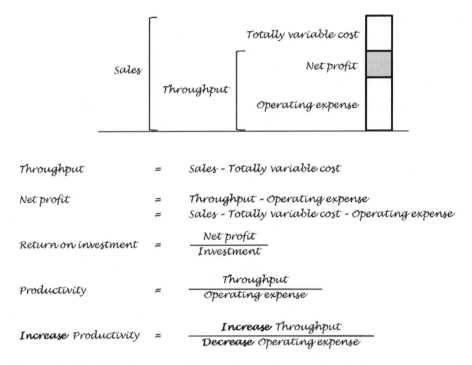

Throughput	=	Sales - Totally variable cost
Net profit	=	Throughput - Operating expense
	=	Sales - Totally variable cost - Operating expense
Return on investment	=	$\dfrac{Net\ profit}{Investment}$
Productivity	≈	$\dfrac{Throughput}{Operating\ expense}$
Increase Productivity	=	$\dfrac{\textbf{Increase}\ Throughput}{\textbf{Decrease}\ Operating\ expense}$

Figure 6-20. *Fundamental operating measurements at a commercial company (Youngman, 2021)*

At a non-profit organization, it looks different with productivity more difficult to measure, at least not directly from financial measurements. On this basis, sales are replaced by funds, and net profit is equal to zero; in practice, there is an operating result that is kept to a minimum but should not become negative, and a financial buffer to cover potential future overruns should be kept as well. The non-profit organization is characteristic for measurement of productivity within SPOM, where the productivity of most generic supplier project objectives (apart from money) is more difficult to measure objectively, and at least not directly from objective financial measurements.

"So, this is what it looks like at a non-profit organization, where there is no profit objective because the profit, or better the operating result, is kept at a minimum. Here it is difficult or even impossible to do a financial productivity measurement based on throughput and operating expense. The productivity measurement at a non-profit organization, or better, the difficulty of productivity measurement, is characteristic of SPOM. The aim is to move toward non-financial goals," Collin explains. (Figure 6-21)

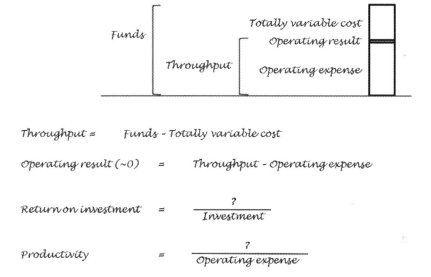

Figure 6-21. *Fundamental operating measurements at a non-profit organization (Youngman, 2021)*

Fundamental Objectives Measurements and the Productivity Check

Although the difficulty of productivity measurement at a non-profit organization is characteristic of the difficulty of productivity measurement within SPOM, I do, however, return to the measurements and productivity check for the *for-profit* organization (Figure 6-20) as a basis for similar measurements and productivity check within SPOM (Figure 6-22).

- **Effort in project actions** within SPOM can be compared with total variable cost at a commercial company or for-profit organization. Total variable costs, such as raw materials, are basically what you process in line with the total quantity of the project result and are not fixed.

    If you process less, you basically use less, apart from inventory cost. Apart from optimization of the quantity of raw materials used, for example, variable cost does not directly impact throughput or productivity. Within the method, this also consists of effort without direct impact on the throughput and productivity of the supplier project objectives and its actions, as it is linked to the project actions of executing the project and delivering the project result to the customer (direct impact to the customer).

    These project actions act as a catalyst for the project objective actions, the key element within the method. Any positive or negative results of project actions for the supplier are covered instead in the relevant generic supplier project objectives (such as customers, employees, money, and lessons learned) and thereby covered by the other fundamental objectives measurements, the result and effort in objective actions.

- **Effort in objective actions** can be compared with the operating expense. Operating expenses are all costs necessary to generate the added value (or profit) by changing the variable cost items into complete project results (product, services, or a combination). Similar to operating expenses, this also consists of the effort required to generate actual results.

- **Result of objective actions** can be compared with the profit. The profit within a commercial company is the added value. Likewise, the result consists of all productive changes that take the project supplier closer to its goal to secure its future. As with profit, which can also be negative or a loss, this result of objective actions can also be none or very limited, in which case there is only effort (operating expense) without a surplus or added value.

- **(Future) throughput of objective actions** is simply the sum of the result and effort in objective actions.

- **Productivity** can be calculated by dividing that (Future) throughput by the effort in objective actions.

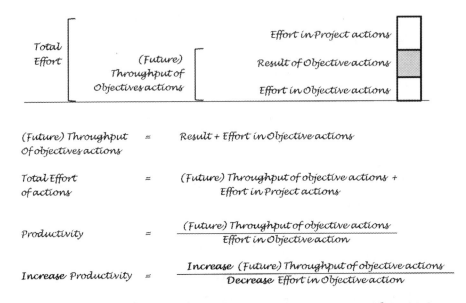

Figure 6-22. *Fundamental operating measurements within SPOM*

Although profit and operating expense can have various magnitudes relative to each other, the result of objective actions should have a higher or at least equal value to the effort within the method. Productivity values at a commercial company in case of actual profit should be minimum, for example, 1.1 in case of profit being 10 percent of operating expense. However, within the method, the productivity value should be significantly higher than one to fulfill minimum expectations, for example, 1.9 or higher, depending on the method used to calculate the result and effort.

As with money or sales, which can also be seen as positive (profit) or negative (covering cost, including the cost for waste, mistakes, defects, etc.), effort or total effort also consists of positive and negative parts; it also covers all the effort an organization needs to do to drive bottom-line productivity that moves the project toward securing the future of the company.

The comparison indicates that by nature of both fundamental measurement systems, there are differences in how the respective measurements can be retrieved (from the financial statements), calculated, or only measured. Where throughput is calculated from sales minus total variable cost, (future) throughput of objective actions can only be calculated by adding the result and effort in objective actions. Likewise, where profit is calculated from throughput minus operating expense, both the result and effort in objective actions are to be measured.

Finally, where sales can be retrieved from the financial statements, total effort can only be calculated by adding the effort in project actions to the result and effort in objective actions (Table 6-4).

Table 6-4. *Fundamental Objectives Measurements vs. Fundamental Operating Measurements*

Fundamental Operating Measurements		Fundamental Objectives Measurements	
Sales	Retrieved	Total effort	Calculated: = Effort in project actions + (Future) throughput of objective actions
Total variable cost	Retrieved	Effort in project actions	Measured
(Future) throughput	Calculated	(Future) throughput of objective actions	Calculated: = Total effort – Effort in project actions
Net profit	Calculated	Result of objective actions	Measured
Operating expense	Retrieved	Effort in objective actions	Measured
Productivity	Calculated	Productivity	Calculated: = (Future) throughput of objective actions / Effort in objective actions

Table 6-5 lists the fundamental objectives measurements connected to the generic supplier project objectives and their impact on the relevant fundamental operating measurements (or financial measurements) according to Goldratt and Youngman.

Table 6-5. *Fundamental Objectives Measurements at the Project Objectives Level*

Generic Supplier Project Objectives	Fundamental Objectives Measurements	Impact on Relevant Fundamental Operating Measurements (Goldratt, Youngman)
Competence		
Increase and improve project employee knowledge and experience	Increase in competence (knowledge and experience) of employees	Increase in throughput, decrease in inventory, decrease in operating expenses
Customers		
Satisfy project customers now or in the future	Increase in satisfaction (of customers)	Increase in throughput
Employees		
Provide project employees with secure and satisfying project work	Increase in security and satisfaction (of employees)	Increase in throughput, decrease in operating expenses
Innovation		
Innovate project products, services, or other results	Increase in innovation of project results	Increase in throughput
Lessons learned		
Identify and feed back project lessons learned to the organization	Increase in identified and feed back lessons learned	Decrease in operating expenses

(continued)

Table 6-5. (*continued*)

Generic Supplier Project Objectives	Fundamental Objectives Measurements	Impact on Relevant Fundamental Operating Measurements (Goldratt, Youngman)
Money		
Generate project profit or secured funds now and in the future	Increase in generated profit or secured funds	Increase in throughput, decrease in operating expenses
Process assets		
Increase, improve, and innovate project process assets	Increase in improved or innovative process assets	Decrease in operating expenses
Resources		
Utilize project resources effectively and efficiently	Increase in effectiveness or efficiency (of resources)	Decrease in inventory, decreased operating expense
Rules and values		
Enhance project compliance with legislation, regulation, and society and organizational values	Enhanced compliance (of rules and values)	Increase in throughput
Stakeholders		
Satisfy project stakeholders now or in the future	Increase in satisfaction (of customers)	Increase in throughput

Based on these fundamental objectives measurements or their impact on the relevant fundamental operating measurements, different methods can be adopted for measuring productivity toward the goal of securing the future of the organization, with or without weighing (by applying a weighting factor) based on the priorities of the organizational supplier project objectives (as established in the organizational definition activity).

Points can be assigned to the effort for each of the fundamental objective measurements against a certain measurement points scale. In the case of a desired financial assessment, the effort for the fundamental objectives measurements could be translated into the relevant fundamental operating measurements in terms of money value. Both steps are difficult due to the various principles this could be done; however, instead of trying to develop the best principle (from a perspective of absolute measurement of points or money), more important and beneficial is the future benefit of comparison with past or other ongoing projects (the perspective of relative measurement of points or money).

The measurement scale for assigning points to the effort for fundamental objective measurements can be divided into different main approaches.

- Assign positive points for both the result and effort in objective actions for each defined organizational supplier project objective, for example, on a scale between 0 and 10. Priorities can next be incorporated by multiplying the points with the weight factor. As per the basic definition of the method's productivity in Figure 6-22, productivity is measured by dividing the sum of all results and effort by the effort. Then, the productivity is evaluated by comparing that productivity value against the base of one and the maximum value of the measurement scale; below one means negative productivity, and above one means positive productivity.

- Assign positive points to the result and negative points to the effort in objective actions for each defined organizational supplier project objective, for example, on a scale between –10 and 10. Priorities can next be incorporated by multiplying the points with the weight factor. In this case, the productivity is evaluated by comparing that value against the base of zero and the maximum value of the measurement scale; below zero is negative productivity, and above zero is positive productivity.

As said, it could be difficult to assign points to the effort in objective actions for a fundamental objectives measurement, such as an increase in employees' competence (knowledge and experience) (Table 6-6). However, when comparing projects and based on experience, assigning a certain value that reflects the effort should be possible. It could be based on the average of multiple assessors and should be backed up by evidence (examples that support the points value). Of course, a high points value will be applicable in case of a clear conclusion and examples of increased satisfaction, and a low points value in case of a clear conclusion and examples of decreased satisfaction. Again, it is more important to have a robust and repeatable assessment system to come up with a certain points value that matches the conclusion than having the absolute correct absolute points value.

Next, translating such fundamental objectives measurement points into a money value for the relevant fundamental operating measurements can also be difficult, such as increased throughput related to increased competence (knowledge and experience) of employees (Table 6-6). This can, for example, be done by developing a baseline of average money values for the fundamental operating measurements throughput, inventory, and operating expense for an average project or project sales volume, which can be matched with the measurement points scale.

Table 6-6. *Assigning Points to Effort for Fundamental Objectives and Operating Measurements*

Generic Supplier Project Objectives	Fundamental Objectives Measurements (measurement points scale: −10 to +10)		Impact On Relevant Fundamental Operating Measurements	
	Measurement	Points	Measurement	Money
		+5		−10,000
Competence	Increase in	**Weight factor**		**Weight factor**
Increase and improve project employee knowledge and experience	competence (knowledge and experience) of Employees	0.2	Decrease in operating expense	−0.2
		Total points		**Total money**
		+2		+2,000
…	…	−3	…	−4,000
…	…	…	…	…
	(scale: −50 to +50)	**Total points**		**Total money**
Total of all objectives		+35		+87,000

The points or money value can also be totaled for the whole organization, and averages calculated, against which the success of each project can be compared again.

"Let's first look at the earlier established priorities of your organizational supplier project objectives at SES. What do we need to do with this as our first step?" Collin explains. (Table 6-2)

"We need to translate this into weight factors that we can use for our fundamental objectives measurements," Julie answers.

"Correct. We can for example, assign fractions of one, starting with 0,1 for lowest priority and increasing with 0,1 with each higher priority," Collin confirms, and after some more work, they come up with a complete table of weight factors for their SES supplier project objectives. (Table 6-7)

Table 6-7. *Weight Factors for the Prioritized Organizational Supplier Project Objectives of SES*

Priority	SES Supplier Project Objectives			Weight Factors
1	Innovation	Employees	Money	0.7
2	Customers	Competence		0.5
3	Rules and values	Stakeholders		0.4
4	Process assets	Lessons learned		0.2
5	Resources			0.1

Together, they work out a proposal for the measurement and final points of their competence objective on the KC Foods project. (Table 6-8)

Table 6-8. *Competence Fundamental Objectives Measurement on KC Foods Project at SES*

KC Foods Project SES Supplier Project Objectives	KC Foods Project Objectives	KC Foods Project Objective Actions	Fundamental Objectives Measurements	
			Measurement	Points
Competence Have SES project team members develop creativity in environmentally friendly, sustainable, and automated building technology	Develop creativity of KC Foods project team members in automation	Senior engineer coaches junior engineer on the project: creativity in automation	Increase in competence (knowledge and experience) of employees	+9
		Result Daniel having successfully developed his creativity skills in automation on the KC Foods project. Daniel assigned on West Lake project, as responsible Engineer for automation.		
			Weight factor 0.5	
			Total points +4.5	

Organizational Objectives Dashboard

For an integral overview and control of supplier project objective management within the organization, in addition to monitoring on project level, a corporate database can be of high value for organizational success. Which, depending on the size of the organization, can be just a centrally accessible Excel list for a small organization, up to a central database on the organization's intranet or a specially tailored system for large organizations.

The main success factor of such a database is its ability to track the status or progress of each item at both the project and organizational levels. The following are important items to track.

- organizational project objectives at the organizational level

- specific project objectives for each project at the project level

- project objective actions at the project level

- potential/realized organizational benefits within the organization at the organizational level

Information can be filtered and ranked within the database in many ways, such as per generic objective or per project. Furthermore, overall status and results can be visualized, such as the number of completed or open objective actions and the number of successfully completed objective actions.

"Another dashboard?!" Jr. exclaims, disappointed.

"Well, yes and no," Collin answers. "But first of all, it is important to point out that you do need to measure somehow your performance to enable adaptations if required, otherwise the productive changes within the organization might be less effective."

"Yes of course, but another dashboard?"

"It is new information; however, it doesn't have to be another or an additional dashboard. It should be possible to integrate such new information in one of your existing organizational dashboards?" Collin asks Julie.

Julie thinks for a bit and then answers. "Yes, you are right, I guess we could do that. I will discuss this with our continuous improvement team and our IT group."

After further planning and preparation work the continuous improvement team has released two types of pilot dashboards accessible to all employees of SES, a high-level dashboard with colors indicating the status and a more detailed dashboard. (Table 6-9)

Table 6-9. Example of SES Project Objectives Management Dashboard

SES Project Objectives Management Dashboard

Project	Reporting Items			Status	Description
	Objective	Specific Project Objective	Project Objective Action	-/—/ 0/ +/++	
KC Foods	Competence	Develop creativity of project team members in automation on the KC Foods project	Senior engineer coaches junior engineer on the project on creativity in automation	0/+	Junior engineer transferred to project and kick-off meeting conducted; in progress; first results to be awaited
West Lake	Competence	...	...	...	...
KC Foods	Innovation	Develop and implement automated solar roof on the KC Foods project to maximize solar energy generation	Design and build automated moving solar panels on KC Foods factory roof, to increase solar energy generation with 10 percent	+	Previous phase detailed simulations estimated 12.1 percent increase, first tests with the test scale model estimates 11.6 percent
West Lake	Money	...	...	...	...
West Lake	Process assets	...	...	...	...

Redefinition of Project-Specific Supplier Project Objectives Necessary?

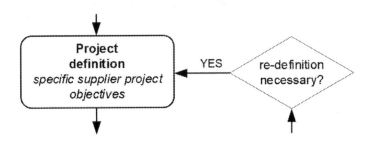

As with organizational supplier project objectives, likewise, the defined (project) specific supplier project objectives might require redefinition, caused by internal or external project changes. For example, the cancellation of an innovative development scope (internal or external) or a change of a project team member with less experience (internal).

> *"Did you ever need to conduct crisis management on a project, for example, if a major problem might turn into a significant loss?*
>
> *"Yes, of course," John answers Collin.*
>
> *"And did that shift the focus of the project team fully on that 'negative' thing or risk on the project."*
>
> *"Uh ... yes," Jr. answers with a bit of hesitation.*
>
> *"Don't worry. I am not trying to trick you into saying something wrong. I just want to bring up that by this natural reaction to focus on negatives automatically the focus on positives or other risks decreases.*
>
> *"Yes, but that is good, isn't it? Focus on the major issue and not on many other issues?"*

"Yes, but wouldn't it be better to do this, such focus on one thing, one objective, more determined within an overall strategy, instead of just as it happens?" Collin asks rhetorically. "And, the intermediate redefinition of the innovation and customer project objectives and objective actions for the automated solar roof pilot project on the KC Foods project together with your customer KC Foods, is a perfect example of such intermediate redefinition."

Within the method, in case required or a new opportunity comes up, a redefinition (possibly temporary) should or could be initiated to redefine one or more specific supplier project objectives. To make it a conscious decision, although in the example, it does not immediately require a hold on all other project objectives, it might also mean an adjustment or partial hold or a temporary transfer of an objective to another project team.

Embedding Organizational Benefits

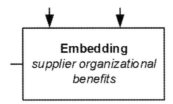

Finally, the organization actively embeds the achieved project objectives as actual realized supplier organizational benefits within its organization as input for its next project. In this activity, it is important to keep in mind that these objective actions should match with the strengths, weaknesses, opportunities, and threats of the organization and its project, and how the organization and its projects with its organizational benefits can create productive change within the organization to secure the future of the organization. This embedding within its organization is critical to turn potential into actual realized supplier organizational benefits, which are productive changes, by the organization (staff department and management).

The "give and take" principle is an important driver of this process step. It means that many project success factors, received or taken by the project, must be established first by the organization based on results from or created by preceding projects, provided or given by these projects based on their project objectives (a measurement of project success criteria). Therefore, many typical project success factors are indirectly linked to project success criteria via project objectives within the project.

I repeat the key importance of the *embedding* process activity as the critical step toward success for the project supplier. To emphasize this, the definition of a project objective from the supplier perspective, as opposed to the customer perspective, is repeated in the following. (Figure 4-18)

> In project objectives management at a project supplier, supplier project objectives are potential supplier organizational benefits achieved by actively fulfilling supplier project objective actions, along with and through supplier project actions (which execute the project and deliver the project result—product(s), service(s), other result(s), or a combination—to the customer. These potential supplier organizational benefits turn into productive changes; however, only when embedded by the organization as actual realized supplier organizational benefits within itself, which take the project supplier closer to its goal to secure its own future.

Without such successful embedding *by the organization as actual realized supplier organizational benefits within itself,* all potential of those potential supplier organizational benefits achieved by actively fulfilling supplier project objective actions might get lost within the project and never reach the organization. In other words, multiple successful projects do not directly result in a successful organization. Even multiple projects with multiple fulfilled objective actions and potential organizational benefits will not directly result in a successful organization without such active embedding.

Based on the generic supplier project objectives, potential supplier organizational benefits are translated into core examples of actual realized supplier organizational benefits, bottom-line added value, and examples of such bottom-line added value of actual realized supplier organizational benefits are listed in Table 6-10. The examples include reference to the fundamental financial measurements (throughput, inventory, and operating expense) within for-profit organizations, to indicate financial health as a measurement of overall success to secure the future. However, it is now clear that not everything can be measured in financial measurements, even in a for-profit organization.

Table 6-10. *Generic Examples of Embedded Actual Realized Organizational Benefits Within an Organization*

Potential Supplier Organizational Benefit	Actual Realized Supplier Organizational Benefit (Embedded Within the Organization)	Examples of Bottom-Line Added Value in Fundamental Operating Measurements
Competence		
Increased and improved project employee knowledge and experience	Successful redeployment of organizational employees with increased and improved knowledge and experience on the next project or assignment within the organization	Limited cost involved in negatives such as repair or redo work caused by employee, extensive training cost of employee, etc. (Decreased inventory or operating expense) or higher output of employee with impact on sales (future increased throughput)

(*continued*)

Table 6-10. (*continued*)

Potential Supplier Organizational Benefit	Actual Realized Supplier Organizational Benefit (Embedded Within the Organization)	Examples of Bottom-Line Added Value in Fundamental Operating Measurements
Customers		
Satisfied project customer now or in the future	Future organizational customer for the next project	Increased satisfaction of customers, leading to future new projects for that customer (future increased throughput)
Employees		
Project employees with secure and satisfying project work	Increased loyalty and commitment of organizational employees on the next project or assignment within the organization	Less cost involved in faults or replacement cost of employees, higher effectiveness, and efficiency of employees' work (decreased inventory or operating expense, increased throughput)
Innovation		
Innovated project products, services, or other results	New organizational products, services, or other results on the next project	(future increased throughput)
Lessons learned		
Identified project lessons learned, fed back to the organization	Implemented improvements on the next project or organizational processes	Implementation of lessons (processes, tools, or process assets to continue to do, to do differently or not to do anymore; or other things to do) into the organization or new projects (future decreased inventory or operating expense)

(*continued*)

Table 6-10. (*continued*)

Potential Supplier Organizational Benefit	Actual Realized Supplier Organizational Benefit (Embedded Within the Organization)	Examples of Bottom-Line Added Value in Fundamental Operating Measurements
Money		
Generated project profit or secured funds now and in the future	Actual realized profit or secure funds, based on actual received sales or funds on bank account of organization	Actual transferred money to bank accounts based on successful submitted and paid invoices (increased throughput)
Process assets		
Improved or innovated project process assets	Implemented and actual used improved or innovated organizational process assets on next projects or organizational processes	(future decreased inventory or operating expense)
Resources		
Effectively and efficiently utilized project resources	More organizational resources made available for other projects	Decreased inventory or operating expense, due to effective and efficient use of organizational resources
Rules and values		
Enhanced project compliance with legislation, regulation, and society and organizational values	Increased reputation and satisfaction at relevant organizational stakeholders leading to less future cost or more efficient work	Increased reputation at and increased satisfaction of regulatory organization (stakeholder), leading to future easier approval process or authorization for a future license (decreased operating expense)

(*continued*)

Table 6-10. (*continued*)

Potential Supplier Organizational Benefit	Actual Realized Supplier Organizational Benefit (Embedded Within the Organization)	Examples of Bottom-Line Added Value in Fundamental Operating Measurements
Stakeholders		
Satisfied project stakeholders now or in the future	Increased satisfaction of organizational stakeholders leading to new projects, availability of resources, or other advantages for the organization or the next project	Future new projects for satisfied stakeholder (future increased throughput) Future available resources or other support from relevant stakeholders (future decreased inventory or operating expense)

"Well, Elena, it has been quite a challenge for you and your KC Foods project team, with changes in the team and the challenge with the automated solar roof pilot," Julie says to Elena during the KC Foods project progress meeting, while looking at Christos as well. Collin is also present in the room, sitting in the back, quietly listening.

"However, you managed to pull it all off with a very committed project team, I must say. That did not go unnoticed here on the fourth floor."

"Thanks John, much appreciated to hear from you. Yes, it was quite a busy and hectic couple of months," Elena answers.

"Although the swap with Daniel made it a lot harder for you, losing your experienced automation engineer, however, in the end the impact on the project was acceptable and a major gain for the company was the strong development of Daniel himself. To speak in SPOM words, by fulfilling this specific

project objective action to develop Daniel's creativity in automation, we achieved the linked potential supplier organizational benefit. And of course, we had the additional benefits from the automated solar roof pilot project as well!"

Collin looks satisfied to Julie. She really starts to take ownership for the implementation of the method within SES. They continue discussing the status and progress of the project and at the end decide to ask Daniel to join in as well.

Julie warmly welcomes Daniel into their meeting.

"Daniel, thanks for joining us, and don't worry, it will be all good news today. You do know Collin, of course, and we were already discussing the overall progress of the KC Foods project with Elena and Christos."

"I heard that you are now working on the close out of the KC Foods project, completing the as-built documentation and lessons learned. And I understood that some good progress has been made on your personal development as well, Daniel?" Collin joins in.

"Well," Daniel hesitates a second but then continues confidently. "I had a good click with Christos and together we came up with some good design ideas, some of which we have implemented in the project. So yes, this gave me quite some confidence, way better than classroom training, I guess, and I am looking forward to my next project."

Julie nods to Elena, and she steps in as discussed.

"Daniel, you know that I have already started preliminary preparations on the West Lake project, that new residential development near West Lake that is about to become a contract. It is a higher segment development, and the developers aim for the latest housing automation technology, and well we would like to have you in the project team, responsible for the automation part of it. We think you are ready for this next challenge."

Daniel is shocked and a bit scared but doesn't show any of that and manages to keep a straight face. He already starts thinking about all the details coming up in the new West Lake project. In the background, he vaguely hears Julie explaining something about what they are now doing with him is actually the activity of turning the competence objective action into a productive change by embedding it as an actual realized supplier organizational benefits within SES that takes SES closer to its goal to secure its own future. He is surely interested in that as well, but first champagne at home, he can't wait to tell the good news to Jenny, his girlfriend!

"Ladies, gentlemen, let's have a look at the detailed results of the KC Foods project and productive change within SES. A nice result for a first pilot project with SPOM within SES," Collin says to all gathered in the room while pointing at the slide presented on the large screen at the front of the room. (Table 6-11)

Table 6-11. *Embedded Actual Realized Organizational Benefits from the KC Foods Project Within SES*

KC Foods Project Objective Actions	Potential SES Organizational Benefits	Embedded Actual Realized SES Organizational Benefits
Competence		
Senior engineer coach junior engineer on the project: creativity in automation	Daniel having successfully developed his creativity skills in automation on the KC Foods project	Daniel assigned on West Lake project, as responsible engineer for automation
Customers		
Locate KC Foods engineer temporary within engineering team, and involved in design of the automated solar roof	KC Foods engineer happily located at SES' office for two months, successfully involved in definition of design requirements of the automated solar roof	KC Foods highly satisfied with SES involving them in the design of the SES innovation, the automated solar roof, strengthening the long-term partnership
Employees		
Organize two project team-building sessions during the project, one including our customer KC Foods	Two successful and fun team-building sessions conducted, one including enthusiastic KC Foods project team members	Good feedback received from both SES and KC Foods project team members, good lessons learned for future sessions on other projects, and an informal commitment from KC Foods exists for sessions on potential future projects

(*continued*)

Table 6-11. (*continued*)

KC Foods Project Objective Actions	Potential SES Organizational Benefits	Embedded Actual Realized SES Organizational Benefits
Innovation		
Design and build automated moving solar panels on KC Foods factory roof to increase solar energy generation with 10 percent	Achievement of a minimum 10 percent increase in solar energy generation from the automated moving solar panels, with a measured of 12.8 percent after three months	Decision made by SES to develop the automated moving solar panels prototype into a full project within the portfolio, and customer KC Foods expressing the intent to install more systems at its other factories
Lessons learned		
Organize two intermediate lessons learned sessions with the project team, one including our customer KC Foods	Successfully completed interviews by continuous improvement department of all KC Foods project team	Multiple expertise entries in the expertise database, ready to be used by new project teams, to consult KC Foods project team members for specific expertise
Money		
Book and accept (generic) design cost of potential new product (automated solar roof) on KC Foods project	Due to the good profit margin, the design cost of the automated solar roof has been booked on KC Foods project, instead of on generic innovation account	Innovation cost of the automated solar roof has been booked in one time on a running project, allowing new projects to select the new product without significant cost to cover investments

(*continued*)

Table 6-11. (*continued*)

KC Foods Project Objective Actions	Potential SES Organizational Benefits	Embedded Actual Realized SES Organizational Benefits
Process assets		
Have junior engineer develop a generic solar energy optimization tool for moving solar panels	Solar energy optimization tool for moving solar panels developed on the KC Foods project, ready for handover to the organization as a corporate process asset	Generic solar optimization tool has been checked and approved by a senior engineer and included in the SES corporate toolbox
Resources		
Rearrange responsibilities within project team to allow senior engineer to coach junior engineer without adding additional experienced engineer	Successfully rearranged the project team, so that senior engineer could coach junior engineer without additional resources	Efficient use of SES' human resources on the KC Foods project
Rules and values		
Have senior and junior engineer together present the new automated solar roof development during the next municipal/ industry environmental conference	New automated solar roof development successfully presented during the next municipal/industry environmental conference	Positive exposure of SES within the municipality and industry, as leader in environmentally friendly and sustainable solutions

(*continued*)

Table 6-11. (*continued*)

KC Foods Project Objective Actions	Potential SES Organizational Benefits	Embedded Actual Realized SES Organizational Benefits
Stakeholders		
Organize quarterly steering group meeting with management and customer KC Foods	SES and customer KC Foods' management successfully and positively informed and involved in the progress and results of the KC Foods project	SES and KC Foods management aligned and satisfied with joined partnership, having established a framework agreement for future innovative developments and projects

Summary

How can the required change be implemented within the project supplier's organization and its project execution practices?

Implement the change by executing the five process activities of SPOM, to take the supplier closer to its goal. These process activities include defining project objectives by the organization; planning, implementation, and measurement and control of objective actions by the project team; and embedding of supplier organizational benefits by the organization.

## CHAPTER 7

Management: How to Integrate Change?

How do you integrate change with existing management processes within the project supplier's organization and its project execution practices?

After introducing the method for implementing change in the previous chapter, this chapter addresses how to integrate the method with existing management processes within the organization.

Project Controls

Existing Organizational Management Processes

Supplier project objectives management (SPOM) is not meant to replace a project supplier's existing (project) management processes, such as the project controls (e.g., cost, time, quality, organization, and information

© Reitse van der Wekken 2024
R. van der Wekken, *Project Objectives Management*,
https://doi.org/10.1007/979-8-8688-0956-9_7

control), or an implemented generic project management method (such as Prince2 or Agile), or an existing employee competence and appraisal management process. The method manages the organization's project objectives, but no other parts of the full scope of (organizational) project management, and therefore is no substitute for these processes or methods. The method should, therefore, be integrated with, but not replace, existing (project) management processes or methods.

What about implementing the new method within the organization while already having several existing management processes or methods in place? Yet another process makes the daily work of the organization and the project team even more laborious. However, the integration and alignment of the method with existing management processes can and should be done as effectively and efficiently as possible, avoiding double processes and work providing a bottom line added value instead of added work. The detail and depth to which the method is integrated with existing management processes and methods should align both with the organization's process culture and with, for example, the type of generic project management method used, which, as we will see later, varies from very detailed and fixed up to very generic and flexible.

Furthermore, at some (small to medium) project suppliers no generic project management method might be implemented within the organization, instead executing projects using project controls only. In other organizations where a generic project management method is fully or partly implemented within its organizational management process, the management of the project controls will usually also be embedded within that method and not a separate process.

> *"I am still concerned about implementing yet another addi-tional process within SES, with major changes and a lot of extra work for our employees and ourselves!" John Jr. explains his concern to Collin and looks worried.*

> *"John," Collin answers, relaxed. "You don't need to worry about this anymore. You know from our sessions that the method provides a productive complement to your existing*

processes at SES and can be integrated without major changes or a significant additional workload. We have learned that many items of the method are already present within SES. The method is all about awareness and focus, and doing it purposely and actively instead of unconsciously, to provide the most benefit to your organization, to SES."

And Collin continues.

"This is actually all there is to it! The only thing left is to guide you toward integrating this method within your existing management and project management processes and to conclude with a summary of how to benefit from this change within SES."

"You're right. I, we, should not doubt and second guess anymore. In fact, you have already convinced us long ago." John smiles and looks at Julie who nods in agreement as well.

The two remaining sections of this chapter address integration with generic project management methods and integration with employee competence and appraisal management processes.

Integration with Project Controls

Project subjects or objectives directly related to project cost, time, and scope (the project result) remain the domain of traditional project controls, such as cost, time, quality, organization, and information control. These project controls control the "project actions" of the supplier, consisting of "executing the project and delivering the project result to its customer" (project execution).

The *iron triangle* defines the triple constraints of project management: time, cost, and quality. Prince2 defines six control variables involved in any project and, therefore, six aspects of project performance to be managed: cost, timescale, quality, scope, risk, and benefit.[1] G. Wijnen and P. Storm define in their Dutch book *Projectmatig werken* (project-based working) that time, money, quality, information, and organization control is the task, responsibility, and authority to timely, profitably, qualitatively, unequivocally and by the responsible people execute the project plan to fulfill the project objectives; which means in such a way that the project result is available at the agreed time, is finished within the agreed budget, meets the required quality, and is documented and handed over to the user for management, operation, and maintenance. These are called *project controls* to manage a project.[2]

Project controls are also involved in the distinction between project success and project management success, with the measurement of project success criteria, measured against the performance on overall objectives of the project, and measurement of project management success criteria, measured against the performance of project management objectives or project controls. Project success deals with goal and purpose, and project management success deals with inputs and outputs.

Although various sources define various controls, the basis always consists of cost, time, and quality control (the Iron triangle) of the project result (scope) delivery. These project controls are linked with and covered by the following generic supplier project objectives to ensure the right balance and priority setting among the defined specific supplier project objectives (Figure 7-1).

Scope control is central within the iron triangle.

- time control is linked with the resources and customers

- cost control is linked with resources and money

- quality control is linked with customers and rules and values

---

[1] Prince2, 2017
[2] Wijnen et al, 1984

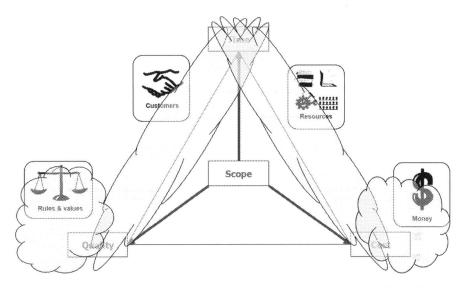

Figure 7-1. *Links between the iron triangle project controls and generic supplier project objectives*

So, the project quality, time, and cost control objectives are set by the project-specific supplier project objectives, as defined in the project team process activity "project definition of project-specific supplier project objectives." This links and aligns the project controls and the supplier project objectives management.

Furthermore, keeping the project controls active next to the method, managing the project via the project controls is important to remain in line with the method of internal reporting to management and the external reporting to the customer, which is usually focused on items such as cost (e.g., variation orders), or time (planning), or quality (of scope), or organization (resources), or information (data) of the project result delivery. However, with the method, internal reporting will be supplemented with reporting on the achievement of potential supplier organizational benefits by fulfilling supplier project objective actions within the project and the successful embedding of actual realized supplier organizational benefits within the organization to take the organization closer to its goal to secure its future.

"But how to avoid overlap between the two, for example between the project control 'cost' and the supplier project objective 'money'?" Jr. asks Collin.

"That is a good question and a perfect example indeed," Collin answers and continues.

"There is a difference because where the project control 'cost' focuses on the direct finance part of the project (topics such as project payment terms, revenue, cost, profit, invoicing, or variation orders) the method will focus on money-related objectives that are not directly related to the project or the customer, but which can still be influenced or developed by the project or the project team. Or the opposite, the project might create future negative financial impact on the organization, which might not be managed by the cost project control."

The method provides a structure to manage such indirect benefits, which might not be directly managed through the project control costs. Although all generic project objectives have the purpose of creating productive change that might result in monetary benefits as well (such as cost reductions by innovations or more effective and efficient use of resources such as machines or project employees), the project objective money focuses more on objectives directly related to money. More important, it guides the prioritization of money vs. other objectives within the organization, such as the core goal of non-profit organizations, or special vision on other goals, such as innovation or a certain type of human resource management at for-profit organizations. But other direct money-related objectives can also be defined, such as cost savings within the organization created by the project.

The best way to explain how the method can be integrated with the project controls without a negative impact on the organization is to refer to the introduction of the supplier project objective actions. Such objective actions are executed through the project actions of executing the project and delivering the project result. With this, the supplier project actions that execute the project and deliver the project result (external focus) act as a catalyst for the supplier project objective actions (internal focus) that achieve the supplier project objectives within the supplier's organization. The project controls focus on the supplier project actions. Supplier project objectives management focuses on the supplier project objective actions. Therefore, both do not interfere with or overlap but similarly enhance each other (Figure 7-2).

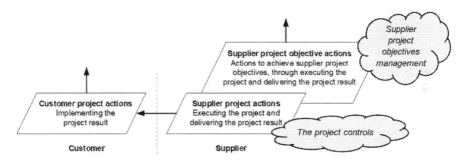

Figure 7-2. *Project objective actions (managed by supplier project objectives management) through project actions (managed by the project controls)*

Generic Project Management Methods

Project Management Methods

A project management methodology (or method in short) is a system of practices, techniques, procedures, and rules to conduct project management in a structured way. According to Wikipedia,[3] project management methods can be applied to any project. However, it is often tailored to a specific type of project based on project size, nature, industry, or sector. Common among all the project management types, they focus on three important goals: time, quality, and budget. Successful projects

---

[3] Wikipedia, 2022

are completed on schedule, within budget, and according to previously
agreed quality standards, or meeting the iron triangle for projects to be
considered a success or failure. For each type of project management,
project managers develop and utilize repeatable templates specific to the
industry they are dealing with. This allows project plans to become very
thorough and highly repeatable, with the intent to increase quality, lower
delivery costs, and lower time to deliver project results. Various types
of categorizations of project management methods exist. Both Wrike[4]
and The Digital Project Manager[5] share insightful categorizations and
descriptions of the most common project management methodologies,
and Wikipedia[6] lists several other common project methods in addition
as well.

Founded in 2006, Wrike provides work management platforms
for organizations (e.g., implementing a chosen project management
methodology within the organization's operations). According to Wrike,
project management methodologies are essentially different approaches to
a project. Each one has a unique process and workflow. Wrike categorizes
the top project management methodologies grouped by similarity and
popularity.

- **Traditional, sequential methods**: Waterfall and
  critical chain project management (CCPM). The
  most common way to plan a project is to sequence
  the tasks that lead to a final deliverable and work
  on them in order. This process is also known as the
  Waterfall methodology, the traditional method for
  managing projects and the simplest to understand.
  You must complete one task before the next begins in

---

[4] Wrike, 2022
[5] DPM, 2021
[6] Wikipedia, 2022

a connected sequence of items that add to the overall deliverable. It is an ideal method for projects that result in physical objects (buildings, computers), and you can easily replicate project plans for future use.

The power of this methodology is that every step is pre-planned and laid out in the proper sequence. While this may be the simplest method to implement initially, any changes in stakeholders' needs or priorities will disrupt the tasks, making them very difficult to manage. This methodology excels in predictability but lacks flexibility.

- **Agile family**: Agile, Scrum, Kanban, and extreme project management (XPM). Agile project management methodologies are gaining popularity thanks to a highly competitive business environment and increased innovation. In general, Agile methodologies prioritize shorter, iterative cycles and flexibility. Agile project management methods are part of the broader Agile family, including software development methods such as extreme programming (XP) and adaptive project framework (APF).

"This is really a fascinating story, but I give it to you in a nut-shell," Collin says to Julie and Johan Jr.

"After initial meetings in 2000, during February 2001, representatives from various adaptive-based software development methods such as extreme programming, Scrum, and adaptive software development, came together in a ski resort in Utah, USA, to try to find common ground. And what emerged was the Agile software development manifesto."

The Agile software development manifesto[7] follows the following 12 principles.

- Our highest priority is to satisfy the customer through early and continuous delivery of valuable software.

- Welcome changing requirements, even late in development. Agile processes harness change for the customer's competitive advantage.

- Deliver working software frequently, from a couple of weeks to a couple of months, with a preference for a shorter timescale.

- Business people and developers must work together daily throughout the project.

- Build projects around motivated individuals. Give them the environment and support they need and trust them to do the job.

- Face-to-face conversation is the most efficient and effective method of conveying information to and within a development team.

- Working software is the primary measure of progress.

- Agile processes promote sustainable development. The sponsors, developers, and users should be able to maintain a constant pace indefinitely.

- Continuous attention to technical excellence and good design enhances agility.

- Simplicity, the art of maximizing the amount of work not done, is essential.

---

[7] Agile, 2022

- The best architectures, requirements, and designs emerge from self-organizing teams.

- The team regularly reflects on how to become more effective, then tunes and adjusts its behavior accordingly.

"So, Agile is not a formal method itself?" Julie asks.

"Indeed, it started from a set of principles initiated by a representative of various 'light' or adaptive-based methods. However, in the years since various developments such as Agile-based software development and project management principles evolved after the manifesto." Collin says.

- **Change management methodologies**: Event chain methodology (ECM) and extreme project management (XPM). Some methodologies deal with managing projects, but with an extra focus on change management, especially planning for risks and taking control of change when it happens.

- **Process-based methodologies**: Lean and Six Sigma. Process-based project management methods overlap with business process management (BPM), where each approach focuses on work as a collection of processes. Lean, developed in the 1980s in the Japanese industry, such as Toyota and Six Sigma, developed in the 1980s at Motorola, have many similarities and specific differences. Lean Six Sigma combines both methods to combine both strengths for process improvement. Lean focus on just in time, build in quality and respect for employees. Six Sigma focus on quality improvement and decrease defects based on data analysis.

- **Other methodologies**: Prince2, PRiSM, and benefits realization management (BRM). Other methodologies are different from or form a combination of project management methods.

Founded in 2011, the Digital Project Manager (DPM) is a platform for digital project management information and thought leadership, providing (e.g., project management guidance and training).

According to DPM,[8] some project management methodologies simply define principles, like Agile. Others define a full-stack methodology framework of themes, principles, and processes, such as Prince2. Some are an extensive list of standards with some processes, like the Project Management Institute's (PMI) Project Management Body of Knowledge (PMBOK) methodology. Some are very light and simply define the process, like Scrum.

DPM categorizes the most popular project management methodologies in delivering projects, with increasing method specificity, applying either or combined (Figure 7-3).

- **Themes**: Prince2 and Lean

- **Principles**: Prince2 and Agile

- **Processes**: Waterfall, Scrum, PMBOK, and XP

- **Standards**: PMBOK and XP

---

[8] DPM, 2021

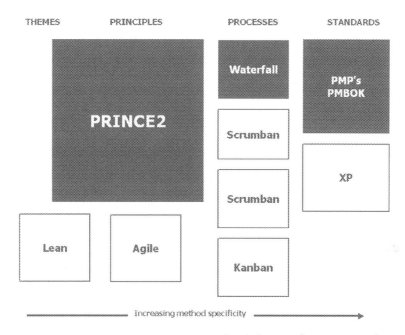

Figure 7-3. *Project management methodologies (DPM, 2021)*

In addition to these methods, Wikipedia[9] lists the following project management methods.

- **Process-based methods**: Guidance on Project Management (ISO 21500) and Capability Maturity Model Integration (CMMI)

- **Construction industry method**: Construction Management (CM)

The International Project Management Association (IPMA), a federation of more than 70 national member associations, maintains the Individual Competence Baseline (ICB) certification for project managers.

---

[9] Wikipedia, 2022 (https://en.wikipedia.org/wiki/Project_management)

As described by Boehm and Turner, project management methods can also be categorized on a scale from adaptive to predictive.[10] On this scale, Agile methods are located on the adaptive side, and methods such as Prince2, PMBOK, or Guidance on Project Management (ISO 21500) toward the predictive side.

Adaptive methods focus on adapting quickly to changes. When the needs of a project change, an adaptive team changes as well. An adaptive team has difficulty describing exactly what will happen in the future. The further away a date is, the less concrete an adaptive method is about what will happen on that date. An adaptive team cannot report exactly what tasks they will do next week but only which features or objectives they plan for the next month.

Predictive methods instead, focus on analyzing and planning the future in detail and plan for known risks. A predictive team can accurately report what features and tasks are planned for the entire length of the project (e.g., based on the detailed project plan). Predictive methods rely on effective early phase analysis; if this is incorrect, the project might have difficulty changing direction. Predictive teams often install a change control board within their organization to ensure only the most important changes are considered.

Traditionally, predictive development approaches and lifecycles for conducting projects were ahead of other adaptive, incremental, and iterative methods. However, changes within the project management field and its approaches during the last decades required a different perspective to react to the many changes in the requirements of the project and its stakeholders. According to PMI, over the past few years, emerging technology, new approaches, and rapid market changes have changed the project management field, driving the profession to evolve.

---

[10] Boehm and Turner, 2004

PMI has updated the latest edition of its *Guide to the Project Management Body of Knowledge* (*PMBOK Guide*)[11] to meet these challenges and to better align with how projects are conducted today. With its tailoring approach, organizations or projects must be tailored to the most suitable approach according to their characteristics. As one of the first steps of the preparation phase of a project, the planned deliverables of a project need to be evaluated carefully. To grant the eventual success of project outcomes, the development approach chosen should be compatible with the nature of the deliverables.

PMBOK categorizes the most common project management approaches or methods as predictive, adaptive, or hybrid development approaches. The (traditional) predictive—also called Waterfall—approach is the most familiar one, as it was the focus of former PMBOK guides. It is based on planning as much as possible prior to performing the project activities. It is useful to define, collect, and analyze the requirements at the beginning of a project. When uncertainty exists at the beginning of a project, then the adaptive approach is the most applicable. In this type of project, requirements change frequently, and the project must adapt to changing requirements. The third most common development approach is the hybrid approach, somewhere between the predictive and adaptive approaches, depending on the specific method.

Recent developments work toward hybrid methodologies, for example, the combination of adaptive and predictive methods and, more concrete the inclusion of Agile principles within the Waterfall project management method.

Finally, it is worth noting that many project management methods originate from and are specifically used in software development, such as the Agile family of methods and Prince2.

Appendix I further introduces each of these methods in alphabetical order.

---

[11] PMI, 2021

Integration with a Project Management Method

Implementing supplier project objectives management within the organization should not make the daily work of both the organization and the project team even more complex and demanding. Therefore, integrating the method with the existing project management method (for example, one of the previously introduced generic methods) should be as effective and efficient as possible, providing a bottom-line added value instead of added work. The detail and depth to which the method is integrated should align with the organization's process culture and the generic project management method used, which varies from very detailed and constrained to very generic and flexible.

As with project controls, the best way to explain how the method can be integrated with the existing project management method without negatively impacting the organization is to reference the supplier project objective actions. The existing project management method focuses on the supplier project actions. Supplier project objectives management focuses on the supplier project objective actions. Therefore, they do not interfere with or overlap each other; instead, they similarly enhance each other (Figure 7-4).

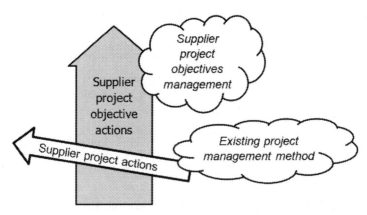

Figure 7-4. *Project objective actions (managed by supplier project objectives management) through project actions (managed by the existing project management method)*

Most project management methods and project organizations release a project initiation document (also called a *project brief* or *project charter*) that provides the project manager with the authority to apply resources to project activities. It formally authorizes a project and documents the business needs (the business case, explaining how the project supports the business strategy), such as measurable project objectives and related success criteria. Sometimes, the focus is on the business strategy of the user of the project result, the customer. Within supplier project objectives management, the focus should be on the project supplier itself, thereby covering the objectives of the user/customer as well.

To integrate the method, the project's relevant objectives can be split into two sections in the initiation document (hard copy, scanned or online version) during the project's initiation phase.

- the original objectives related to the project controls, such as cost, time, scope, and quality

- the project-defined specific supplier project objectives

Within the method, this project definition activity of the specific supplier project objectives in the initiation document coincides with the initiation phase of the project according to the project management method.

During the project execution, the process activities of the method, such as execution, measurement, and control of the project objective actions, can be aligned with the processes of the project management method as well. The periodic project progress report (the internal report) can be extended by reporting the status and planning of the project's objective actions. For example, align with a simple reporting method on the status of project controls (such as cost, time, quality, and other controls) with colors (red, orange, green), plus/minus (-, --, 0, +, ++) or another type of indicator, and a comments box.

"The simplest way to integrate the status reporting on the project's objective actions would be to add these to your existing internal progress report under an additional heading," Collin explains.

After some further pre-discussions, they invite Elena, the project manager of the KC Foods project, into the session and work out a preliminary update of her current progress report template. (Table 7-1)

Table 7-1. *Example of Internal Progress Reporting on Project Control and Project Objective Actions*

Internal Project Progress Report		
KC Foods Project		
Reporting Items	**Status**	
	–/––/ **0/** **+/++**	**Description**
Project Control		
Cost	+	Plus and minus on various cost positions, overall less forecasted planned cost; invoicing and scheduled payments; profit margin improved by 0.4 percent.
Time	–	Long deliveries 2W delayed, under discussion with supplier.
Quality	0	NTR

(continued)

Table 7-1. (*continued*)

Internal Project Progress Report				
KC Foods Project				
Reporting Items			**Status**	
			–/––/	**Description**
			0/	
			+/++	
SES Project Objectives Management				
Objective	**KC Foods Project Objective**	**KC Foods Project Objective Action**		
Competence	Develop creativity of project team members in automation on the KC Foods project	Senior project engineer coaches junior engineer on creativity in automation	0/+	Junior engineer transferred to project and kick-off meeting conducted; in progress; first results to be awaited

A corporate database is of high value for an integral overview and control of supplier project objective management within the organization, not only for the embedding activity, however, for all process activities. Depending on the organization's size, such an organizational objectives dashboard can just be a centrally accessible Excel spreadsheet list for a small organization, up to a central database for large organizations.

Competence and Appraisal Management

It should be avoided that by implementing the method within the organization, the daily work of the organization and the project team becomes even more complex and extensive. Integrating the method with the existing employee competence and appraisal management should be done as effectively and efficiently as possible, avoiding overlap and providing a bottom-line added value instead of added work. The detail and depth to which the method is integrated should align with the organization's process culture and the type of competence and appraisal management process.

Another type of process within organizations, with many interactions with supplier project objectives management, consists of employee competence and appraisal management. Part of the supplier project objective actions defined for a specific project can be personalized incentivized for a respective project team member, to further strengthen the method's full integration within the organization.

The following needs to be secured to integrate the method with the existing competence and appraisal process with a minimum impact or change and create further synergy.

- Align the wording and definitions used within the existing competence and appraisal process system with supplier project objectives management.

- Ensure that all supplier project objective actions of the projects that the concerned employee is working on are covered in his competence and appraisal document or online system.

Daniel is in his appraisal meeting with his line manager to discuss Daniel's last and upcoming year. The section on personal targets now includes all the method's related targets, such as his competence objective action on the KC Foods project.

"So, Daniel, your result on your competence objective action on the KC Foods project is scored unanimously as plus-plus, or above expectations." Daniel's line manager concludes. (Table 7-2)

Table 7-2. *Section of Daniel's Competence and Appraisal Form*

Competence and Appraisal Form

Daniel

Competences and Targets

Competence	Assessment	Comments
Result orientation	Meets expectations	Daniel shows a high focus on getting results and does not spend too long time on too much detail
Customer orientation	Improvement possible	Daniel could make more personal contact with customers and develop a constructive relationship
...	...	...

(continued)

Table 7-2. (*continued*)

Competence and Appraisal Form

Daniel

SES Project Objectives Management

Project	Objective	Specific Project Objective	Project Objective Action	Status -/--/ 0/ +/++	Comments
KC Foods	Competence	Develop creativity of project team members in automation on the KC Foods project	Senior project engineer coaches junior engineer on creativity in automation	++	Daniel has successfully developed his creativity skills in automation on the KC Foods project, and therefore has been assigned on the West Lake project as responsible engineer for automation
...	...	...	...	...	...

Not all personal targets involving a project should be defined as project objective action. Only when the execution of that objective action has a (significant) impact on the concerned projects does it make sense to incorporate; otherwise, it can just be defined as a regular personal target in the competence and appraisal form.

For successful implementation of the method within the organization, the senior project managers' involvement, support, and commitment is a major success factor. Implementing change within an organization is usually already a challenge. Change implementation within an organization is a field and process on its own. Where you might give junior or even experienced project managers the benefit of the doubt, organizations should expect from senior project managers that they can look beyond the success of their project and that they look at the organization's success. They should lead by example in subordinating the project to the organization.

"I am still struggling with the concrete and practical implementation of this," John says to Collin, and then asks, "If there is one suggestion you could give me, what would it be?"

Collin thinks for a moment and then answers.

"Well, what I also see within project organizations is that the most experienced and senior project managers have, or can have, a decisive impact on the success of implementing the method. It will be difficult if they do not give the right example or support the method."

"Yes, we have talked about that before, but I am still not sure what to really do with that. I am not looking for advice to find this out myself. Tell me. What do we have to do?"

"OK, if you are open to my strongest suggestion. If you really want to make this implementation a success, you should concretely define as an objective for your senior project managers that they demonstrate the subordination of their project to the organization. For example, if they have a conflict with a

colleague senior project manager about the planning of a crit-ical resource on their projects, they should not escalate to management however, resolve this among the group of senior project managers. If you reach that stage within your organi-zation, within SES, you are really implementing the philoso-phy of project objectives management."

Junior listens closely and says, "But this is not only between senior project managers, this can also be relevant for a conflict between the project manager and the lead engineer on our projects. Sometimes, we see that both escalate to their line manager and that then both line managers are expected to, and many times do, resolve the conflict. We should expect them as leads within the project team, to lead by example and resolve between each other instead of escalating!"

"Yes, and you, as management, have to lead by example," Collin concludes. John and Julie glance at each other, and both think back to their frequent quarrels in front of personnel. They both nod in agreement but say nothing more.

Senior Project Management Philosophy

To underline the importance of the senior project managers' active involvement, support, and commitment for successful implementation of the method within the organization, the senior PM philosophy is a driving principle within the method. The level of junior up to senior is meant relative to the organization, subject to its size and number of project managers.

In general, and specifically within the method, the main difference between junior (project) and senior managers is their expected interest in the project and its environment, such as its organization and other projects. Where the (junior) project manager focuses his or her interest mainly on their project, a senior project manager should unquestionably focus their interest on both his or her project and its organization and its other projects, independent of whether the method is implemented or not (Figure 7-5).

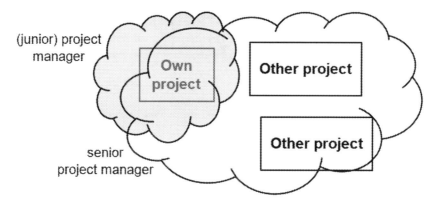

Figure 7-5. Interest of (junior) project managers vs. senior project managers

Within the method, however, each employee (and all project managers) is expected to behave and act to subordinate the project to its organization. But again, it is also expected from senior project managers to fully behave and act according to this principle, and to lead by example. An example is that senior project managers of different projects should actively discuss the best overall interest of the organization in case of a resource conflict, independent of an organizational process. Of course, such conflicts could be properly managed within a mature organization. However, senior project managers should naturally show such behavior and actions as part of their seniority. Senior project managers should never escalate a resource conflict to management for resolution on their behalf. However, management involvement is appropriate in case a conflict cannot be resolved within the group of senior project managers.

Collin explains.

"For example, you can stimulate and incentivize a culture within SES for project managers to resolve resource or other conflicts between projects with their colleagues instead of escalating resolutions to management. And as part of that culture, you can agree with your most 'senior' project managers

as one of their personal targets for the upcoming year, that they specifically lead by example and actively show this behavior."

Julie thinks for a couple of seconds and responds.

"We can literally strengthen a resource-related supplier project objective action on his project—to utilize project resources effectively and efficiently on his project—by including this in his personal targets as well."

"So, it is not either supplier project objectives management or our competence and appraisal process, but both?" John Jr. adds.

"Correct, they can and should be aligned to strengthen each other and create a strong synergy within SES!" Collin concludes.

Such seniority of project managers can, therefore, be seen as the highest competence level, integrated within the competence and appraisal process of the project supplier.

Summary

How do you integrate change with existing management processes within the project supplier's organization and its project execution practices?

Integrate change with existing management processes by aligning with the organization's existing project controls, generic project management method, employee competence, and appraisal management.

CHAPTER 8

Benefits: How to Benefit from Change?

How does a project supplier benefit from the changes to the organization and its project execution practices?

Chapter 6 established how to implement change, and Chapter 7 addressed integrating the method with existing management processes. This chapter focuses on how an organization can benefit from the change to the organization and its project execution practices.

Principles

Benefits realization management (BRM) offers organizations a way to measure how projects and programs add true value to the enterprise. It consists of the following three phases: identify benefits, execute benefits, and sustain benefits. BRM focuses on managing benefits linked to (project) objectives. Furthermore, the focus on the measurement of added value has a link to the measurement of success, by success criteria.[1] Various principles are therefore involved in how a project supplier benefits the most from the change of implementing supplier project objectives management within its organization, such as give and take, resources, the balancing act, push/pull, now and in the future, and balance in the multi-project environment.

Give and Take

As analyzed earlier, the project's inputs (project success factors) must be created first as outputs (project success criteria) from a preceding project by the organization. In other words, outputs "given" by a preceding project are "taken" as inputs by the next project. (Figure 8-1). A good example is using lessons learned and process assets as output from a project and input into the next project.

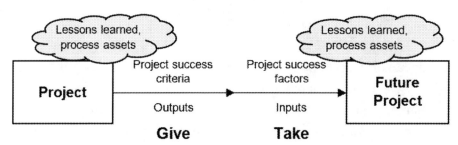

Figure 8-1. *Give (outputs) by a project, taken (inputs) by the next project*

This input/output and give/take relationships between projects seem logical; however, it is not a guaranteed result. It must be created.

---

[1] BCG, 2016

"We should draw it like this instead," Collin says while he draws a new flip chart. (Figure 8-2)

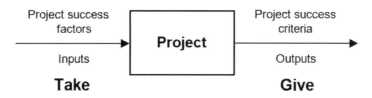

Figure 8-2. *Give (outputs) and take (inputs) by the same project*

"Do you see the difference?" Collin asks while pointing at both flip charts.

"Is it not the same?" Julie questions.

"Where do you think that the priority of a project team will be, taking or giving?"

Then it hits her, and she confirms. "I guess I understand. The priority is likely with the taking, and perhaps less or not on the giving."

"Yes." Collin confirms and draws a cloud around the 'taking' side of the project. (Figure 8-3)

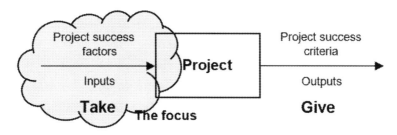

Figure 8-3. *Give (outputs) and take (inputs) by the same project*

"And if the project gives nothing, there is also nothing to pass on to be taken by the next project through the organization."

"Give and take! It is a chain from one project to the next that only works if a project and its project team are willing or motivated to spend time and effort to give and take."

Then Collin asks Jr. "How could a project team be willing or motivated to focus on the giving side as well?"

If there are no proper incentives in place within the organization, or even in an extreme example, only negative incentives and no positive incentives, the project team might not be motivated and thereby willing to spend time and effort on the giving; or there can also be negative causes within the project team itself without negative incentive from the organization or environment of the project. However, positive exceptions occur where a project team or project manager is driven by personal motivation (positive causes) to do so even without positive incentives from the organization. Positive incentives can be various, such as a positive personal appraisal for the project team member, a positive culture in which urgency and importance for the give-and-take principle are key, or positive examples where productive new process assets are used by a project team on a new project from which they know that other colleagues have spent significant time and effort to create it. Negative incentives can be various as well, such as a negative personal appraisal for the project team member for getting distracted from the primary project controls, time, cost, and quality of the project result, or not getting sufficient time to be able to spend effort on creating a productive process asset.

"Perhaps the organization and the project team should see it like this." And Collin draws another flip chart. (Figure 8-4)

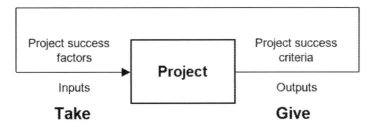

Figure 8-4. *Give (outputs) to take (as inputs) into the project itself*

The urgency and importance can be recognized by imagining that the process where the project, and thereby ultimately its organization, benefits from inputs only works when it provides productive outputs into itself. In other words, no productive outputs or productive inputs (Figure 8-5).

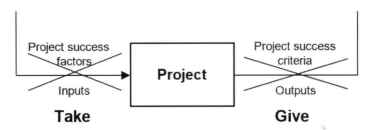

Figure 8-5. *No productive outputs, no productive inputs*

"Give and take" is an important benefit principle within the method, explaining how a project can benefit the most from productive change, specifically as a prerequisite for the method.

Resources

Effective and efficient use of the project's or the organization's resources is a key benefit principle. Utilization of resources on the project (such as human resources or production capacity) should be managed and, even more important optimized, at an organizational level, to provide the most benefit to the organization. This is opposed to every project requesting

resources and the organization trying to accommodate this on a project
and case-to-case basis. Although case-to-case management will involve
some alignment between projects, it can result in large resource peaks
by overlapping projects if not managed from an overall optimization
perspective. Even before the project award, the project delivery timing
could and should be optimized where possible to manage (or plan)
resource peaks between multiple projects and, after that, further optimized
during the project execution phase.

A Balancing Act

In his book, *The Future of Management*, Gary Hamel introduces the
balancing act related to precedent-breaking management innovation as
a critical trade-off where one side always seems to prevail at the expense
of the other.[2] Within a project supplier this balancing act is the trade-off
between the project's and the organization's interests, a potential for
friction within the organization, when not actively managed. The method
manages this by subordinating the project to the organization and its
goal. The project has no goal of its own, no sole interest of its own, and
therefore, no interests of the project can be impaired; only the interests of
the organization can be impaired.

Push/Pull

Push/pull is a key benefit principle of the method. To *push* means acting
on the project level: the project (team) should push the planned supplier
project objective actions, independent of the pull by the organization
at an organizational level. Simultaneously, to *pull* means acting on the
organization level: the organization pulls the planned supplier project

---

[2] Hamel, 2007

objective actions by the defined supplier project objectives. It creates opportunities for turning this potential into realized project supplier organizational benefits by embedding changes within the organization.

Now and in the Future

The saying "now and in the future" regarding customers, money, and stakeholders highlights a key benefits principle of the method: the fact that the project itself has no goal of its own, that the project is subordinate to the organization and its goal to "secure the future of the organization," which contains the important term future. The goal of the organization is to secure the future, by that also securing the *now* of the organization. As the project subordinates to the organization by aligning its supplier project objectives toward the goal, the project also requires a primary focus on the future within supplier project objectives. Although all objectives require attention for the future, the "now and in the future" definition is specifically included within the objectives related to people (customers, employees, and stakeholders) and money.

> *"An extreme example of the now vs. future conflict is a short-term (now) organizational benefit such as a maximized project profit that actually takes the organization away from instead of toward its goal, to secure the future of the organization," Collin explains.*

> *"But how can a good project profit ever take our organization away from our goal?" John Jr. asks Collin.*

> *"Well, for example, if this profit was realized at the expense of a customer that will never contract new business again, unsatisfied and feeling mistreated due to, in his opinion (too) rigorous claim management on your project by your highly motivated and tough project manager." Collin answers and immediately continues.*

"Another example is to secure a guaranteed future income source by current, now, successful project results; or just the opposite, to secure future business by acceptance of a project with a certain accepted profit loss."

In his famous book *The Seven Habits of Highly Effective People*, Stephen Covey explains that effectiveness lies in the balance, what I call the *P/PC balance. P* stands for production of desired results, the golden eggs, and *PC* stands for production capability, the ability or asset that produces the golden eggs.[3] There are three kinds of assets: physical, financial, and human. *Balance* means proper investment in the asset instead of short-term production maximization, ensuring long-term (future) asset (resource) returns.

Balance in the Multi-Project Environment

As you have learned, one successful project and even the sum of multiple successful projects does not guarantee a successful project supplier organization. There is more involved in securing the future of the project supplier organization then one or more successful projects. However, this focus on delivering successful projects might be the practical approach for running a multi-project-based department or organization troubled by its day-to-day challenges. The project team and project manager have their direct project-related objectives, and the department or organization has its higher-level objectives; these might not be aligned and, thereby, often cause friction within the organization.

Sometimes, it is assumed that the organization and its management shall facilitate and support the project (team) so that the project team can execute the project optimally and that all available conditions for a successful project are fulfilled. However, this is not the right balance and

---

[3] Covey, 1989

approach to secure the future of the organization. At the method's core, the project (team) should subordinate to the organization and be executed by the project team with the right balance to fully subordinate and contribute to the organization's goal.

> *"What about assigning an inexperienced employee to one of your projects? A disadvantage for the project but a benefit for the organization. How does that work here?" Collin asks John.*

> *"I know what you are getting at, which is also what we sometimes discuss with involved project managers. This is indeed a typical example that now and then happens with us," Julie answers and continues.*

> *"We do explain that giving this project only the experienced employees results in sub-optimizations; optimum for this project but sub-optimum for other projects, which have inexperienced resources. But it is difficult to convince when there is, or was, no corporate philosophy behind such discussions."*

> *"Exactly, that is what we implement with the method! A corporate philosophy, a corporate urgency, to strengthen such approach and expectations from the project." Collin agrees.*

Independent management of project results is sub-optimization; instead, overall optimization and integrated management of ongoing projects (multi-projects, program, or portfolio management) at the organizational level is a prerequisite to provide the highest benefit to the organization. Such management in the multi-project environment is provided by the method.

Benefits of the Method

The Project Supplier That Benefits the Most from the Method

Although the method is applicable for all project suppliers, also referred to as a *supplier* and a *supplier organization*, it is specifically applicable and beneficial for the characterized by the following.

- a for-profit (commercial) company or a non-profit (non-commercial) organization (e.g., institute, association)

- a project execution and delivery department delivering the project result to a receiving and using department (the internal customer or user) within one corporate organization; or a corporate organization delivering to another corporate organization (the external customer), or a corporate organization delivering to an (external) private person

- a multi-project environment with limited resources (e.g., human resources) for all ongoing projects

- small to medium-sized organizations

- or without extensive and matured organizational procedures embedded within their organization to manage their projects

- growing fast (e.g., size or revenue)

- in a turbulent or changing business field

- has many competitors

Collin steps to one of the flip charts and flips through it, look-ing for one of his earlier charts. He finds it, points at the first bullet, and explains: "Examples of such typical project suppli-ers are an IT department developing and implementing new software at the procurement department of a commercial company; a painting company doing all paintwork at an office construction project; or a local house construction com-pany building a new house for a private person; or a steel fab-rication company fabricating steelwork for another commercial company."

Benefits from Implementing Supplier Project Objectives Management

The structure of the systematic method provides an effective and efficient process to proactively and continuously (fully) utilize all potential supplier organizational benefits for the project supplier. Although various concepts of the method seem logical, not special, and partly already being conducted within many project supplier organizations, the transparency of the method's core principles and aim provides a strong "urgency" upon executing the supplier project objective actions among the daily normal organizational actions by the organization and the normal supplier project actions (executing the project and delivering the project result) by the project team.

"For example," Collin says to John and Julie "It should be clear to your project manager that an employee who is trained on his project becomes a benefit for his organization, right?"

"However," he continues, "if, at the same time, he is only bound and judged by tight project controls such as scope, time, and cost control, it might remain difficult for him to set or keep the right priority for the organization."

Within the method, the transparency and aim provide the context and urgency, and the systematic process provides the effectiveness and efficiency to pursue the objectives according to the defined priorities.

"Based on the method's core principles, it can be concluded that training the inexperienced employee on his project provides more benefits for the organization in the long term (the future), as opposed to the short-term achievement of project controls (the now)."

And Collin further explains.

"However, instead, it might also be that for one of your other projects, you will define that the most (future) benefit for your organization is to exploit a potentially large profit on a project by using the most experienced employee while training an inexperienced employee on another project with less potential for a large profit. It is all a matter of defining specific supplier project objectives for the project in question."

The method focuses on potential supplier organizational benefits that might otherwise get less, limited, or no attention within the supplier organization during its day-to-day business. The method does not conflict with the existing organizational management processes within the organization; instead, it strengthens such processes. The method can and should be integrated with, and thereby strengthening, the existing organizational management processes such as the project controls time, quality, scope, and cost management (which control the direct management of the project execution and delivery of the project result to the customer), or the existing generic project management method (which organizes the detailed process of project management execution within the organization), or the existing employee competence and appraisal management process. However, even if the supplier does not fully integrate the method with its existing organizational management processes or implements just parts of the method, this will provide more focus on supplier project objectives next to the project controls, providing more benefit to the supplier organization.

In its totality, supplier project objectives management (SPOM) provides an effective and efficient process to proactively and continuously (fully) utilize all potential supplier organizational benefits for the project supplier to take the supplier closer to its goal of securing its future.

> *"This was our last session," Collin says finally after some awkward small talk.*
>
> *John Jr. and Julie look at each other, sad and uneasy, although they knew this was coming.*
>
> *"Yes, I know, Collin," Julie answers reluctantly. "But don't you think we should do one more session to recapture the key points?"*
>
> *"No, Julie, you are ready to continue your journey to secure the future of SES! And I am sure you will adjust along the way to some of these newly implemented learnings further to your SES culture. You will likely remove certain elements we invented together and add new elements of your own instead. And that is all right. That is what it is all about—learning and continuous improvement!"*
>
> *Suddenly, Collin stands up and says dramatically, "Farewell!"*
>
> *He turns around and walks out of the room, taking Julie and John off guard, staring in amazement at each other. But to their comfort, they hear him shout from the hallway.*
>
> *"See you tonight for dinner. It's my treat!"*

Summary

How does a project supplier benefit from the changes to the organization and its project execution practices?

Based on benefit (principles), SPOM provides an effective and efficient process to proactively and continuously (fully) utilize all potential supplier organizational benefits for the project supplier, thereby taking the project supplier closer to its goal to secure its future.

APPENDIX A

Current Reality Tree: Process Assets

For explanation on the current reality tree method and the specific example for 'Process Assets', refer to Chapter 1, Section 'A Current Reality Tree of Process Assets'.

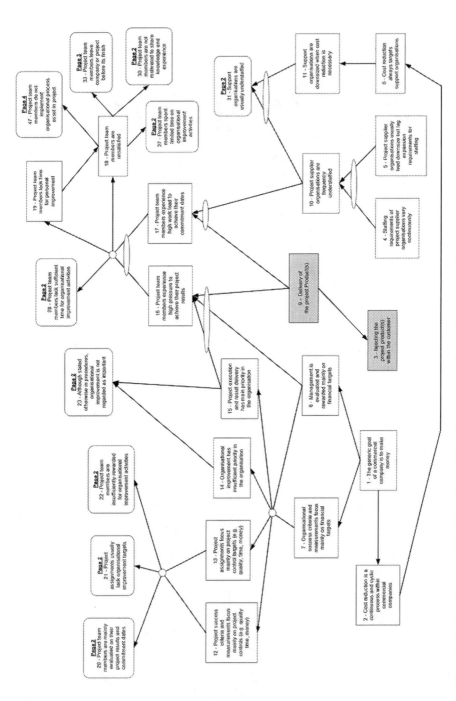

Figure A-1. *Current Reality Tree (CRT) Process Assets (Page 1/4)*

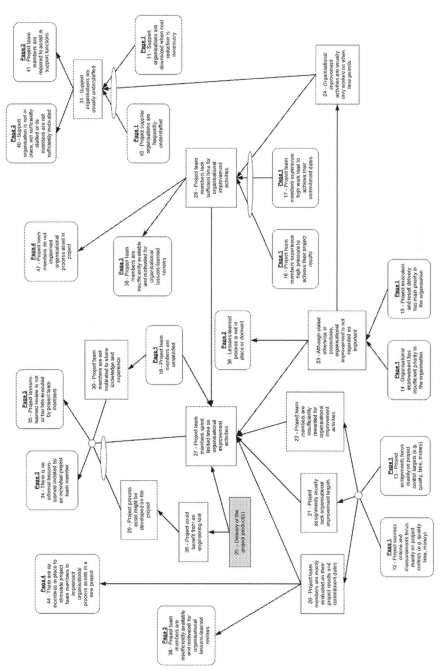

Figure A-2. *Current Reality Tree (CRT) Process Assets (Page 2/4)*

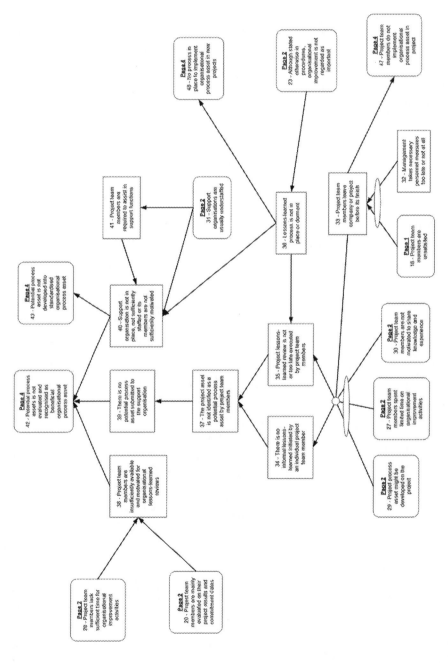

Figure A-3. Current Reality Tree (CRT) Process Assets (Page 3/4)

Figure A-4. *Current Reality Tree (CRT) Process Assets (Page 4/4)*

APPENDIX B

Generic Project Management Methods

Agile

Agile software development and project management are part of the Agile family of project management methodologies. In 2004, Jim Highsmith, co-author of the Agile software development manifesto, published his book *Agile Project Management: Creating Innovative Products*,[1] in which he sets out the principles of Agile project management. In his introduction, Highsmith states that project management needs to be transformed to move faster, be more flexible, and be aggressively customer-responsive. Agile project management (APM) answers this transformational need, which brings together a set of principles, practices, and performance measures that enable project managers to catch up with the realities of modern product development. The Agile software development manifesto's core values and principles actuate APM: delivering value over managing tasks; leading the team over managing tasks; and adapting to change over conforming to plans.

---

[1] Highsmith, 2004

© Reitse van der Wekken 2024
R. van der Wekken, *Project Objectives Management*,
https://doi.org/10.1007/979-8-8688-0956-9

APM is furthermore structured in an enterprise framework (project governance, project management, iteration management, and technical practices) and the phases of a delivery framework (envision, speculate, explore, adapt, and close).

1) **Envision.** Determine the product vision, project objective and constraints, the project community, and how the team will work together.

2) **Speculate.** Develop a capability or feature-based release plan to deliver on the vision.

3) **Explore.** Plan and deliver running tested stories in a short iteration, constantly seeking to reduce the risk and uncertainty of the project.

4) **Adapt.** Review the delivered results, the current situation, and the team's performance, and adapt as necessary.

5) **Close.** Conclude the project, pass along key learnings, and celebrate.

Benefits Realization Management (BRM)

Benefits realization management (BRM)[2] allows organizations to measure how projects and programs add value to the enterprise. BRM consists of a collective set of processes and practices for identifying benefits and aligning them with formal strategy, ensuring benefits are realized as project implementation progresses and finishes. The benefits are sustainable—and sustained—after project implementation is complete. BRM consists of the following three phases.

---

[2] BCG, 2016

1) **Identify benefits** to determine whether projects, programs, and portfolios can produce the intended business results.

2) **Execute benefits** to minimize risks to future benefits and maximize the opportunity to gain additional benefits.

3) **Sustain benefits** to ensure that whatever the project or program produces continues to create value.

Capability Maturity Model Integration (CMMI)

Capability Maturity Model Integration (CMMI)[3] describes how to make project management processes capable of performing successfully, consistently, and predictably to enact the strategies of an organization. CMMI is a proven set of global best practices that drive business performance through building and benchmarking key capabilities. CMMI was originally created for the US Department of Defense to assess the quality and capability of their software contractors. However, their models have expanded beyond software engineering to assist any organization in any industry in building, improving, and measuring their capabilities and improving performance.

For over 25 years, high-performing organizations around the world have achieved demonstrable, sustainable business results with CMMI. The best practices of CMMI focus on what needs to be done to improve performance and align operations to business goals. Designed to be understandable, accessible, flexible, and integrated with other methodologies such as Agile, CMMI models help organizations

---

[3] CMMI, 2007

understand their current capability and performance and offer a guide to optimize business results. How capable is your organization? This is the primary question of CMMI. All organizations have capabilities. Many do not have a process by which they can measure their different capabilities against best practices and pinpoint which ones are driving higher performance.[4]

Construction Management

Construction Management Association of America (CMMA)[5] is a professional service that provides a project's owner(s) in the construction industry with effective management of the project's schedule, cost, quality, safety, scope, and function. Construction management is compatible with all project delivery methods. No matter the setting, a construction manager's responsibility is to the owner and a successful project. CMMA is an industry association in the USA dedicated to professional construction management. CMMA represents more than 16,000 members, including federal/state/local government and private sector owners, construction consultants, technology suppliers, academia, and legal organizations, all with a common goal: to improve the nation's infrastructure.

Critical Chain Project Management (CCPM)

Critical chain project management (CCPM)[6] is a method of planning and managing projects that emphasize the resources required to execute project tasks, such as people, equipment, and physical space. CCPM was developed from the ideas of Eliyahu M. Goldratt about project

---

[4] CMMI Institute, 2021
[5] CMMA, 2021
[6] Leach, 2014

management, which he initially called a *critical chain*, according to his business novel from 1997 with the same name. CCPM involves key features of the Theory of Constraints (TOC), such as the core conflict, leading to all project undesirable effects, is between the individuals and the project management system; the core conflict derives from how the project system manages (or fails to manage) uncertainty by allocating contingency to buffers; the constraints for single projects is the critical chain; a system to exploit this constraint aggregates individual task uncertainty into buffers at the end of activity chains; buffer management provides real-time information; the system constraint in a multi-project environment is a resource shared across multiple project buffer; exploiting the multi-project resource constraint requires eliminating bad multitasking of all project resources; you must subordinate resource efficiency measures to the multi-project constraint. CCPM describes the project delivery process value stream, consisting of the project system, leading people, charter, the right solution, managing variation, managing risks, project planning, and execution.

Event Chain Methodology (ECM)

The underlying idea behind the *event chain methodology* (ECM)[7] is that potential risks often lie outside the project's scope. It is, therefore, essential to prepare for these risks and plan your responses since unexpected events will impact your project's schedule, deliverables, and potentially its success. ECM is a network analysis and uncertainty modeling schedule technique focused on identifying and managing events and the relationship between them (event chains) that affect project schedules. ECM is an extension of quantitative project risk analysis with Monte Carlo simulations and is considered the next advance beyond the critical path

---

[7] Virine and Trumper, 2007

method (CPM) and critical chain project management (CCPM). ECM tries to mitigate the effect of motivational and cognitive biases in estimating and scheduling. It improves risk assessment accuracy and helps generate more realistic risk-adjusted project schedules.

Individual Competence Baseline (ICB)

The Individual Competence Baseline (ICB)[8] is a global competence standard defined by the International Project Management Association (IPMA) and describes the competencies that project, program, and portfolio managers should possess to certify at four levels of increasing competence.

D) certified project management associate

C) certified project manager

B) certified senior project manager

A) certified projects director

The ICB manual outlines 29 competence elements divided into three subcategories: perspective, people, and practice.

Perspective

- **Strategy** describes how corporate strategy is transformed into manageable elements using projects.

- **Governance, structures, and processes** provide support for the project.

---

[8] IPMA, 2018

- **Compliance, standards, and regulations** interpret and balance the restrictions in a country, company, or industry.

- **Power and interest** recognize and understand the informal personal and group interests and the resulting politics and use of power.

- **Culture and values** to be aware of the organization's corporate culture and values and those of the wider society in which the project operates.

People

- **Self-reflection and self-management** to be aware of and reflect on how emotions and values guide our decision-making. Competent project managers are aware of their primary reactions and are open to the possibility of changing and improving their behavior.

- **Personal integrity and reliability** to be in accordance with your moral and ethical values and principles, fostering consistent behavior in project management decisions. It supports an environment of trust that makes others feel secure and confident.

- **Personal communication** as effective communication is essential to strong project management. The content of each communication and the means (tone of voice, channel, and amount of information) must be clear and appropriate to the target audience. Formal communication, such as presentations, meetings, and written forms, must be used according to their value and limitations.

- **Relationships and engagement** as the quality of relationships is one of the most important success factors in project management. Both one-to-one relationships and a relationship network are important competence elements resulting in high performance. Strong relationships allow for easier engagement, decision-making, and leadership.

- **Leadership** is important for the project manager throughout the lifecycle of a project. There are many different leadership styles available. Which ones, and how they are implemented, are an important driving factor in the steps to project success.

- **Teamwork** allows project teams to carry out the project's technical work and accomplish the project objectives. They often encompass multiple disciplines and personal experiences. Managing the team requires selecting the right team members, keeping them motivated, and giving them the tools to succeed.

- **Conflict and crisis** can occur between project team members, stakeholders, or the project manager. How these conflicts are handled can result in positive outcomes or significant, long-term negative effects on the project.

- **Resourcefulness** is the application of techniques and ways of thinking to find alternatives and problem-solving. It is utilized when unique problems, difficult situations, and risks occur. Resourcefulness motivates the project team to work together to develop a workable solution.

- **Negotiation** is required on all projects, between the project team and its customer, the project, and its parent organization, or within the project. Because of this, the project manager must be familiar with negotiation strategies and tactics.

- **Results orientation** requires the project manager to focus on the project's result. All project activities must support results, or they should not be part of the project. Likewise, all project decisions must consider how they impact the result.

Practice

- **Project design** details the processes and steps the project will take to ensure its success. Aspects such as perceived benefits, team and stakeholders, and stakeholder communication are analyzed and planned to ensure project success. The blueprint or overall architecture of the project is laid out and managed.

- **Requirements, objectives, and benefits** address why the project is being undertaken. Every project produces a product or service, but on a deeper level, those products benefit the organization. The project manager must realize those benefits and seek to maximize them.

- **Scope** is one of the highest sources of project issues. Scope defines what is part of the project and what is not, and when the boundaries of the project are not well understood (or change without well-defined parameters), problems almost always arise. Thus, the project manager must understand, define, and manage the scope.

- **Time** includes project scheduling, planning for an acceptable time frame, and ensuring that the project deliverables are produced within that time frame. The project must be divided into tasks, and each task must be estimated to determine its duration. During project execution, project control mechanisms are implemented to warn the project manager of behind-schedule situations and take appropriate action.

- **Organization and information** require the project manager to define, implement, and manage the temporary organization. They must also create the project documentation, storage facilities, reporting structures, and communication flows.

- **Quality** encompasses the whole project, from its planning to the final touches. Quality is about determining the right specifications and ensuring that the products are produced to those specifications.

- **Finance** requires the project manager to estimate the project during the planning phase, and control the financial expenditures of the project during the execution phase. Also, ensuring the financial resources are in place to complete the project is extremely important to successful project outcomes.

- **Resources** define, acquire and control resources is where a project manager spends most of their day. Resources include people, expertise, facilities, equipment, materials, infrastructure, tools, and any other assets required to complete the project tasks.

- **Procurement** means that most projects must purchase (procure) goods, services, or resources to carry out their mandate. The types of contracts, roles and responsibilities, supplier selection processes, and the like are core to the project manager's expertise.

- **Plan and control** require the project manager must create a plan for the project and exercise project control to ensure that the project remains within the plan. The plan is a moving document, updated regularly to ensure it is relevant and progress is sufficient.

- **Risk and opportunity** require project managers to identify and prioritize risks, including creating risk response plans and project control during the execution phase. The opposite of risks are opportunities (positive risks) and should be tracked for potential exploitation.

- **Stakeholders** are anyone interested in the project, whether positive or negative. Stakeholders have expectations that must be managed; otherwise, a small stakeholder can often trip up a project. Project managers must identify each stakeholder and ensure they are familiar with their needs and wants. There needs to be a stakeholder engagement strategy.

- **Change and transformation** refers to projects attempting to institute change within an organization. How the organization responds to that change and how the project manager must manage that change is the focus of this competence element.

- **Select and balance** applies only to program and portfolio management.

Guidance on Project Management (ISO 21500)

ISO standard 21500[9] provides guidance on project management and specifies the organizational context and underlying concepts for undertaking project, program, and portfolio management. It also guides organizations to adopt or improve project, program, and portfolio management. The standard applies to most organizations, including public and private organizations, and does not depend on the size and type of the organization. It also applies to any project, program, and portfolio, regardless of complexity, size, or duration.

According to the standard, governance, and management of projects, programs, and portfolios operate within an overall context: in addition to ongoing operations, project, program, and portfolio management provide an integrated management framework to deliver value. Projects, programs, and portfolios exist within the organizational environment, and the organization exists within the larger external environment. Opportunities and threats can be identified through organizational strategy and objectives. The opportunities and threats can be evaluated and further developed into requirements and business cases. Based on those business cases and using portfolio management or another management structure, the organization selects and authorizes projects and programs that provide operations deliverables, outputs, and outcomes. When used in operations, deliverables, outputs, and outcomes should contribute to realizing benefits for internal and external stakeholders. The benefits can also further develop the organization's strategy and objectives.

---

[9] ISO, 2021

Organizations perform work to achieve objectives. This work can be performed as ongoing operations, a project, or a program, or organized as a portfolio with other related work. The focus of each of these organizational activities can be summarized as follows.

- **Relatively stable teams conduct operations** through ongoing, repetitive processes focused on sustaining the organization.

- **Projects** are performed by temporary teams and provide deliverables, outputs, outcomes, and benefits. A project can be managed as a stand-alone work effort within an organization or as part of a larger program or portfolio.

- **Programs** are groups of program components managed and coordinated to provide advantages and synergies, contribute to the achievement of common strategic and operational objectives, and realize benefits.

- **Portfolios** are the sets of projects, programs, and other related work undertaken to contribute to meeting an organization's strategic objectives.

The ISO standard identifies the recommended project management processes to be used during a project, for individual phases, or both. These project management processes are appropriate to projects in all organizations. Project management requires significant coordination and, as such, requires each process to be appropriately aligned and connected with other processes. Some processes may be repeated to fully define and meet stakeholder requirements and reach an agreement on the project objectives. The project management processes may be viewed from two different perspectives.

- process groups for the management of the project

- subject groups for collecting the processes by subject

The following lists and describes the process groups.

- **Initiating process group**: Initiating processes are used to start a project phase or project, define the project phase or project objectives, and authorize the project manager to proceed with the project work.

- **Planning process group**: Planning processes are used to develop planning details. This detail should be sufficient to establish baselines against which project implementation can be managed, and project performance can be measured and controlled.

- **Implementing process group**: Implementing processes are used to perform the project management activities and to support the provision of the project's deliverables in accordance with the project plans.

- **Controlling process group**: Controlling processes are used to monitor, measure, and control project performance against the project plan. Consequently, when necessary, preventive, and corrective actions may be taken and change requests made to achieve project objectives.

- **Closing process group**: Closing processes are used to formally establish that the project phase or project is finished and to provide lessons learned to be considered and implemented as necessary.

The following lists and describes subject groups.

- **Integration**: The integration subject group includes the processes required to identify, define, combine, unify, coordinate, control, and close the various activities and processes related to the project.

- **Stakeholder**: The stakeholder subject group includes the processes required to identify and manage the project sponsor, customers, and other stakeholders.

- **Scope**: The scope subject group includes the processes required to identify and define the work and deliverables and only the work and deliverables required.

- **Resource**: The resource subject group includes the processes required to identify and acquire adequate project resources such as people, facilities, equipment, materials, infrastructure, and tools.

- **Time**: The time subject group includes the processes required to schedule the project activities and to monitor progress to control the schedule.

- **Cost**: The cost subject group includes the processes required to develop the budget and to monitor progress to control costs.

- **Risk**: The risk subject group includes the processes required to identify and manage threats and opportunities.

- **Quality**: The quality subject group includes planning and establishing quality assurance and control.

- **Procurement**: The procurement subject group includes the processes required to plan and acquire products, services, or results and to manage supplier relationships.

- **Communication**: The communication subject group includes the processes required to plan, manage, and distribute information relevant to the project.

Kanban

Kanban (project management) is part of the Agile family of project management methodologies. Kanban originates from Japanese car manufacturer Toyota's factories during the 1940s. The departments used a visual system of cards called Kanban to signal that their team was ready for more raw materials and had more capacity to produce. Today, this visual approach to managing a project is well-suited for work that requires steady output. Project teams create visual representations of their tasks, often using sticky notes and whiteboards or online Kanban boards, moving the notes or tasks through predetermined stages to see progress as it happens and identify where bottlenecks could occur. Toyota has formulated six rules for the application of Kanban.[10]

- Each process issues requests (Kanban) to its suppliers when it consumes its supplies.

- Each process produces items according to the quantity and sequence of incoming requests.

- No items are made or transported without a request.

- The request associated with an item is always attached to it.

---

[10] Taiichi, 1978

- Processes must not send out defective items to ensure that the finished products will be defect-free.

- Limiting the number of pending requests makes the process more sensitive and reveals inefficiencies.

Lean

Lean project management is adapted from lean principles, which were developed in the Japanese industry. Lean was introduced by John Krafcik in his 1988 dissertation titled "Triumph of the Lean Production System," arising from the results of his research. Krafcik was a quality engineer at a joint venture of Toyota and General Motors before going to MIT for his MBA.

Krafcik's research was continued at MIT, leading to the book *The Machine That Changed the World* by Jim Womack, Daniel Jones, and Daniel Roos in 1990. Womack and Jones refined their strategy over the years and published in 1996 their book *Lean Thinking: Banish Waste and Create Wealth in Your Corporation*. This book provides a set of management principles, tools, and best practices designed to identify and eliminate waste in work processes and increase efficiency.

The goal is to help organizations achieve operational excellence. To be lean is to provide what is needed, when needed, with the minimum quantity of materials, equipment, labor, and space. In their book, they introduce the five core principles.

- **Specify value in the eyes of the customer.** The first lean principle is to specify the value of a product or service, which is a capability provided to a customer at the right time at an appropriate price, as defined in each case by the customer. The challenge here is to focus on what the customer is willing to pay.

- **Identify the value stream for each product.** The value stream includes all the actions, both value-added and non-value-added, currently required to bring a product from raw material to the customer or through the design flow from concept to launch. A value stream map is created that reflects the current state of the process. This map is then analyzed for waste and value creation, and a future-state map is created, which represents how the process could and should operate.

- **Make value flow by eliminating waste.** Once the value is defined and the value stream is identified, the next step is to create continuous flow by eliminating backflows, scrap, rework, and interruptions. In analyzing value streams, work will fall into one of three categories.

  - **Value-added work**: This category consists of essential changes to products and services. This category must be maximized as it provides customer value (form, fit, and function).

  - **Value-enabling work**: This category has potential for future elimination (with identified improvements) but cannot be eliminated immediately. This category is necessary to run the current process and it needs to be assessed if it can be minimized.

  - **Non-value-added work**: This category can usually be eliminated quickly and is not dependent on the improvement of other areas. This is the work nobody needs, and it is pure waste. This category of work needs to be eliminated.

According to lean principles, all types of waste in a process, pure or necessary, can be classified as one of the following seven types.

- **Overproduction**: Producing more than is needed before it is needed

- **Waiting**: Any non-work time waiting for approval, supplies, parts, and so forth

- **Transportation**: Wasted effort to transport materials, parts, or finished goods into or out of storage or between processes

- **Overprocessing**: Doing more work than is necessary (customer requirements) or double work

- **Inventory**: Maintaining excess inventory of raw materials, parts in process, or finished goods

- **Motion**: Any wasted motion to pick up parts or stack parts, also wasted walking

- **Defects**: Repair or rework

Let the customer pull the flow. The challenge here is to avoid delivering value before the customer requests it. Also, you should not provide the customer with more than the agreed initial scope. In manufacturing, the customer should pull the flow using a Kanban system. Kanban allows the implementation of a just-in-time system. It uses cards to signal the need for an item by triggering a unit's movement, production, or supply.

Continuously improve in the pursuit of perfection. The final step is pursuing perfection, leading to a lean culture. The pursuit of perfection implies process improvement is endless. The value of all activities should be constantly questioned. Perfection will certainly not be achieved, but it must be constantly strived for to get closer.

Prince2

Prince2[11] is a structured project management method and practitioner certification program emphasizing dividing projects into manageable and controllable stages. Prince2 was developed as a UK government standard for information systems projects. Ownership of the rights of Prince2 was transferred in July 2013 to Axelos Ltd, a joint venture by the UK government and a private company. Prince was derived from an earlier developed method and was later renamed as an acronym for PRojects IN Controlled Environments. Prince2 is the second edition of the earlier Prince method and was released in 1996 as a generic project management method.

Prince2 comprises principles, control themes, a process lifecycle, and guidance on matching the method to the project's environment. Prince2 provides a process model for managing a project. This consists of a set of activities that are required to direct, manage, and deliver a project.

The seven Prince2 principles are the guiding obligations for best practice that a project should follow if it uses Prince2. These are derived from good and bad lessons that have affected project success. The principles provide a framework of best practice for those involved in a project, ensuring that the method is not applied in an overly prescriptive way or in name only but in a way sufficient to contribute to the project's success. The following describes the seven Prince2 principles.

- **Prince2 project teams learn from previous experience.** Lessons are sought, recorded, and acted upon throughout the life of the project.

- **Continue business justification**. A Prince2 project has continued business justification.

---

[11] Prince2, 2022

- **Define roles and responsibilities**. A Prince2 project has defined and agreed on roles and responsibilities with an organizational structure that engages the business, user, and supplier stakeholder interests.

- **Manage in stages**. A Prince2 project is planned, monitored, controlled, and managed stage by stage.

- **Manage by exception**. A Prince2 project has defined tolerances for each project objective to establish limits of delegated authority.

- **Focus on products**. A Prince2 project focuses on the definition and delivery of products, particularly their quality requirements.

- **Tailor to suit the project environment**. Prince2 is tailored to suit the project environment, size, complexity, importance, team capability, and risk.

The seven Prince2 themes are those aspects of project management that need to be addressed continually throughout the project lifecycle (i.e., not once only). They provide guidance on how the process should be performed. For example, numerous processes in Prince2 involve creating or approving plans and explanatory guidance in the plans theme. The set of Prince2 themes describes how baselines for benefits, risks, scope, quality, cost, and time are established (in the business case, quality and plans themes). How the project management team monitors and controls the work as the project progresses (in the progress, quality, change, and risk themes). The organization theme supports the other themes with a structure of roles and responsibilities with clear paths for delegation and escalation. The following are seven the Prince2 themes.

- Business case: Why?
- Organization: Who?

- Quality: What?

- Plans: How? How much? When?

- Risk: What if?

- Change: What's the impact?

- Progress: Where are we now? Where are we going?

Prince2 provides a process model for managing a project. This consists of a set of activities that are required to direct, manage, and deliver a project. (Figure B-1)

1) **Starting a project**: The pre-project activities required to commission the project and to gain commitment from corporate or program management to invest in project initiation by answering a question: Is this a viable and worthwhile project?

2) **Directing a project**: The project board's activities in exercising overall project control. The activities focus on the decision-making necessary for project board members to fulfill their accountabilities successfully while delegating the day-to-day management of the project to the project manager.

3) **Initiating a project**: The project manager must lead activities to establish the project on a sound foundation. Every Prince2 project has an initiation stage. The key deliverable from this stage is the project initiation documentation, which includes an overall project plan and defines baselines for the six project performance targets of time, cost, quality, scope, risk, and benefits.

4) **Managing a stage boundary**: The activities the project manager must undertake to provide the project board with sufficient information to enable it to review the success of the current stage, approve the next stage plan, review the updated project plan, and confirm continued business justification and acceptability of the risks.

5) **Controlling a stage**: How the project manager manages the project execution/delivery activity during a stage and reports progress and exceptions to the project board.

6) **Managing product delivery**: The team manager supervises the detailed work of creating the project's products and provides the link between the project manager and the teams undertaking the project work.

7) **Closing a project**: The closure activity is toward the end of the final stage of the project. The project manager leads the process for orderly decommissioning, including any remaining project acceptance and handover requirements.

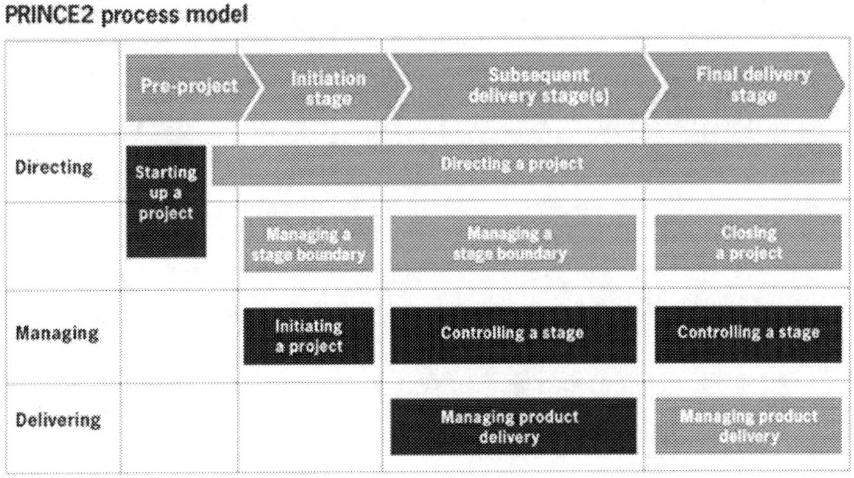

PRINCE2 process model

Figure B-1. *Prince2 process model (Prince2, 2022)*

Projects Integrating Sustainable Methods (PRiSM)

PRiSM (Projects integrating Sustainable Methods) is developed by Green Project Management,[12] a project management method based on sustainable development. The aim is to enable organizations to manage their projects while integrating environmental sustainability into their processes, reducing their negative ecological and social impact when executing their projects. PRiSM is a principles-based, sustainable project management methodology. Its key difference from traditional approaches is that it incorporates a value maximization model that focuses on the total asset lifecycle. PRiSM is a structured, process-based methodology. PRiSM is based on the P5 standard for sustainability in project management. It is effective in reducing project-level risk from an environmental, social, and

---

[12] GPM, 2022

economic perspective while expanding the range of benefits to be gained. The main purpose of P5 is to identify potential impacts to sustainability, both positive and negative, that can be analyzed and presented to management to support informed decisions and effective resource allocation. P5 expands on the triple bottom line of people, planet, and prosperity—as developed by John Elkington[13]—by considering product and process impacts. Thus, P5 stands for product, process, people, planet, and prosperity.

- **Product**: A product may be a physical item (such as a traffic bridge), a service (such as a consulting report or a training course), or another type of asset (such as a research report). The outputs of a project are one or more products and are used to build capabilities that will eventually benefit the organization.

- **Process**: According to the ISO 9000 series of standards, a process is "a set of interrelated or interacting activities that transforms inputs into outputs." These interrelated or interacting activities apply mechanisms to inputs to generate outputs while subject to constraints.

  Processes used in projects can be categorized into three major types.

  - **Project management–oriented processes** are concerned with identifying, describing, and organizing the work of the project.

  - **Product-oriented processes** are concerned with specifying and creating the project product (physical items, services, or other assets).

---

[13] Elkington, 1994

- **Support-oriented processes** provide relevant and valuable support to the other processes in disciplines such as logistics, finance, accounting, and safety.

- **People** The people (social) category of sustainability concerns the impacts a project's activities and results may have on individuals, society, and communities. The people category focuses on operating ethically and maintaining mutually beneficial relationships with employees, customers, suppliers, supply chains, and the wider community in general.

  The people category contains the following subcategories: labor practices and decent work, society and customers, human rights, and ethical behavior.

- **Planet** The planet (environmental) sustainability category concerns the impacts a project's activities and results may have on living and non-living natural systems. These systems include land, air, and water, as well as the flora, fauna, and people that live in them. The planet category focuses on preserving, restoring, and improving these natural systems.

  The planet (environmental) category contains the following subcategories: transport; energy; land, air, and water; and consumption. While these subcategories are detailed as part of the environmental domain, most have social and economic impacts that may need to be accounted for in those domains.

- **Prosperity** The prosperity (economic) category of sustainability concerns the impacts that a project's activities and results may have on the finances of the project's stakeholders. The prosperity category focuses on maximizing positive returns for as many stakeholders as possible.

The prosperity category contains the following subcategories: business case analysis; business agility; and economic stimulation.

P5 is explicitly focused on projects. Most projects will be part of one or more programs and portfolios. Although there may be some differences in how sustainability impacts are identified and responded to at the program or portfolio level, the vast majority of the contents of P5 can be applied as is by simply changing the word project to program or portfolio. Within PRiSM, benefits realization is captured in a structure from business (sponsor/permanent organizations) to benefits and useful life via preparing the high-level business case and the business case after that. PRiSM extends beyond the typical project lifecycle with a phased approach.

1. Pre-project

2. Discovery

3. Design

4. Delivery and closure

5. Post-project

Finally, the six principles of sustainable change delivery within PRiSM, derived from the UN global compact's ten principles, consist of 1) commitment and accountability; ethics and decision-making; integrated and transparent; principle and values based; social and ecological equity; economic prosperity.

Project Management Body of Knowledge (PMBOK)

It is debated whether a true project management methodology; however, some organizations use the Project Management Body of Knowledge[14] (PMBOK) method for managing their projects. While not an official methodology, this system involves breaking down projects into the five process groups agreed upon by the Project Management Institute (PMI) and documented in the *Guide to the Project Management Body of Knowledge* (*PMBOK Guide*). A major change in the PMBOK's seventh edition is the significant shift from process-based project management (such as the traditional waterfall method) to principle-based project delivery, supporting every type of project delivery process (including adaptive methods such as Agile and Scrum). The sixth edition was based on five project process stages: initiating, planning, executing, controlling, and closing.

It was also based on ten knowledge areas: project integration management, project scope management, project schedule management, cost management, project quality management, project resources management, project communications management, project risk management, project procurement management, and project stakeholder management.

Another important change is the shift in scope that addresses project delivery apart from project management. A fundamental aspect of the PMBOK is the principles of the value delivery system, an all-inclusive approach through which projects accomplish business value. Organizational value is typically associated with tangible and intangible advantages from users, employees, and other business professionals. Projects are the key

---

[14] PMI, 2021

method to deliver business value by reaching corporate objectives. This is primarily achieved by defining organizational strategies and identifying objectives that later become practical initiatives.

Key within the current PMBOK are the twelve principles of project delivery and the eight performance domains. The twelve principles of project delivery focus on the what and why of project management and the thought process and behavior of people involved in project delivery.

- Be hardworking and respectful.

- Create a culture of responsibility.

- Actively engage stakeholders to comprehensively understand their interests and requirements.

- Emphasize on value.

- Acknowledge team interactions and respond accordingly.

- Encourage, influence, teach, and learn.

- Customize the delivery strategy.

- Ensure quality in procedures and outcomes.

- Take notice of complications involved in knowledge and experience.

- Report prospects and threats.

- Be flexible.

- Allow change to accomplish the predicted future state.

The PMBOK's eight performance domains consist of team, stakeholders, lifecycle, planning, navigating uncertainty and ambiguity, delivery, performance, and project work.

Scrum

Scrum (project management) is part of the Agile family of project management methodologies. Scrum specifically addresses the development of complex products, such as software. Scrum is based on working in a small team led by a Scrum master, conducting the project work in short cycles called *sprints*. The Scrum master can be the project manager or any other team member experienced in the method or an external specialist supporting the team with the Scrum process. The scrum team meets daily in scrum sessions to discuss the current tasks and any obstacles that need to be cleared. Scrum is a method for managing projects that allows for rapid development and testing, especially within a small team.[15] Ken Schwaber, a leader of the Agile process revolution and co-creator of Scrum, introduced the Scrum methodology in his book *Agile Project Management with Scrum*,[16] published in 2004. Scrum follows a heuristic approach where the project result under development or preparation is discovered through systematic conduct of the method. This is as opposed to prescribing methods where the development or preparation is being pre-planned. Scrum is founded on empirical process theory where knowledge develops from experience and step-by-step improvement of predictability and control of the risks. The starting point is that within product development, the project outcome and activities are uncertain by nature and, therefore best to be dealt with by the self-organizing and problem-solving capabilities of capable and motivated team members.

The Scrum process is outlined in Figure B-2.

---

[15] Wrike, 2022
[16] Schwaber, 2004

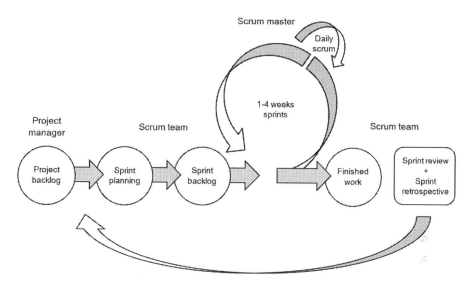

Figure B-2. *Scrum project management process*

The Scrum process is described as follows.

- **Project backlog**: A project starts with the backlog, a list of all project features to be implemented during the development or engineering phase or all activities to be executed for the project. Every feature, called a *user story*, is assigned a unique identification number and ordered by priority.

- **Sprint planning**: The first step of sprint planning is to determine the goal and duration of the respective sprint. As a rule, a Scrum sprint lasts about two to four weeks. Based on the goal, the sprint is filled with features or activities.

- **Sprint backlog**: The sprint backlog contains the features or activities chosen to reach the sprint goal.

319

- **Daily scrum**: The objective of the daily scrum meeting is to ensure that all team members are fully informed about the current sprint status and aligned. During a scrum meeting, every team member tells what he or she has done for the sprint goal, which task will be the next, and what problems they face during work. A task board is commonly used to track the current progress and planning of the scrum, containing single tasks linked to each feature or activity. During the scrum, these tasks are moved from to do, via in progress, to done.

- **Sprint review and retrospective**: In the sprint review after each sprint, the overall results can be demonstrated and analyzed. The stakeholders can decide on further project changes and plan the next sprint based on all this info. Furthermore, in the retrospective, the sprint process and results are reviewed, and improvements of the next sprint are determined and incorporated into the next sprint's planning. The work and team interaction processes are discussed to improve the work of the scrum team as a whole. The team should conclude what went well during the working process and what can be done better during future sprints.

Six Sigma

Six Sigma[17] comprises a set of techniques and tools for process improvement, developed within Motorola in the 1980s and followed in the 1990s by early adopters such as Honeywell and General Electric. Six Sigma improves manufacturing or process quality by identifying and removing the causes of defects and minimizing variability in the processes. This is done using empirical and statistical quality management methods and hiring people who serve as Six Sigma experts. Six Sigma creates an environment of continuous process improvement, enabling businesses to provide better products and services to customers. There are five main principles of Six Sigma.

- **Focus on the customer.** The main objective is to maximize the benefits for customers. Therefore, a business must understand the needs of its customers and the drivers of sales. It requires establishing quality standards according to the market or customer demands.

- **Assess the value chain and find the problem.** Detail a process's steps to find undesired effects and gather related data. Then, find out the problem and its root cause.

- **Eliminate defects and outliers.** After identifying the problem, make appropriate modifications to eliminate the defects. Eliminate any activity in the given process that does not contribute to the customer value. If the

---

[17] Chowdhury, 2001

value chain cannot reveal the problem area, various tools are used to find the problem areas and outliers. Eliminating the outliers and defects removes the bottlenecks in a given process.

- **Involve stakeholders.** A structured process should be adopted where all stakeholders collaborate and contribute to finding solutions to complex issues. The team needs to achieve proficiency in the methodologies and principles applied. Therefore, specialized knowledge and training are required to lower project failure risks and ensure optimal performance of the processes.

- **Maintain a flexible and responsive system.** When an inefficient or faulty process is eliminated, the employee approach and work practices must be changed. A flexible and responsive environment to the changes in processes can lead to the efficient implementation of the projects.

Apart from the DMAIC (define, measure, analyze, improve, control) main methodology, which focuses on optimizing and improving existing processes, the project-related DMADV methodology focuses on developing an entirely new process, product, or service and consists of the following five phases.

- **D**efine the purpose of the project, product, or service.

- **M**easure the crucial components of a process and product capabilities.

- **A**nalyze data and develop design alternatives, ultimately selecting the best design.

- **D**esign the selected best alternative and test the prototype.

- **V**erify the effectiveness of the design through several simulations or a pilot program.

Extreme Project Management (XPM)

Extreme programming or project management is part of the Agile family of project management methodologies. In his book *eXtreme Project Management*,[18] Doug DeCarlo introduces the principles and methods of XPM, a method of managing very complex and uncertain projects. XPM focuses on the human factor within project management, such as managing stakeholders, rather than planning techniques or extensive procedures. XPM is short and flexible, whereas traditional project management is not. Traditional project management means creating and sticking to a plan, usually for long-term projects. XPM allows to alter the project plan, the budget, and the outcome to fit changing needs, no matter what stage the project is in, and usually involves projects that last only a few weeks or even just days. XPM is said to be specifically suited for extreme projects characterized by fast-paced work; highly complex project needs and outcomes; frequent changes to the project requirements as the project progresses; trial-and-error approach to see what works; self-correcting process when things go wrong to get back on track; a move away from hierarchy in decision-making; people-driven projects, instead of process-driven (people do not adapt their projects to fit the model, they adapt models to fit the project).

---

[18] DeCarlo, 2004

According to DeCarlo, XPM is meant to be fast and adept, started by gathering a team of people willing and ready to embrace this Agile approach and mind set. After assembling the star team, the following steps are to be followed.

1) **Create a project plan.** Create a project plan with extreme project management in mind. That means expecting change, acknowledging that timelines may change, and leaving room for error.

2) **Ensure success.** To ensure success, your plan should answer all the critical questions. Who needs what, and why? What will it take to do it? Can we get what it takes to finish? Is it worth it?

3) **Schedule.** Plan the work in short cycles of a maximum of a few weeks.

4) **Have a kick-off.** Have a project kick-off meeting to give everyone the full rundown of the work involved and get people excited to work on a great, new project. Answer every question and communicate expectations. Make project visibility a priority starting from day one.

5) **Communicate.** Communicate with your client frequently, listen closely to their wants and needs, and immediately relay their feedback to your team.

6) **Develop work cycles.** Do follow-up work cycles with check-ins, review sessions, and realignment meetings if the project seems off-track.

7) **Celebrate.** When projects or cycles finish, celebrate every win. Make teams feel appreciated to keep them excited about the demanding work. Consider starting every meeting by listing team accomplishments since the last meeting, or going around to have everyone list one accomplishment they are proud of.

The project should not set up more processes than needed to complete the project. Extreme project management advises the KISS principle (keep it simple, stupid). Each project will probably require different steps and different templates, so customization of each project is required.

Waterfall

Waterfall is the traditional sequential or predictive project management methodology based on the waterfall model (serial flow from one phase to the next) described in the 1970s. According to Wrike,[19] the basis of the waterfall approach is that the project proceeds sequentially from its conception, each phase leading into the next. The waterfall model originates from the strict processes used in industries like construction and manufacturing. It is an approach focused on creating the best possible final product, with little room for adjustments or upgrades following the project completion. Since today's technology makes it feasible to adopt a more flexible methodology, other ways of developing software and other products or project management have become popular, such as the Agile family of methods; however, waterfall remains highly influential and used. The basic model breaks down into the following six basic phases, as illustrated in Figure B-3.

---

[19] Wrike, 2022

1) **Requirements**: The requirements phase defines the system's intended functions and qualities.

2) **Design**: Developers create the software architecture during the design phase.

3) **Construction**: During the construction phase, the software is developed and integrated.

4) **Testing**: During testing and debugging, the team finds and addresses flaws in the software.

5) **Installation**: The product is implemented in this phase.

6) **Maintenance**: The last phase is maintenance, which involves supporting the product and keeping it working properly for the customer.

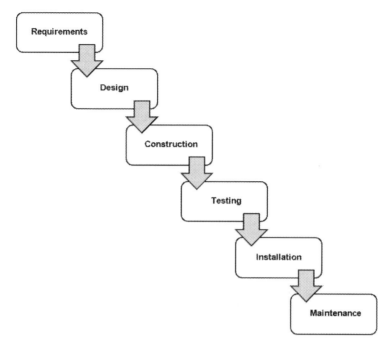

Figure B-3. *Waterfall model*

Although the Waterfall methodology might be perceived as restrictive for certain projects, it can be a solid approach to keep a well-defined, predictable project from exceeding time and budget guidelines. A clear and detailed organization can provide a strong basis during complex projects involving many people working toward a clearly outlined goal. Recent developments do apply adaptive (Agile family) based practices with Waterfall-based methods.

References

Agarwal, N., Rathod, U., 2006. "Defining success for software projects: An exploratory revelation," *International Journal of Project Management*, vol. 24, 2006, pp. 358–370.

Agile, 2022. "Manifesto for Agile Software Development." Retrieved January 2022, from `http://agilemanifesto.org/`.

Ahimbisibwe, A., Cavana, R.Y., Daellenbach, U., 2015. "A contingency fit model of critical success factors for software development projects," *Journal of Enterprise Information Management*, 2015, vol. 28, no. 1, pp. 7–33.

Ahola, T., Vuori, M., Viitamo, E., 2017. "Sharing the burden of integration: An activity-based view to integrated solutions provisioning," *International Journal of Project Management*, vol. 35, no. 6, August 2017, pp. 1006–1021.

Ahonen, J.J., Savolainen, P., 2011. "The Presence of the Customer and the Supplier Perspectives in Studies on Software Development Project Success," *Scientific Journal of Riga Technical University Computer Science*, Applied Computer Systems, vol. 46, 2011.

Almarri, K., Boussabaine, H., 2017. "Interdependency of the critical success factors and *ex-post* performance indicators of PPP projects," *Built Environment Project and Asset Management*, 2017, vol. 7, no. 5.

Al-Tmeemy, S.M. H.M., Abdul-Rahman, H., Harun, Z., 2010. "Future criteria for success of building projects in Malaysia," *International Journal of Project Management*. 11 March 2010.

Andersen, E.S., Birchall, D., Jessen, S.A., Money, A.H., 2006. "Exploring project success," *Baltic Journal of Management*, vol. 1, no. 2, pp. 127–147.

© Reitse van der Wekken 2024
R. van der Wekken, *Project Objectives Management*,
https://doi.org/10.1007/979-8-8688-0956-9

REFERENCES

Atkinson, R., 1999. "Project management: cost, time and quality, two best guesses and a phenomenon, it's time to accept other success criteria," *International Journal of Project Management*, 1999, vol. 17, no. 6, pp. 337–342.

Baccarini, D., 1999. "The Logical Framework Method for Defining Project Success," *Project Management Journal*, Project Management Institute, vol. 30, no. 4, pp. 25–32.

Basu, R., 2012, *Managing quality in projects*, Gower Publishing Limited, Surrey, England, Chapter 4, Project success criteria and factors.

BCG, 2016. *Connecting Business Strategy and Project Management— Benefits realization management (BRM)*. Boston Consulting Group (BCG), Report, November 2016.

Be CC, 2013. Sector Forum: *Be Collaborative Contract*, Collaborating for the Built Environment, Constructing Excellence, Retrieved February 2013, http://www.constructingexcellence.org.uk/sectorforums/buildingestatesforum/bcc

Belassi, W., Tukel, O.I., 1996. "A new framework for determining critical success/failure factors in projects," *International Journal of Project Management*, vol. 14, no. 3, pp. 141–151.

Beleiu, I., Crisan, E., Nistor, R., 2015. "Main factors influencing project management," *Interdisciplinary Management Research*, 2015, vol. 11, pp. 59–72.

Birkenshaw, J., Foss, N.J., Lindenberg, S., 2014. "Combining purpose with profits," *MIT Sloan Management Review*, 2014, Reprint no. 55315.

Blindenbach-Driessen, F., 2006. "Innovation management in project-based firms," Doctoral thesis, School of Management Erasmus University, Rotterdam.

Boehm, B., Turner, R., 2004. *Balancing Agility and Discipline: A Guide for the Perplexed*, Boston, MA: Addison-Wesley.

Carvalho, M.M. de, Patah, L.A., Bido, D. de S., 2015, "Project management and its effects on project success: Cross-country and cross-industry comparisons," *International Journal of Project Management*, vol. 33 (2015), pp. 1509–1522.

Chan, A., & Chan, A., 2004. "Key performance indicators for measuring construction success," B*enchmarking: An International Journal*, vol. 11, no. 2, April 2004, pp. 203–221.

Chowdhury, S., 2001. *The Power of Six Sigma*, Kaplan Publishing, UK.

CMAA, 2021. Construction Management. Construction Management Association of America. Retrieved January 2021 from https://www.cmaanet.org/

CMMI, 2007. CMMI for development, version 1.2, Second Edition. Capability Maturity Model Integration, Software Engineering Institute (SEI), Carnegie Mellon, Pittsburgh, USA.

CMMI Institute, 2021. Schaumburg, Illinois. Retrieved April 2021, from https://cmmiinstitute.com/.

Collins, A., Baccarini, D., 2004. "Project Success—A Survey," *Journal of Construction Research*, vol. 5, no. 2, pp. 211–231.

Collins, J.C., 2001. *Good to Great*. Collins Business, Random House Business Books, London.

Collins, J.C., Porras, J.I., 1994. *Built to Last—Successful habits of visionary companies.* HarperCollins Publishers, New York.

Cooke-Davies, T.J., 2002. "The "real" success factors on projects," *International Journal of Project Management*, vol. 20 (2002), 185–190.

Cooper, R.G., Kleinschmidt, E.J., 2007. Winning business in product development, Research Technology Management, 2007.

Covey, S.R., 2004. *The seven habits of highly effective people*, Free Press, USA.

Dalcher, D., 2012. "The nature of project management: A reflection on the anatomy of major projects by Morris and Hough," *International Journal of Managing Projects in Business*, 643–660.

REFERENCES

Davis, K., 2014. "Different Stakeholder groups and their perceptions of project success," *International Journal of Project Management*, 2014, vol. 32, pp. 189–201.

DeCarlo, D., 2004. *eXtreme Project Management*, Jossey-Bass, San Francisco, CA.

De Wit, A., 1988. "Measurement of project success," *International Journal of Project Management*, vol. 6, no. 3, pp. 164–170.

DNV, 2003. *DNV-RP-H101—Risk Management in Marine and Subsea Operations*, January 2003, Det Norske Veritas, Recommend Practice, Retrieved October 2012, from http://www.dnv.com/, section: DNV Rules and Standards.

DPM, 2021. The Digital Project Manager. Retrieved February 2021 from https://thedigitalprojectmanager.com.

Drucker, P.F., 2001. *The Essential Drucker: The Best of Sixty Years of Peter Drucker's Essential Writings on Management*, Collins Business Essentials.

Ebbesen, J.B., Hope, A.J., 2013. "Re-imagining the Iron Triangle: Embedding Sustainability into Project Constraints," *PM World Journal*, 2013, vol. 2, no. 3.

Elattar, S., 2009. "Towards developing an improved methodology for evaluating performance and achieving success in construction projects, *Scientific Research and Essay*, vol. 4, no. 6, June 2009, pp. 549–554.

Elkington, J., 1994. "Towards the Sustainable Corporation: Win-Win-Win Business Strategies for Sustainable Development," *California Management Review*, vol. 36, no. 2, 1994, pp. 90–100.

Frödell, M., 2011. "Criteria for achieving efficient contractor-supplier relations," *Engineering, Construction and Architectural Management*, vol. 18, no. 4, pp. 381–393.

Gemunden, H.G., 2015. "Foundations of Project Management Research: Stakeholders and Agile," *Project Management Journal*, 2015, vol. 46, no. 6, pp. 3–5.

Goldratt, E.M., Cox, J., 1984. *The Goal.* Aldershot, England. Gower Publishing Limited.

Goldratt, E.M., Fox, R.E., 1986. *The Race.* North River Press, Great Barrington, USA.

Goldratt, E.M., 1994. *It's Not Luck.* Aldershot, England: Gower Publishing Limited.

Goyette, P., 2016. "6 Types of Corporate Culture (And Why They Work)," *Eagle's Flight*, November 9, 2016. Retrieved February 2022 from https://www.eaglesflight.com.

GPM, 2022. "Green Project Management." Retrieved February 2022 from https://www.greenprojectmanagement.org.

Hamel, G., Breen, B., 2007. *The future of management.* Harvard Business School Press, Boston, USA.

Haried, P., Ramamurthy, K., 2009. "Evaluating the success in international sourcing of information technology projects: the need for a relational client–vendor approach," *Project Management Journal*, 40, no. 3, pp. 56–71.

Heemstra, F.J., Ketel, L., Jonker, A. 2011. Sturen op project succes (project success control). KWD Resultaatmanagement.

Heiskanen, A., Newman, M., Eklin, M., 2008. "Control, Trust, Power, and the Dynamics of Information System Outsourcing Relationships: A Process Study of Contractual Software Development," *The Journal of Strategic Information Systems*, 2008, vol. 17, no. 4, pp. 268–286.

Hellström, M., Gustafsson, M., Wikström, R., Luotola, H., 2016. "The value of project execution services: a problem and uncertainty perspective," *Construction Management and Economics*, vol. 34, no. 4, April 2016, pp. 1–14.

Highsmith, J., 2004. *Agile Project Management: Creating Innovative Products.* Pearson Education Inc., USA.

Hyväri, I., 2006. "Success of Projects in Different Organizational Conditions," *Project Management Journal.* Project Management Institute. vol. 37, no. 4, pp. 31–41.

REFERENCES

Ika, L.A., 2009. "Project success as a topic in Project Management Journals," *Project Management Journal*, 2009, vol. 40, no. 4, pp. 6–19

Infolific, 2013. Retrieved March 2013, from `http://infolific.com`, section: /technology/definitions/pm-definitions/project-objective.

IPMA, 2018. Individual Competence Baseline (ICB) for project management. International Project Management Association (IPMA), Version 4.0. Retrieved January 2022 from `http://www.ipma.world`.

Irvine, R.J., 2013. "Success Factors for Organisational Information Systems Development Projects: A Scottish Suppliers' Perspective," Edinburgh Napier University, Thesis Doctor of Philosophy, June 2013.

ISO, 2021. Guidance on Project Management, 21500:2021, ISO (International Organization for Standardization), http:/`www.iso.org`.

JISC, 2013. Joint Information Systems Committee, UK. Retrieved October 2013, from `http://www.jisc.ac.uk/fundingopportunities/ projectmanagement/planning/objectives-outputs-outcomes.aspx`.

Kassc, T., Johansen, J., 2014. "Maturity differences between customer and supplier—challenges, problems, and possible solutions," *Journal of Software: Evolution and Process*, Special no.: Software Process Assessment and Improvement, March 2014, vol. 26, no. 3, pp. 295–305.

Kerzner, H., 2009. *Project Management: Systems Approach to Planning, Scheduling, Controlling*, John Wiley & Sons Inc., Hoboken, NJ, 10th edition.

Khosravi, S., Afshari, H., 2011. "A Success Measurement Model for Construction Projects. 2011 International Conference on Financial Management and Economics, IPEDR vol. 11 (2011).

Kim, J., Wilemon, D., 2007. "The learning organization as facilitator of complex NPD projects," *Creativity and Innovation Management Journal*, vol. 16, no. 2, pp. 176–191.

Kim, S., Mabin, V.J., Davies, J., 2008. "The theory of constraints thinking processes: retrospect and prospect, *International Journal of Operations & Production Management*, 2008, vol. 28, no. 2, pp. 155–184.

Knowledgerush, 2012. Retrieved October 2012, from `http://www. knowledgerush.com` [not active anymore].

Korbijn, G., 2014. "Success criteria and critical success factors for contractors of urgent and unexpected projects," Erasmus University, Rotterdam School of Management, September 2014.

Kotter, J.P., 2008. *A sense of urgency*. Harvard Business Press, Boston, MA.

Kylindri, S., Blanas, G., Henriksen, L., Tanev, S., 2012. "Measuring project outcomes: A review of success effectiveness variables," Management of international business and economic systems (MIBES) Conference, Oral, 25–27, May 2012.

Leach, L.P., 2014. *Critical chain project management (CCPM)*, Artech House, Boston/London.

Lehtimäki, T., Komulainen, H., Oinonen, M., Salo, J., 2018. "The value of long-term co-innovation relationships: Experiential approach," *International Journal of Business Innovation and Research*, 2018, vol. 16, no. 1.

Levina, N., Ross, J.W., 2003. "From the Vendors Perspective: Exploring the Value Proposition in Information Technology Outsourcing," *MIS Quarterly*, 2003, vol. 27, no. 3, pp. 331–364.

Lindhard, S., Larsen, J.K., 2016. "Identifying the key process factors affecting project performance," *Engineering, Construction and Architectural Management*, vol. 23, no. 5, pp. 657-673.

Machado, F.J., Martens, C.D.P., 2015. "Project management success: A bibliometric analysis," Revista de Gestão e Projetos—GeP, 2015, vol. 6 (1), Janeiro/Abril.

MacKerron, G., Kumar, M., Benedikt, A., Kumar, V., 2015. "Performance management of suppliers in outsourcing project: Case analysis from the financial services industry," *Production Planning and Control*, vol. 26, no. 2, pp. 150–165.

Manana, M.M., Waveren, C.C., Chan, K.Y., 2011. "Does regulation have an impact on project success? An empirical study in the construction industry in South Africa," *African Journal of Business Management*, 2011, vol. 6, no. 6, pp. 2115–2125.

REFERENCES

Mao, J., Lee, J., Deng, C., 2008. "Vendors' Perspectives on Trust and Control in Offshore Information Systems Outsourcing," *Information & Management*, 2008, vol. 45, no. 7, pp. 482–492.

Martinsuo, M., Ahola, T., 2010. "Supplier integration in complex delivery projects: comparison between different buyer-supplier relationships," *International Journal of Project Management*, vol. 28, 2010, pp. 107–116.

Müller, R., Jugdev, K., 2012. "Critical success factors in projects: Pinto, Slevin, and Prescott—the elucidation of project success," *International Journal of Managing Projects in Business*, vol. 5 no. 4, pp. 757–775.

Newbold, R.C., 1998. *Project Management in the Fast Lane—Applying the Theory of Constraints*, CRC Press LLC, Boca Raton, FL.

Ofman, D.D., 1995. Bezieling en kwaliteit in organisaties (Inspiration and quality in organizations), Kosmos Uitgevers, Utrecht, The Netherlands.

Osorio, P.C.F., Quelhas, O.L.G., Zotes, L.P., Shimoda, E. França, S., 2014. "Critical Success Factors in Project Management: An Exploratory Study of an Energy Company in Brazil," *Global Journal of Management and Business*, vol. 14 (10), 2014.

Oxford (2020), Oxford Dictionaries Online, Retrieved December 2020, from http://oxforddictionaries.com

Pankratz, O., Basten, D., 2018. "Opening the Black Box: Managers' Perceptions of IS Project Success Mechanisms," *Information & Management*, vol. 55, no. 3, April 2018, pp. 381–395.

Patah, L.A., 2010. "Evaluation of the relationship between the use of methods and training in project management and the success of projects through a contingency perspective: a quantitative analysis," PhD in Production Engineering, Dissertation, Universidade de São Paulo, São Paulo.

Patanakul, P., Milosevic, D., 2009. "The effectiveness in managing a group of multiple projects: Factors of influence and measurement criteria," *International Journal of Project Management*, vol. 27, no. 3, April 2009, pp. 216–233.

Peters, T.J., Waterman, R.H., Jr., 1982. *In search of excellence*. Harper & Row (HarperCollins), New York.

Peters T., Austin, N., 1985. *A passion for excellence*. Random House, New York.

Pinto, J.K., Prescott, J.E., 1988. "Variations in critical success factors over the stages in the project life cycle," *Journal of Management*, vol. 14, no. 1, pp. 5–18.

PMAJ (2001), *A Guidebook for Project and Program Management for Enterprise Innovation (P2M)*, Revision 3, October 2005, Representative author Prof. Shigenobu Ohara, Project Management Association of Japan.

PMI, 2021. *A Guide to the Project Management Body of Knowledge (PMBOK Guide)*, 7th Edition, 2021. Project Management Institute, USA.

PMI, 2014. *Implementing organizational project management: a practice guide*, 2014. Project Management Institute, USA.

Pokorny, J., Repa, V., Richta, K., Wojtkowski, W., Linger, H., Barry, C., Lang, M., 2011. *Information Systems Development—Business Systems and Services: Modeling and Development, Springer Science & Business Media*, Springer, 2011.

Pollack, J., Adler, D., 2018. "What is the Iron Triangle, and how has it changed?," *International Journal of Managing Projects in Business*, 2018, vol. 11, no. 2.

Porter, M.E., 1985. *Competitive Advantage: Creating and Sustaining Superior Performance*, 1985. Free Press.

Prabhakar, G.P., 2008. "What is Project Success: A Literature Review," *International Journal of Business and Management*, September 2008.

Prince2, 2017. *Managing Successful Projects with Prince2*, 6th edition. The Stationery Office (TSO), UK.

Prince2, 2022. "Prince2 in one thousand words white paper." Axelos, Retrieved January 2022, from https://www.axelos.com/resource-hub/white-paper/prince2-in-one-thousand-words-white-paper.

Projectmanager.com, 2021. Projectmanager.com Inc., Austin, Texas, USA. Retrieved January 2021 from http://www.projectmanager.com.

REFERENCES

Ram, J., Corkindale, D., 2014. "How 'critical' are the critical success factors (CSFs)?" *Business Process Management Journal*, vol. 20, no. 1, 2014, pp. 151–174.

Saadé, R.G., Dong, H., Wan, H., 2015. "Factors of Project Manager Success," *Interdisciplinary Journal of Information, Knowledge, and Management*, vol. 10, 2015, pp. 63–80.

Sadeh, A., Dvir, D, Shenhar, A.J., 2000. "The role of contract type in the success of R&D defense projects under increasing uncertainty," *Project Management Journal*. 2000, vol. 31, no. 3, pp. 14–21.

Sariola, R., 2018. "Utilizing the innovation potential of suppliers in construction projects," *Construction Innovation*, vol. 18, no. 2, pp. 167–182.

Savolainen, P., Ahonen, J.J., Richardson I., 2012. "Software development project success and failure from the supplier's perspective: A systematic literature review," *International Journal of Project Management*, vol. 30, no. 4, May 2012, pp. 458–469.

Schwaber, K., 2004. *Agile Project Management with Scrum (Developer Best Practices)*. Microsoft Press, USA.

Shenhar, A.J., Dvir, D., Levy, O., 1995. "Project Success: A Multidimensional, Strategic Concept," Research paper, University of Minnesota, MN, June 1995.

Shenhar, A.J., Renier, J.J., 1996. "Improving PM: Linking success criteria to project type." Creating Canadian Advantage through Project Management Symposium, Southern Alberta Chapter, Project Management Institute, Calgary, May 1996.

Shenhar, A.J., Levy, O., Dvir, D., 1997. "Mapping dimensions of project success," *Project Management Journal*, Project Management Institute, no. 2, vol. 28, June 1997.

Shenhar, A.J., Dvir, D., 2007. *Reinventing project management: the diamond approach to successful growth and innovation*, Harvard Business School Press, Boston, MA.

Shokri-Ghasabeh, M., Kavousi-Chabok, K., 2009. "Generic Project Success and Project Management Success Criteria and Factors: Literature review and survey," *WSEAS transactions on business and economics*, vol. 6, no. 8, pp. 456–468. World Scientific and Engineering Academy and Society.

Siddique, L., Hussein, B.A., 2016. "A qualitative study of success criteria in Norwegian agile software projects from suppliers," *International Journal of Information Systems and Project Management*, vol. 4, no. 2, 2016, pp. 63–79.

Simsit, Z.T., Gunay, N.S., Vayvay, O., 2014. "Theory of Constraints: A Literature Review," *Procedia, Social and Behavioral Sciences*, vol. 150, 15 September 2014, pp. 930–936. Part of special issue: 10th International Strategic Management Conference 2014.

Sköld, D., Fornstedt, H., Lindahl, M., 2018. "Dilution of innovation utility, reinforcing the reluctance towards the new: An upstream supplier perspective on a fragmented electricity industry," Energy Policy, no. 116, May 2018, pp. 220–231.

Slevin, D.P., Pinto, J.K., 1986. "The Project Implementation Profile: New Tool for Project Managers," *Project Management Journal*, Project Management Institute, September 1986, pp. 57–58.

Smartsheet, 2021. Smartsheet Inc., Bellevue, Washington, USA. Retrieved January 2021 from `http://www.smartsheet.com`.

Stonehouse, G., Snowdon, B., 2007. "Competitive Advantage Revisited: Michael Porter on Strategy and Competitiveness," *Journal of Management Inquiry*, September 2007, vol. 16, no. 3, pp. 256–273.

Sudhakar, G.P., 2016. Understanding the meaning of project success, Binus Business Review, vol. 7, no. 2, August 2016, pp. 163–169.

Taiichi, O., 1978. *Toyota Production System: Beyond Large-Scale Production*, Productivity Press, Portland, OR.

Taylor, H., 2007. "Outsourced IT Projects from the Vendor Perspective: Different Goals, Different Risks," *Journal of Global Information Management*, 2007, vol. 15, no. 2, pp. 1–27.

REFERENCES

Techt, U., 2015. *Goldratt and the Theory of Constraints: The Quantum Leap in Management*, Ibidem Press, Stuttgart, Germany.

Thomas, G., Fernández, W., 2008. "Success in IT projects: A matter of definition, *International Journal of Project Management*, 2008, vol. 26, no. 7, pp. 733–742.

Too, E.G., Weaver, P., 2014. "The management of project management: A conceptual framework for project governance," *International Journal of Project Management*. vol. 32, no. 8, November 2014, pp. 1382–1394.

Turner, J.R., 2009. *The handbook of project-based management*. The McGraw-Hill Companies Inc., New York, USA.

Turner, J., Zolin, R., 2012. "Forecasting success on large projects: Developing reliable scale to predict multiple perspectives by multiple stakeholders over multiple time frames," *Project Management Journal*, vol. 43(5), October 2012, pp. 87–99.

Velayudhan, D.P., Thomas, S., 2016, "Measuring Project Success: Emergence of Dimensions," *The International Journal of Business & Management*, April 2016, vol. 4, no. 4, pp. 48–53.

Virine, L., Trumper, M., 2007. *Project Decisions: The Art and Science*, Berrett-Koehler Publishers, Oakland, CA.

Waddock, S., Graves, S.B., 2002. "Beyond Built to Last ... Stakeholder Relations in "Built-to-Last" Companies," *Business and Society Review*, December 2002, vol. 105, no. 4, pp. 393–418.

Walker, L.W., 2008. "Learning lessons on lessons learned," Conference paper. Project Management Institute, USA.

Westerveld, E., 2003. "The Project Excellence Model: linking success criteria and critical success factors," *International Journal of Project Management*, 21 (2003), pp. 411–418.

Wikipedia, 2022. "Wikimedia Foundation Inc.," Retrieved January 2022 from http://www.wikipedia.org.

Wijnen, G., Storm, P., 1984. Projectmatig werken. Spectrum.

Williams, P., Ashill, N.J., Naumann, E., Jackson, E., 2015. "Relationship quality and satisfaction: Customer-perceived success factors for on-time projects," *International Journal of Project Management*, 2015, vol. 33, pp. 1836–1850.

Womack, J.P., Jones, D.T., 1996. *Lean Thinking: Banish Waste and Create Wealth in Your Corporation*. Free Press, New York, USA.

Wrike, 2022. Retrieved February 2022 from `https://www.wrike.com`.

Youngman, Dr. K.J., 2021. *A Guide to Implementing the Theory of Constraints (TOC)*. Retrieved March 2021, from `http://www.dbrmfg.co.nz`.

Terms and Abbreviations

APM	Agile project management
aspect	a particular part or feature of something (of a subject)
BRM	benefits realization management
CCPM	critical chain project management
CF	cash flow
competence	the combination of knowledge and experience
compliance	the action or fact of complying with a wish or command
CM	construction management
CMMI	capability maturity model implementation
CRT	current reality tree
CSF	critical success factor
DE	desirable effect
ECM	event chain methodology
effective	successful in producing a desired or intended result
efficient	(of a person) working in a well-organized and competent way, or (of a system or machine) achieving maximum productivity with minimum wasted effort or expense
employee	a person employed for wages or salary, especially at a non-executive level

(*continued*)

© Reitse van der Wekken 2024
R. van der Wekken, *Project Objectives Management*,
https://doi.org/10.1007/979-8-8688-0956-9

experience	practical contact with and observation of facts or events (in a positive context)
for-profit	a type of organization, also called a *company*, with the aim to earn profit for its shareholders
FRT	future reality tree
FT	(future) throughput
fund	a sum of money saved or made available for a particular purpose (Oxford Dictionaries Online)
goal	an aim or objective that you work toward with effort and determination
I	inventory
ICB	individual competence baseline
IPMA	International Project Management Association
ISO	International Organization for Standardization
knowledge	facts, information, and skills acquired through experience or education; the theoretical or practical understanding of a subject (in a positive context)
KPI	key performance indicator
legislation	laws, considered collectively
money	any item or medium of exchange that people accept for the payment of goods and services, as well as the repayment of loans
NP	net profit
non-profit	a type of organization with a non-financial aim
OE	operating expense

(*continued*)

OPM	organizational project management (PMI)
organization	an organized group of people with a particular purpose, such as a business or a government department
organizational benefit	(at customer) change within its organization that takes the customer closer to its goal
	(at supplier) productive change, when embedded as actual realized organizational benefits within itself, that takes the supplier closer to its goal
perspective	a particular attitude toward or way of regarding something; a point of view
PMBOK	Guide to the Project Management Body of Knowledge
PMI	Project Management Institute (USA-based)
Prince2	PRojects IN Controlled Environments, second edition
PRiSM	projects integrating sustainable methods
process asset	any or all process related assets, from any or all the organizations involved in the project that can be used to influence the project's success
profit	a financial gain, especially the difference between the amount earned and the amount spent in buying, operating, or producing something
project	a temporary endeavor designed to produce a unique product, service, or result with a defined beginning and end, usually time-constrained and often constrained by funding or staffing, undertaken to meet unique goals and objectives, typically to bring about beneficial change or added value
project customer	customer or user of the project result, also referred to as a *customer*

(*continued*)

project management	the process of leading the work of a team to achieve goals and meet success criteria at a specified time
project objective	(at customer) organizational benefit achieved by project action (project implementation)
	(at supplier) potential organizational benefit achieved by project objective action
project objective action	(at customer) none
	(at supplier) action to achieve project objectives through project actions (project execution)
project supplier	supplier of the project result to the customer or user, also referred to as a *supplier*
regulation	a rule or directive made and maintained by an authority
resource	a stock or supply of money, materials, staff, and other assets that a person or organization can draw on to function effectively
ROI	return on investment
rule	one of a set of explicit or understood regulations or principles governing conduct or procedure within a particular area of activity
SES	Smith Electrical Services
SMART	Specific, Measurable, Attainable, Relevant and Timely
society	the aggregate of people living together in a more or less ordered community
SPOM	supplier project objectives management
stakeholder	a person with an interest or concern in something, especially a business

(continued)

subject	a person or thing that is being discussed, described, or dealt with
supplier organizational benefit	productive change, when embedded as actual realized organizational benefits within itself, that takes the supplier closer to its goal
supplier goal	secure the future of the organization
supplier project objective	potential organizational benefit achieved by project objective action
supplier project objective action	action to achieve project objectives through project actions (project execution)
standard	something established by authority, custom, or general consent as a model, example, or point of reference
SWOT (analysis)	analysis method to identify strengths, weaknesses, opportunities, and threats (SWOT) of an organization of subject
synergy	the interaction or cooperation of two or more organizations, substances, or other agents to produce a combined effect greater than the sum of their separate effects
TBL	triple bottom line
TOC	Theory of Constraints
UDE	undesirable effect
user	a person who uses or operates something
values	principles or standards of behavior
XPM	extreme project management

Index

A

Abbreviations, 343–347

Adaptive project framework (APF), 251

Agile project management (APM), 289, 290

APF, *see* Adaptive project framework (APF)

APM, *see* Agile project management (APM)

B

Benefits realization management (BRM), 254, 290
  balancing act, 274
  future objectives, 275, 276
  give/take relationships, 270
  identify/execute/sustain benefits, 269
  inputs/outputs projects, 270–273
  multi-project environment, 276, 277
  optimization perspective, 274
  push/pull, 274
  resources, 273

BPM, *see* Business process management (BPM)

BRM, *see* Benefits realization management (BRM)

Business process management (BPM), 253

C

Capability maturity model implementation (CMMI), 147

Capability Maturity Model Integration (CMMI), 291

CCPM, *see* Critical chain project management (CCPM)

CMMA, *see* Construction Management Association of America (CMMA)

CMMI, *see* Capability maturity model implementation (CMMI); Capability Maturity Model Integration (CMMI)

Construction Management Association of America (CMMA), 292

© Reitse van der Wekken 2024
R. van der Wekken, *Project Objectives Management*,
https://doi.org/10.1007/979-8-8688-0956-9

T